FREE MONEY®
for Small Businesses
and Entrepreneurs

Fourth Edition

FREE MONEY® BOOKS BY LAURIE BLUM

The Complete Guide to Getting a Grant (Simon & Schuster)

Business

Free Money® for Small Businesses & Entrepreneurs (John Wiley)
Free Money® When You're Unemployed (John Wiley)
Free Money® from the Federal Government for Small Businesses & Entrepreneurs (John Wiley)

Childcare/Education

Free Money® for Athletic Scholarships (Henry Holt & Company)
Free Money® for College (Facts-on-File)
Free Money® for College from the Government (Henry Holt & Company)
Free Money® from Colleges & Universities (Henry Holt & Company)
Free Money® for Day Care (Simon & Schuster)
Free Money® for Graduate School (Henry Holt & Company)

Healthcare

Free Money® for Childhood Behavioral & Genetic Disorders (Simon & Schuster)
Free Money® for Diseases of Aging (Simon & Schuster)
Free Money® for Heart Disease & Cancer Care (Simon & Schuster)
Free Money® for Infertility Treatments (Simon & Schuster)
Free Money® for Mental/Emotional Disorders (Simon & Schuster)

The Arts

Free Money® for People in the Arts (Macmillan)

FREE MONEY®
for Small Businesses and Entrepreneurs

Fourth Edition

Laurie Blum

John Wiley & Sons, Inc.
New York · Chichester · Brisbane · Toronto · Singapore

Library of Congress Cataloging-in-Publication Data:
Blum, Laurie.
    Free money for small businesses and entrepreneurs / Laurie Blum. – 4th ed.
      p.   cm.
    Includes index.
    ISBN 0-471-10388-8 (cloth). – ISBN 0-471-10387-X (pbk.)
      1. Small business–United States–Finance–Directories.
2. Commercial loans–United States–Directories.   3. Endowments–
United States–Directories.   4. Federal aid to community
development–United States–Directories.   I. Title
HG4027.7.B58   1995
658.15'224–dc20   94-43280

Printed in the United States of America

10 9 8 7 6 5 4 3 2 1

It isn't money that sustains me–it's the faith I have in myself, in my own powers. In spirit I'm a millionaire–maybe that's the best thing about America, that you believe you'll rise again.

–Henry Miller

Contents

Introduction

Are you a small business person frustrated by lack of investment capital or by lenders unwilling to take risks? Are you a would-be entrepreneur with no idea of how you are going to raise the needed capital to start your business? Or do you own a medium-sized business that is looking for expansion capital? Believe it or not, the nonprofit community has billions of dollars available to entrepreneurs and profit-making businesses. The money takes the form of outright grants (which is money that does not have to be paid back), equity investments, letters of credit, and direct loans (often at extremely low interest rates, and often with extended time periods and flexible terms for repayment).

The information presented in this book demonstrates that there is a large yet untapped source of alternative venture and expansion capital available to both profit and nonprofit organizations. Remember, however, that funding sources are not without restrictions. Do you just walk up, hold out your hand, and expect someone to put money in it? Of course not. It takes time, effort, and thought on your part. You are going to have to find out who is giving away the money, and you are going to have to fill out applications. You may experience frustration or rejection at some point, but the odds are in your favor that you will qualify for some sort of funding.

The hardest part has always been finding the sources of money. That is why I wrote this book. I have written books on grant monies for students and individuals in the arts, and I have written three previous editions of this book. This new edition of *Free Money*® includes updated funding information that I have been using very successfully for my clients. Much of the information in this book has never been made available to the general public.

I wanted to make this book as easy to use as possible. The listings are divided into three sections: Program-Related investments, Flow-Through Funding, and Federal Money. Within these sections the listings are arranged by geographic location (where you or your business is located) and type of business (for example, real estate, import/export). Check all three sections to see which grants apply to you.

You'll find all the details you'll need, including the total amount of money that is awarded, the number of grants or loans given, the range of monies given, and the average size of an award. Note that the word "minority" in this book refers to people who are either African American, Hispanic, Asian American, American Indian, or female.

By the time this book is published, some of the information contained here will have changed. No reference book can be as up-to-date as the reader (or author) would like. Names, addresses, dollar amounts, telephone numbers, and other data are always in flux; however, most of the information will not have changed. Good luck.

HOW TO APPLY

Applying for nonprofit money takes work, as well as some thought and organization. First, begin with the sorting-out process. Go through each section of the book and mark all the foundations that could potentially give you money. (Don't be dissuaded from applying if the money given is a low-interest loan or if the award is donated technical services). Pay close attention to the restrictions and eliminate those foundations for which you don't qualify. You should apply for a number of grants and awards (the same material you use for one application can be used for most, if not all, of the other applications.) Although none of the foundations in this book requires an application fee, the efforts required to meet all the requirements will probably limit you to no more than eight applications. (If you are ambitious and want to apply to more than eight foundations, go right ahead.)

Write or call those foundations that you've identified as possible funders to obtain a copy of their guidelines. In cases where the contact's name is not listed, begin your letter: To Whom It May Concern. If you call the foundation, limit yourself to a request for the guidelines; do not cross-examine the person who answers the phone.

Grant applications take time to complete. Quite often you will be required to write one or more essays. Be neat! You may very well prepare a topnotch proposal, but it won't look good if it's done in a sloppy manner.

Proposals should always be typed and doubled spaced. Be sure to make a copy of the proposal. I've learned the hard way that there is nothing worse than having the foundation or governmental agency lose your proposal and then having to reconstruct it because you didn't have a copy. You may be asked for your tax return and other financial records. (Don't worry, you won't be penalized for having money in the bank or having run an effective business.) You may be asked to include personal references. Be sure to get strong references; call each person you plan to list, and ask them if they feel comfortable giving you a reference. Remember, you have to sell yourself; you have to convince the grantors to give the money to you and not to someone else.

The Proposal

A grant proposal will include a concise and tight narrative description of the project or business that you are attempting to fund. Remember, it is essential that you sell your project to the potential grantor in the very first paragraph. The following outline should give you a good idea of how to put together the necessary components of a good proposal:

1. **Title page:** Name of applicant (organization, business, or nonprofit organization) and, where necessary, fiscal sponsor. (See appropriate chapter introduction for explanation.)

2. **First paragraph:** A clear and precise statement of purpose. Your statement of purpose should answer the following three questions:

   a. What do you hope to accomplish?

   b. How do you plan to accomplish you goals? (What activities, programs, or services will you undertake to accomplish your goals? Would you characterize these efforts as service related, advocacy focused, or public education related?)

c. For whose benefit does your organization or business exist? (Whom does your organization or business currently serve or plan to serve? Specifically, how do you define your prime constituents by age, sex, geography, minority group status, or income?)

3. **Body of narrative:** Try to keep this to two or three double-spaced paragraphs at the most. Brevity is the key! The body of this narrative should include a vary specific indication of the proposed goals of the project and how the objectives will be met.

4. **Attachments:**

   a. For a profit-making business, the following items should be attached to the narrative:
      1. Use of loan or grant (working capital, land, and so forth)
      2. Balance sheets
      3. Profit and loss statements (for 90 days and three years)
      4. Accounts receivables
      5. Earnings projections (for one year)
      6. Business and personal IRS returns (last three years)
      7. Resumes of management
      8. Any machinery or equipment owned (cost and name of seller)
      9. Any lawsuits or bankruptcies

   b. For nonprofit organizations or profit-making businesses working with a fiscal sponsor, the following items should be attached to the narrative:
      1. A copy of the nonprofit organization's 501(C)(3) IRS letter that documents tax-exempt status
      2. A list of the board of directors
      3. A list of past and present funding support (government, corporate, and foundation)
      4. Budgets (last year, current year, and projected)
      5. One or two good press articles on the organization, if available

The following are examples of two excellent proposals–one for a profit-making enterprise and the other for a nonprofit organization.

Sample Proposal: Profit

Contact
Company
Address

Dear   ,

Year after year, medical insurance premiums spiral upward and the complexity of filing claims increases. Medicare's budget has become an enormous black hole where money falls in but little or no correlation can be made to the quality of medical care that is received in turn. The American Medical Association (AMA) has come under frequent attack for protecting doctors who have been negligent. The burdens on the system raise the cost of medical care for all Americans, causing us all to suffer the effects and costs.

Medinet is a high-speed information system designed to link medical services and related industries. Medinet could be the cornerstone of a comprehensive evolution of medicine, revolutionizing the medical industry with the same convenience and efficiency that the ATM card brought to the banking industry. Through the application of technological advances in networking data storage/access, transmission, and communications combined with medical expertise, Medinet will vastly improve the delivery, tracking, and availability of medical information, billing, and medical treatment utilization.

Medicine still lags far behind many other fields in the use of computer information systems. To improve its control over itself, its costs, and its vulnerabilities or irregularities in fees and services, Medinet will benefit doctors, patients, insurance companies, and government medical agencies by providing a unified standard network and efficiency of information. There are numerous advantages to this system, since its function is the reliable and timely management and distribution of information. Medinet can serve as a secured archive for medical information. This information may be utilized by insurance companies, government agencies, or universities to typify or track trends in the population. This information can also determine relative concentrations of certain diseases and injuries, and it can establish standards for treatment or cost of medical care. Short- and long-term medical problems can be identified, and adjustments can be made more gradually to ensure rates and premium standards for medical care. Medinet could be used to reduce the number of lawsuits due to wrongful deaths and other forms of negligence by showing that a minimum and a maximum level of competent treatment do exist in the medical industry.

Physically, Medinet is a network of computer systems. Each system consists of building blocks of fast RISC (Reduced Instruction Set Computer) -based computers. With this architecture, Medinet can provide several times the performance of the most powerful single computer designs over a distribution link that minimizes redundancy and allows high reliability, low purchase and maintenance costs, and geographical flexibility.

Our computer system will be linked to a high-speed network to provide fast transfer and sharing of data among distant locations. Networks are designed for fast, efficient communications among different hosts and client sites. By using localized networks feeding into larger systems, networks can minimize the amount of redundant hardware and phone costs. At the same time, we can provide flexible systems that adapt themselves to the amount of traffic and work load needed. Medinet will be an efficient data management system that will radically improve the delivery and quality of medical care coverage for the insurance company, the patient, and the provider.

Medicare is by far the most significant potential Medinet user. Our capacity to collect, verify, and store information in a timely fashion and with greater accuracy will exceed any current technology. Medicare will have access to obtain information on medical costs and treatments. There will be an opportunity to control the rising costs of medical care and to observe trends in costs and participation in different programs. Insurance companies will have an opportunity to use similar tracking that will result in better budget control and in the lowering of overall Medicare spending. Patients, doctors, and Medicare all suffer from the lack of uniformity in the quality of medical care, from deep insurance premium hikes, and from spending controls.

Because we feel that (corporation, foundation) would be interested in the implementation of Medinet, we are now approaching you for a contribution of $_____. Medinet will be the system to bring together the patient, the doctors, and the insurance companies, saving valuable time and lives. It will restore the trust in our health care system and practitioners.

We have also enclosed additional materials about Medinet for your information. If you have any questions or need additional materials about Medinet, please do not hesitate to call me at (213) 462-5292.

Sincerely,

Michael Gitter, M.D.

MG/cm
encl.

Sample Proposal: Nonprofit

Contact
Company
Address

Dear

Without the help of corporate and foundation support here in Los Angeles, there is a chance we will have to close our doors for good in the fall of 1988.

Few organizations in Los Angeles have worked as long and as hard as the Inner City Cultural Center has to bridge the gaps between the diverse cultural and ethnic groups that make up this vast city. Since the Center's founding in 1966, it has been dedicated to providing the multicultural communities in Los Angeles performing artists with meaningful statements about them. At the same time, the Center has committed itself to enriching these communities by bringing outstanding works of creative expression, including theater, dance, music, and poetry, to audiences who otherwise would have little or no access to them.

The communities' response to the artistic excellence offered by the Inner City Cultural Center confirms our belief that the Center does serve a deeply felt need. Attendance at the Center's performances and events has increased steadily over the years and, at present, the Center can boast one of the highest number of sold-out houses of any theater in Los Angeles.

Productions at the Center have ranged from the Greek classics to the latest in contemporary theater and dance. The Center has been the site of numerous world premieres, including the first productions of works it has commissioned. All productions are of the highest professional caliber possible within the means of the Center. And the performances—including memorable appearances by such artists as Paul Winfield, Beah Richards, Lawrence Hilton-Jacobs, Carmen Zapata, and the Dance Theater of Harlem—have consistently received critical praise.

In addition to the full spectrum of productions, the Center also has classes, competitions, and training and intern programs designed to broaden the opportunities of talented young people in the performing arts. The Center can point with pride to the large number of performers who have launched their careers in its classrooms and on its stages. They have learned and practiced all aspects of their crafts in the Center's classes and have tested their ability in the Ira Alridge Annual Acting Competition and the ICCC Short Play Competition.

The Inner City Cultural Center is among this country's very few cultural organizations founded and operated by people of color. As such, the Center has, for the past two decades, been a great source of pride to the black, Hispanic, Asian, and white communities. It has demonstrated time and time again the great potential each community has for making a serious, positive contribution to the cultural life of our city and of our country. The Center encourages a true dialogue between the communities, striving for greater understanding that will improve the quality of life for us all.

Since 1972, the Center has been located in its own building near the corner of Pico and Vermont in the section of Los Angeles that is the home of well-established black, Hispanic, and Asian neighborhoods. With its classrooms, rehearsal rooms, library, and three theaters, the Center is viewed as an important cultural resource by the surrounding communities. It has received the majority of its support—both earned and contributed—from those who use it the most.

The Inner City Cultural Center today finds its future in serious jeopardy. The building code for the City of Los Angeles mandates that all large structures within the city limits be able to withstand the force of an earthquake of considerable magnitude. The Center's building is sound and stable (it sustained no damage during October's quake), and it will continue to meet the Center's needs in terms of space. However, if it is not brought up to the City's earthquake standards, the Center will be forced to close its doors.

The Center had been working with local engineers on a gradual renovation that would ease the financial strain that an extensive rebuilding would have on the Center. This renovation was to be done over a number of years. Unfortunately, the city recently revealed its new timetable for the project: it must be finished by fall of next year.

Thus, we are now making this urgent appeal both to corporations and to foundations who share our concern for a cultural life that encompasses all the communities in our city. If we do not reach our goal of raising the estimated $200,000 necessary to meet the city's requirements by next fall, it could bring our two-decade record of accomplishments to an end.

We sincerely hope that, in recognizing the importance of our work and the seriousness of our situation, you will contribute $_____ to our Renovation Fund, thereby helping to ensure that the Inner City Cultural Center can continue serving those who have traditionally been undeserved here in Los Angeles.

Enclosed is some additional information about the Inner City Cultural Center. If you should need more information, please do not hesitate to call us.

Sincerely,

Gene Bolande

GB/blp
encl.

Program-Related Investments

A program-related investment (PRI) is an investment a foundation makes in a nonprofit organization, a profit-making business, or an individual that furthers the charitable objectives of the foundation (for example, housing for low-income residents or expansion capital for a small manufacturing firm, which in turn will allow for the hiring of more workers). PRIs traditionally take the form of outright grants, equity investments, letters of credit, donated services (that can range from copying equipment to consultants), and direct loans (the loans are usually offered at extremely low interest rates and often with extended time periods and flexible terms for repayment).

PRIs, as they exist today, date back only as far as 1968. However, here were a few earlier examples. Benjamin Franklin created a charitable trust in the late eighteenth century to lend money to "young married artificers" at one percentage point below prevailing interest rates to help them in establishing themselves in business. The Russell Sage Foundation invested in innovative garden apartments in the 1920s. However, this instrument of philanthropy, the use of the investing process to carry out a foundation's program purposes, has gone virtually unused for most of American's philanthropic history.

PRIs are invaluable sources of money for established businesses and particularly for start-up situations. Commercial investors usually are unable to invest in many socially beneficial projects because the financial return is too low. Foundations, however, will invest in enterprises that many commercial investors would consider too speculative. They will act as patient investors willing to wait through the difficult and often unprofitable early years of a business's life with the expectation that profitability will come and that investments (if the PRI takes the form of an equity investment) will pay an acceptable return. If a foundation is willing to provide a portion of the needed financing through a PRI with a below-market rate of return (or no return at all), then the recipient may be able to obtain the remainder of the financing from commercial investors or leaders. The main function of the PRI, however, is to fulfill a major charitable objective.

An example of a program-related investment is the loan that was made available at three percent during a time of double-digit interest rates by the Collins Foundation to rehabilitate the Butte Hotel, a single-room-occupancy hotel (SRO) in downtown Portland, Oregon. The hotel was renovated through the Burnside Consortium, a nonprofit umbrella organization of civic groups, businesses, and individuals set up to improve the quality of life in Portland. The Consortium's first housing project had been the rehabilitation of the Rich Hotel, also an SRO. The Consortium worked with the owner to attract Housing and Urban Development (HUD) neighborhood self-help grants and loans provided by the local urban renewal agency. The Collins Foundation seed grant was of great importance because of the Foundation's willingness to "take a chance" on a project that at the start "had no money, no lease with the owner, and no technical assistance money to do a feasibility study."

PRIs can be made directly to profit-making businesses and individuals, though sometimes a foundation will only fund nonprofit organizations. An individual or business can use an established nonprofit corporation as a "flow-through," utilizing their tax-exempt status and thereby eliminating the need to set up a separate nonprofit organization. If possible, it is a good idea to work through a nonprofit organization whose purposes and activities are compatible with your own (for example, if you are building low-income housing in a inner-city neighborhood, work with a foundation that makes grants for community renewal). The established nonprofit organization is usually given three to seven percent of monies raised as a flow-through fee. For further information, see Section II.

1

Program-Related Investments by State

ALABAMA

BellSouth Foundation
c/o BellSouth Corporation
1155 Peachtree Street, N.E., Room 7H08
Atlanta, GA 30367-6000
(404) 249-2396
(404) 249-2429
(404) 249-2428

See full entry under Georgia.

The Christian Workers Foundation
3038 Bankhead Avenue
Montgomery, AL 36106
Mailing address: P.O. Box 457, Wolfeboro, NH 03896

Restrictions: Program-related investments to evangelistic Christian organizations involved in youth work.
Focus of giving: No geographic restrictions.
$ given: $163,980 for 26 grants; average range, $500–$2,000.
Assets: $3 million
Contact: G.R. Lockhart, Trustee
Application information: Applications by invitation only

Jack Eckerd Corporation Foundation
P.O. Box 4689
Clearwater, FL 34618
(813) 398-8318

See full entry under Florida.

Norton Company Foundation
New Bond Street
P.O. Box 15008
Worcester, MA 01615-0008
(508) 795-4700

See full entry under Massachusetts.

The Sonat Foundation, Inc.
1900 Fifth Avenue, North
P.O. Box 2563
Birmingham, AL 35202
(205) 325-7460

Restrictions: Program-related investments and other forms of funding for education, social service agencies, health services, community development, environmental concerns, and cultural programs.
Focus of giving: Limited primarily to Alabama, Connecticut, and Texas.
$ given: $1.4 million for 292 grants; average, $5,000–$25,000.
Assets: $6.2 million
Contact: J. Lisa Burge, Secretary
Application information: Application form required
Initial approach: Letter
Copies of proposal: 1
Deadlines: None
Board meeting dates: As needed
Final notification: Within 2 weeks

ALASKA

Alaska Conservation Foundation
750 W. 2nd Avenue, Suite 104
Anchorage, AK 99501
(907) 276-1917

Restrictions: Support for environment, conservation, wildlife, ecology, and peace. Grants for seed money, continuing support, emergency funds, equipment, technical assistance, loans, and operating budgets.
Focus of giving: Alaska.
$ given: $935,166 for 124 grants.
Assets: $816 million

Contact: Jan Konigsberg, Executive Director
Application information: Application form required
Initial approach: Letter or telephone
Copies of proposal: 16
Deadlines: 6 weeks prior to board meetings
Board meeting dates: 2 annually
Final notification: 2 weeks after board meeting

ARIZONA

Arizona Community Foundation
2122 East Highland Avenue, Suite 400
Phoenix, AZ 85016
(602) 381-1400

Restrictions: Program-related investments and other forms of support for health programs, human services programs (including services for the handicapped), conservation, and community-based economic development.
Focus of giving: Limited to Arizona.
$ given: $1.7 million for grants; average range, $1,000–$10,000.
Assets: $33 million
Contact: Stephen D. Mittenthal, President
Application information: Application form required
Initial approach: Letter
Copies of proposal: 15
Deadlines: February 1, June 1, and October 1
Board meeting dates: Semiannually
Final notification: 60 days

Samuel B. Mosher Foundation
3278 Loma Riviera Drive
San Diego, CA 92110
(619) 226-6122

See full entry under California.

ARKANSAS

Pearl M. and Julia J. Harmon Foundation
P.O. Box 52568
Tulsa, OK 74152-0568
(918) 743-6191

See full entry under Oklahoma.

The Winthrop Rockefeller Foundation
308 East Eighth Street
Little Rock, AR 72202
(501) 376-6854

Restrictions: Program-related investments and other forms of funding for programs designed to encourage local economic development and education.
Focus of giving: Limited primarily to Arkansas and to projects that benefit Arkansas.
$ given: $2.57 million for 127 grants; average range, $1,000–$50,000.
Assets: $55.35 million
Contact: Mahlon Martin, President
Application information: Application form required
Initial approach: Telephone or letter
Copies of proposal: 3
Deadlines: January 1 and July 1
Board meeting dates: First weekend in March, June, September, and December
Final notification: 2 weeks after board meetings

Union Pacific Foundation
Martin Tower
Eighth and Eaton Avenues
Bethlehem, PA 18018
(215) 861-3225

See full entry under Pennsylvania.

CALIFORNIA

American Honda Foundation
P.O. Box 2205
Torrance, CA 90509-2205
(213) 781-4090

Restrictions: Grants for national organizations supporting youth and scientific education. Scholarship funds, fellowships, special projects, operating budgets, continuing support, research, seed money, annual campaigns, internships, matching funds, and program-related investments. No funding to individuals. Please see flow-through funding chapter for application information.
$ given: $816,000 for 16 grants; range, $10,000–$100,000.
Assets: $14.1 million
Publications: Grants list, newsletter, informational brochure (including application guidelines), program policy statement, and application guidelines

Contact: Kathryn A. Carey, Manager
Application information: Application form required
Initial approach: Letter or telephone
Copies of proposal: 1
Deadlines: February 1, May 1, August 1, and November 1
Board meeting dates: January, April, July, and October
Final notification: 2 months

California Community Foundation

606 South Olive Street, Suite 2400
Los Angeles, CA 90014
(213) 413-4042

Restrictions: Program-related investments and other forms of funding for community development, human services, health, education, civic affairs, and culture.
Focus of giving: Limited to greater Los Angeles County, California area.
$ given: $9.4 million for 1,114 grants; average range, $5,000–$25,000.
Assets: $107.9 million
Contact: Jack Shakely, President
Application information: Application form required
Initial approach: Full proposal
Copies of proposal: 1
Deadlines: None
Board meeting dates: Quarterly
Final notification: 3 months after board meeting

CBS Foundation, Inc.

51 West 52nd Street
New York, NY 10019
(212) 975-5791

See full entry under New York.

Fresno Regional Foundation

1999 Tuolumne, Suite 600
Fresno, CA 93721
(209) 233-2016

Restrictions: Program-related investments, seed money, equipment and continuing support for conservation projects, senior citizens, character-building programs, local historical programs, health programs, and education.
Focus of giving: Limited primarily to the central San Joaquin Valley, California—Fresno, Madera, Merced, Tulane, and Kings counties.
$ given: $384,522 for grants.
Assets: $1.3 million
Contact: Annette Leifer, Executive Director

Application information: Application form required
Initial approach: Letter or telephone
Deadlines: February 1
Board meeting dates: Quarterly
Final notification: April

Wallace Alexander Gerbode Foundation
470 Columbus Avenue, Suite 209
San Francisco, CA 94133
(415) 391-0911

Restrictions: Support for innovative programs and projects with a direct
   impact on residents of the five San Francisco Bay Area counties or
   Hawaii. No grants to individuals. Please see flow-through funding chapter
   for application information.
Focus of giving: Limited to programs directly affecting residents of
   Alamada, Contra Costa, Marin, San Francisco, and San Mateo counties in
   California, and to residents of Hawaii.
$ given: $2.2 million for 131 grants; average range, $5,000–$25,000.
Assets: $45.6 million
Contact: Thomas C. Layton, Executive Director
Initial approach: Letter
Copies of proposal: 1
Deadlines: None
Board meeting dates: 4 times a year
Final notification: 2 months–3 months

The Luke B. Hancock Foundation
360 Bryant Street
Palo Alto, CA 94301
(415) 321-5536

Restrictions: Local giving primarily for job training and youth employment.
   Special project grants for consortia with other foundations in areas
   where there is unmet need; some support for technical assistance and
   emergency funding. No funding to individuals. Please see flow-through
   funding chapter for application information.
Focus of giving: Limited to California, particularly the six counties of the San
   Francisco Bay area.
$ given: $909,000 for 31 grants; range, $1,000–$30,000.
Assets: $22.7 million
Contact: Joan H. Wylie, Executive Director
Initial approach: Letter
Copies of proposal: 1
Deadlines: None
Board meeting dates: February, July, and October
Final notification: 3 months–4 months

The James Irvine Foundation
One Market Plaza
Spear Tower, Suite 1715
San Francisco, CA 94105
(415) 777-2244
Southern California office:
777 South Figueroa Street, Suite 740
Los Angeles, CA 90017-5430
(213) 236-0552

Restrictions: Program-related investments and other forms of support for community development, cultural programs, health issues, education, and social concerns.
Focus of giving: Limited to California.
$ given: $22.1 million for 463 grants; average range, $25,000–$150,000.
Assets: $608.9 million
Contact: Luz A. Vega, Director of Grants Program
Application information: No application form required
Initial approach: Letter or full proposal
Copies of proposal: 1
Deadlines: April 15 for universities; no other deadlines
Board meeting dates: March, June, September, October, and December
Final notification: 3 months–6 months

Peter Kiewit Foundation
900 Woodmen Tower
17th and Farnam Streets
Omaha, NE 68102
(402) 344-7890

See full entry under Nebraska.

Komes Foundation
1801 Van Nees Avenue, Suite 300
San Francisco, CA 94109
(415) 441-6462

Restrictions: Program-related investments and several other types of funding support for health services, education, cultural programs, welfare organizations, and legal/justice programs.
Focus of giving: Limited primarily to northern California.
$ given: $245,000 for 68 grants; average award, $2,400
Assets: $2.46 million
Contact: J.W. Komes, President
Application information: No application form required
Initial approach: Letter
Copies of proposal: 1
Deadlines: None

Abe and Frances Lastfogel Foundation
c/o Wallin, Simon, Black and Co.
1350 Avenue of the Americas
New York, NY 10019
(212) 586-5100

See full entry under New York.

Layne Foundation
29214 Whites Point Drive
Rancho Palos Verdes, CA 90274-4644
(213) 544-4700

Restrictions: Program-related investments and conventional loans for
   Christian religious organizations, usually for capital purposes.
Focus of giving: Limited to southern California.
$ given: $1.34 million for grants.
Assets: $8.16 million
Contact: Wesley M. Mason, President
Application information: Application form required
Initial approach: Letter
Copies of proposal: 1
Deadlines: None
Board meeting dates: February

Ludwick Family Foundation
145 North Grand Avenue
Glendora, CA 91740
Application address: P.O. Box 1796, Glendora, CA 91740

Restrictions: Seed money for intercultural relations, ecology, museums,
   education, libraries, child development, and cancer.
Focus of giving: California.
$ given: $105,700 for 7 grants.
Assets: $2 million
Application information: No application form required
Initial approach: Letter
Deadlines: Fall
Board meeting dates: Fall
Final notification: After board meeting

Marin Community Foundation
17 East Sir Francis Drake Boulevard, Suite 200
Larkspur, CA 94939
(415) 461-3333

Restrictions: Program-related investments and several other forms of
   funding support for programs in seven areas: (1) arts and humanities, (2)
   education, (3) environment, (4) housing and community development, (5)
   human needs, (6) religion, and (7) integrative approaches.

Focus of giving: Limited to Marin County, California.
$ given: $29.8 million for grants.
Assets: $548.9 million
Contact: Pamela Lynch, Corporate Secretary
Application information: Application form required
Initial approach: Written request for guidelines
Copies of proposal: 2
Deadlines: November 15 for environment, arts and humanities, and housing and community development; December 14 for education; January 15 for human needs; February 15 for religion
Board meeting dates: Monthly
Final notification: 3 months

The Maxfield Foundation
12930 Saratoga Avenue, Suite B3
Saratoga, CA 95070
(408) 253-0723

Restrictions: Support for cancer research, medical research, and for charitable activities. Grants for seed money, research, and special projects.
$ given: $249,500 for 11 grants.
Assets: $5.47 million
Contact: Robert Maxfield, President

Samuel B. Mosher Foundation
3278 Loma Riviera Drive
San Diego, CA 92110
(619) 226-6122

Restrictions: Program-related investments, building funding, and operating budget funding for educational programs; some funding for cultural and youth-oriented organizations.
Focus of giving: Limited primarily to Arizona and California.
$ given: $226,000 for 16 grants; average range, $10,000–$15,000.
Assets: $3.8 million
Contact: Robert R. Fredrickson, Secretary
Application information: No application form required
Initial approach: Full proposal
Copies of proposal: 1
Deadlines: None
Board meeting dates: Monthly

The David and Lucille Packard Foundation
300 Second Street, Suite 200
Los Altos, CA 94022
(415) 948-7658

Restrictions: Program-related investments and several other forms of funding-locally, for educational, cultural, and community development concerns; on a national and international basis, for conservation, population studies, film preservation, and ancient studies.

Focus of giving: Local funding in the San Francisco and Monterey Bay areas of California, with additional funding in the Pueblo area of Colorado; national funding has no geographic restrictions.

$ given: $29.2 million for 365 grants; average range, $5,000–$500,000.

Assets: $718.1 million

Contact: Colburn S. Wilbur, Executive Director

Application information: No application form required

Initial approach: Full proposal

Copies of proposal: 1

Deadlines: March 15, June 15, September 15, and December 15

Board meeting dates: March, June, September, and December

Final notification: Immediately following board meetings

The Parker Foundation

1200 Prospect Street, Suite 575
La Jolla, CA 92037
(619) 456-3038

Restrictions: Funding for cultural and health-related programs. Giving largely in the form of partial seed money and matching or challenging grants.

Focus of giving: Limited to San Diego County, California

$ given: $746,000 for 67 grants; average range, $5,000–$15,000

Assets: $14.3 million

Publications: Annual reports, informational brochure, and application guidelines

Contact: Robbin C. Powell, Assistant Secretary

Initial approach: Letter

Copies of proposal: 7

Deadlines: None

Board meeting dates: Monthly

Final notification: 2 months

The San Francisco Foundation

685 Market Street, Suite 910
San Francisco, CA 94105-9716
(415) 495-3100
(510) 436-3100

Restrictions: Grants awarded in the categories of the arts, health, education, environment, and urban affairs for operating budgets, seed money, program-related investments, special projects, loans, and technical assistance. No funding to individuals. Please see flow-through funding chapter for application information.

Focus of giving: Limited to the Bay Area, California, counties of Alameda, Contra Costa, Marin, San Francisco, and San Mateo.

$ given: $21.8 million for 1,659 grants; average range, $5,000–$50,000.

Assets: $248.5 million
Contact: Robert M. Fischer, Director
Application information: Application form required
Initial approach: Letter
Copies of proposal: 1
Deadlines: None
Board meeting dates: Monthly except August; applications reviewed 4–6 times each year
Final notification: 3 months–4 months

The Times Mirror Foundation

Times Mirror Square
Los Angeles, CA 90053
(213) 237-3945

Restrictions: Program-related investments and several other forms of funding for education, community service, civic organizations, health, and culture.
Focus of giving: Primarily to southern California.
$ given: $4.2 million for 168 grants; average range, $5,000–$200,000.
Assets: $10.9 million
Contact: Cassandra Malry, Treasurer
Application information: No application form required
Initial approach: 2–3 page letter
Copies of proposal: 1
Deadlines: April 1 and October 1
Board meeting dates: May and November
Final notification: June 30 or January 15

Union Pacific Foundation

Martin Tower
Eighth and Eaton Avenues
Bethlehem, PA 18018
(215) 861-3225

See full entry under Pennsylvania.

COLORADO

Animal Assistance Foundation

455 Sherman Street, Suite 462
Denver, CO 80203
(303) 744-8396

Restrictions: Grants for animal welfare, especially to prevent cruelty to cats and small household pets. Funds for research, building funds, and equipment.

Focus of giving: Limited to Colorado.
$ given: $2.4 million, including $613,276 for 24 grants.
Assets: $26.6 million
Contact: Erik S. Taylor, Executive Director
Application information: No application form required
Initial approach: Letter or telephone
Deadlines: None–applications considered May and November
Board meeting dates: Monthly
Final notification: Varies

The Chamberlain Foundation
P.O. Box 5003
Pueblo, CO 81002
(719) 543-8596

Restrictions: Support for museums, history, the arts, conservation, and
    education. Grants for operating budgets, equipment, and special projects.
Focus of giving: Pueblo County, Colorado.
$ given: $198,171 for 19 grants.
Assets: $5.2 million
Contact: David B. Shaw, Chairman
Application information: No application form required
Initial approach: Letter
Copies of proposal: 1
Deadlines: None
Board meeting dates: March, June, September, and December

Garvey Texas Foundation, Inc.
P.O. Box 9600
Fort Worth, TX 76147-0600

See full entry under Texas.

Gates Foundation
3200 Cherry Creek South Drive, Suite 630
Denver, CO 80209-3247
(303) 722-1881

Restrictions: Grants (primarily for education and youth services) for
    continuing support, building funds, capitol campaigns, endowment funds,
    matching funds, program-related investments, renovation projects, special
    projects, equipment, fellowships, general purposes, land acquisition, and
    publications.
Focus of giving: Limited to Colorado, especially the Denver area except for
    foundation-initiated grants.
$ given: $4.2 million for 131 grants; average range, $5,000–$25,000.
Assets: $110.2 million
Publications: Annual report, informational brochure (including application
    guidelines), program policy statement, and grants list

Contact: Thomas Stokes, Executive Director
Initial approach: Telephone
Copies of proposal: 1
Deadlines: January 15, April 1, July 15, and October 15
Board meeting dates: April 1, June 15, October 1, and December 15
Final notification: 2 weeks following meetings

Lowe Foundation
Colorado Judicial Center
Two East 14th Avenue
Denver, CO 80203
(303) 837-3750

Restrictions: Grants to organizations serving the mentally retarded and
   individuals with cerebral palsy for building funds, equipment, general
   purposes, operating budgets, program-related investments, and seed
   money.
Focus of giving: Limited primarily to Colorado.
$ given: $144,000 for 22 grants; average award, $6,000.
Assets: $3.7 million
Publications: 990-PF, annual report, and application guidelines
Contact: Justice Luis D. Rovira, President
Initial approach: Letter
Copies of proposal: 5
Deadlines: Submit proposal in January; deadline February 1
Board meeting dates: March and November

David and Lucille Packard Foundation
300 Second Street, Suite 200
Los Altos, CA 94022
(415) 948-7658

See full entry under California.

Phillips Petroleum Foundation, Inc.
16 C4 Phillips Building
Bartlesville, OK 74001
(918) 661-6248

See full entry under Oklahoma.

The Piton Foundation
Kittredge Building, Suite 700
511 16th Street
Denver, CO 80202
(303) 825-6246

Restrictions: Funding focuses on improving low-income neighborhoods by
   supporting affordable housing, children's health, education, and self-help

programs. Grants awarded for operating budgets, seed money, emergency funds, technical assistance, and program-related investments.
Focus of giving: Limited to the city of Denver, Colorado.
$ given: $677,000 for 64 grants; average range, $500–$30,000.
Assets: $3.6 million
Contact: Phyllis Buchele, Grants Administrator
Initial approach: Letter
Copies of proposal: 1
Deadlines: None
Board meeting dates: As required
Final notification: Approximately 4 months

Union Pacific Foundation
Martin Tower
Eighth and Eaton Avenues
Bethlehem, PA 18010
(215) 861-3225

See full entry under Pennsylvania.

CONNECTICUT

The Barnes Foundation, Inc.
P.O. Box 1560
Bristol, CT 06011-1560
(203) 583-7070

Restrictions: Program-related investments, seed money, and other forms of support for educational programs.
Focus of giving: Limited primarily to Connecticut.
$ given: $161,000 for 32 grants; average range, $5,000–$10,000.
Assets: $5.3 million
Contact: Carlyle F. Barnes, President, or Sally O'Connor, Executive Director
Application information: No application form required
Initial approach: Letter
Copies of proposal: 1
Deadlines: March 15 and October 15
Board meeting dates: January, May, September, and December
Final notification: May 31 and December 31

The Connecticut Mutual Life Foundation, Inc.
140 Garden Street
Hartford, CT 06154
(203) 727-6500

Restrictions: Largely for education, community development, housing, and

social purposes. Grants given for operating budgets, continuing support, seed money, matching funds, technical assistance, program-related investments, special projects, capital campaigning, and loans.
Focus of giving: Limited primarily to the Hartford, Connecticut, area.
$ given: $1.14 million for 139 grants; average range, $3,000–$6,000.
Assets: $8.66 million
Contact: Astrida R. Olds, Assistant Vice President
Initial approach: Letter or full proposal
Copies of proposal: 1
Deadlines: None
Board meeting dates: March and November
Final notification: 3 months

Dorr Foundation
P.O. Box 281
Bedford, NY 10506
(914) 234-3573
(212) 683-1370

See full entry under New York.

Joseph C. and Esther Foster Foundation, Inc.
1088 Park Avenue
New York, NY 10028

See full entry under New York.

GTE Foundation
One Stamford Forum
Stamford, CT 06904
(203) 965-3620

Restrictions: Program-related investments and several other types of support for educational programs, social service agencies, community funds, and the performing arts.
Focus of giving: Limited to areas of corporate operations.
$ given: $18 million for 1,468 grants.
Assets: $27 million
Contact: Maureen Gorman, Secretary and Director, Corporate Social Responsibility
Application information: No application form required
Initial approach: Letter or full proposal
Copies of proposal: 2
Deadlines: Fall
Board meeting dates: February, May, August, December, and as required
Final notification: After December 15

The Bulkley Foundation Trust

25 Forest Road
Weston, CT 06883-2307
(203) 227-8161

Restrictions: Support for welfare and family services, cancer and heart disease, community funds, homelessness and alcoholism. Funds for capital campaigns, building funds and annual campaigns.
Focus of giving: The greater Norwalk, Connecticut, area.
$ given: $139,561 for 25 grants.
Assets: $3.1 million
Contact: Kenneth M. Park, Trustee
Application information: No application form required
Copies of proposal: 1
Deadlines: Before November 1

Smart Family Foundation

15 Benders Drive
Greenwich, CT 06831
(203) 531-1474

Restrictions: Program-related investments, seed money, and research funding for education projects concerning primary and secondary school children.
Focus of giving: No geographic restrictions.
$ given: $2.3 million for 25 grants; average range, $10,000–$120,000.
Assets: $49.2 million
Contact: Raymond Smart, President
Application information: No application form required
Initial approach: Letter or full proposal
Copies of proposal: 1
Deadlines: 90 days before board meetings
Board meeting dates: Fall and spring
Final notification: 6 weeks after board meetings

The Sonat Foundation, Inc.

1900 Fifth Avenue, North
P.O. Box 2563
Birmingham, AL 35202
(205) 325-7460

See full entry under Alabama.

The John L. Weinberg Foundation

c/o Goldman Sachs & Co.
Tax Department
85 Broad Street, 22nd Floor
New York, NY 10004

See full entry under New York.

The Xerox Foundation
P.O. Box 1600
Stamford, CT 06904
(203) 968-3306

Restrictions: Program-related investments and several other types of funding for science and technology, higher education, social, civic, and cultural organizations, the encouragement of public policy debates, and social responsibility.
Focus of giving: Limited primarily to areas of corporate operations.
$ given: $14.7 million for 1,526 grants; average range, $2,000–$20,000.
Assets: $777,500
Contact: Robert H. Gudger, Vice President
Application information: No application form required
Initial approach: Brief proposal
Copies of proposal: 1
Deadlines: None
Board meeting dates: December, and as needed
Final notification: 3 months

DELAWARE

Crystall Trust
1088 DuPont Building
Wilmington, DE 19898
(302) 744-8421

Restrictions: Funding for higher education and social/family services, as well as cultural programs. Grants awarded for seed money, building funds, equipment, land acquisition, special projects, and program-related investments.
Focus of giving: Limited primarily to Delaware, especially in Wilmington.
$ given: $3.1 million for 48 grants; average range, $10,000–$100,000.
Assets: $66.1 million
Contact: Stephen C. Doberstein, Director
Initial approach: proposal
Copies of proposal: 1
Deadline: October 1
Board meeting date: November
Final notification: December 31

Jack Eckerd Corporation Foundation
P.O. Box 4689
Clearwater, FL 34618
(813) 398-8318

See full entry under Florida.

Marpat Foundation, Inc.
c/o Miller & Chevalier
655 15th Street, N.W., Suite 900
Washington, DC 20005
(202) 626-5832

See full entry under District of Columbia.

Raskob Foundation for Catholic Activities, Inc.
P.O. Box 4019
Wilmington, DE 19807
(302) 655-4440

Restrictions: Funding for Roman Catholic Church activities worldwide. Grants
for operating budgets, seed money, emergency funds, equipment, land
acquisition, matching funds, conferences and seminars, program-related
investments, renovation projects, and special projects. No grants to
individuals. Please see flow-through funding chapter for application
information.
$ given: $3.6 million for 620 grants; average range, $5,000–$10,000.
Assets: $93.7 million
Publications: Biennial report (including application guidelines)
Contact: Gerard S. Garey, President
Application information: Application form required
Initial approach: Letter
Copies of proposal: 1
Deadlines: Applications accepted for spring meeting from December 15 to
February 15; applications accepted for fall meeting from June 15 to
August 15
Board meeting dates: Spring and fall
Final notification: 6 months

DISTRICT OF COLUMBIA

The Coleman Foundation, Inc.
575 West Madison, Suite 4605-11
Chicago, IL 60661
(312) 902-7120

See full entry under Illinois.

Cooperative Assistance Fund
2100 M Street, NW, Suite 306
Washington, DC 20037
(202) 833-8543

Restrictions: Program-related investments and conventional loans to
finance community-based enterprises that will generate jobs, ownership,

capital accumulation, and other socioeconomic benefits for low-income groups and minorities.
Focus of giving: No geographical restrictions.
$ given: $250,000 for foundation-administered programs.
Assets: $4.8 million
Contact: David C. Rice, Executive Vice President
Application information: No application form required
Initial approach: Business plan with analysis of company
Copies of proposal: 1
Deadlines: None
Board meeting dates: Quarterly

The Hitachi Foundation
1509 22nd Street, N.W.
Washington, DC 20037
(202) 457-0588

Restrictions: Funding for community/economics development, arts, education, and technology. Grants for general purposes, program-related investments, seed money, special projects, and technical assistance.
$ given: $1.4 million for 92 grants; average, $5,000–$30,000.
Assets: $25.6 million
Publications: Annual report (including application guidelines), program policy statement, and newsletter
Contact: Felicia B. Lynch, Vice President, Programs
Initial approach: Letter
Deadlines: February 1, June 1, and October 1
Board meeting dates: March, July, and October

Marpat Foundation, Inc.
c/o Miller & Chevalier
655 15th Street, N.W., Suite 900
Washington, DC 20005
(202) 626-5832

Restrictions: Program-related investments and other types of support for established charitable organizations, including those which promote health care and family planning, those which conduct research projects, those which preserve natural resources, and those which encourage volunteer participation.
Focus of giving: Limited primarily to the mid-Atlantic region.
$ given: $754,000 for 59 grants; range, $3,000–$50,000.
Assets: $12.3 million
Contact: Marvin Breckinridge Patterson, President
Application information: Application form required
Initial approach: Letter or full proposal
Copies of proposal: 3
Deadline: October 1
Board meeting dates: November
Final notification: After December 15

MCI Foundation
1133 19th Street, N.W.
Washington, DC 20036
(202) 887-2175

Restrictions: Program-related investments and scholarship funds for
   organizations (usually nonprofit) providing job-related training or educa-
   tion, including those offering opportunities to the disadvantaged.
Focus of giving: No geographical restrictions.
$ given: $1.85 million for 350 grants; average range, $5,000–$25,000.
Assets: $6.9 million
Contact: Dorothy Olley
Application information: No application form required
Initial approach: Full proposal
Copies of proposal: 1
Deadlines: None

FLORIDA

Mary Reynolds Babcock Foundation, Inc.
102 Reynolda Village
Winston-Salem, NC 27106-5123
(919) 748-9222

See full entry under North Carolina.

BellSouth Foundation
c/o BellSouth Corporation
1155 Peachtree Street, N.E., Room 7H08
Atlanta, GA 30367-6000
(404) 249-2396
(404) 249-2429
(404) 249-2428

See full entry under Georgia.

Edyth Bush Charitable Foundation, Inc.
199 East Melbourne Avenue
P.O. Box 1967
Winter Park, FL 32790-1967
(407) 647-4322

Restrictions: Funding for charitable, educational, and health service
   organizations, with emphasis on human services, health, higher education, the elderly, and youth. Provides limited number of program-related

investment loans for construction, land purchase, emergency, or similar purposes to organizations otherwise qualified to receive grants.
Focus of giving: Primarily to local areas within 100 miles of Winter Park, Florida.
$ given: $1.6 million for 47 grants; average range, $20,000–$70,000.
Assets: $51.6 million
Publications: 990-PF, program policy statement, application guidelines, financial statement, and grants list
Contact: H. Clifford Lee, President
Initial approach: Letter
Copies of proposal: 2
Deadlines: September 1 or December 31
Board meeting dates: April, November, and as required
Final notification: 2 weeks after board meeting

CBS Foundation, Inc.
51 West 52nd Street
New York, NY 10019
(212) 975-5791

See full entry under New York.

The Coleman Foundation, Inc.
575 West Madison, Suite 4605-11
Chicago, IL 60661
(312) 902-7120

See full entry under Illinois.

Jack Eckerd Corporation Foundation
P.O. Box 4689
Clearwater, FL 34618
(813) 398-8318

Restrictions: Program-related investments and several other types of support for higher education and health services.
Focus of giving: Limited primarily to areas of corporate operations, including Alabama, Delaware, Florida, Georgia, Louisiana, Mississippi, New Jersey, North Carolina, Oklahoma, South Carolina, Tennessee, and Texas.
$ given: $516,500 for grants.
Assets: $9.41 million
Contact: Michael Zagorac, Jr., Chairman
Application information: No application form required
Initial approach: Letter
Copies of proposal: 1
Deadlines: None
Board meeting dates: Quarterly
Final notification: 4 months–6 months

Grable Foundation
650 Smithfield Street, Suite 240
Pittsburgh, PA 15222
(412) 471-4550

See full entry under Pennsylvania.

James G. Hanes Memorial Fund/Foundation
c/o NationsBank
One NCNB Plaza, TO9-1
Charlotte, NC 28255
(704) 386-8477

See full entry under North Carolina.

Jacksonville Community Foundation
112 West Adams Street, No. 1414
Jacksonville, FL 32202
(904) 356-4483

Restrictions: Program-related investments and other forms of support for
   general charitable giving.
Focus of giving: Limited primarily to northeastern Florida.
$ given: $2.5 million for 755 grants; average range, $100–$20,000.
Assets: $10 million
Contact: L. Andrew Bell III, President
Application information: No application form required
Initial approach: Letter
Copies of proposal: 1
Deadlines: March 1, June 1, September 1, and December 1
Board meeting dates: February, May, August, and November
Final notification: February, May, August, and November

Knight Foundation
One Biscayne Tower, Suite 3800
Two South Biscayne Boulevard
Miami, FL 33131-1803
(305) 539-0009

Restrictions: Program-related investments and other forms of support
   provided through the Education Program and the Cities Program. The
   latter funds a broad spectrum of socioeconomic, cultural, and civic
   organizations in 26 specific communities.
Focus of giving: Cities Program funding is limited to the 26 communities
   where John S. and James L. Knight were involved in newspaper publishing. Education Program funding is limited to small, private liberal-arts
   colleges in the 16 states where the Knights published newspapers.
$ given: $25.1 million for 439 grants; average range, $5,000–$100,000.
Assets: $605 million

Contact: Lee Hills, Chairperson
Application information: No application form required
Initial approach: Letter
Copies of proposal: 2
Deadlines: January 1, April 1, July 1, and October 1
Board meeting dates: March, June, September, and December
Final notification: 2 weeks after board meetings

The McIntosh Foundation
215 Fifth Street, Suite 100
West Palm Beach, FL 33401
(407) 832-8845

Restrictions: Program-related investments and general-purpose funding to support environmental lawsuits brought by public interest groups; additional funding for education.
Focus of giving: No geographic restrictions.
$ given: $1.45 million for 58 grants; range, $400–$278,300.
Assets: $28.3 million
Contact: Michael A. McIntosh, President
Application information: No application form required
Initial approach: Letter or full proposal
Copies of proposal: 1
Deadlines: None
Board meeting dates: Bimonthly
Final notification: 60 days–90 days

Meyer Family Foundation
(formerly The Meyer-Ceco Foundation)
P.O. Box 3098
Oakbrook, IL 60522-3098

See full entry under Illinois.

The Dr. P. Phillips Foundation
60 West Robinson Street
P.O. Box 3753
Orlando, FL 32802
(407) 422-6105

Restrictions: Program-related investments and other forms of support for community development, education, and youth/elderly welfare.
Focus of giving: Limited to Orange County, Florida, and the central Florida area.
$ given: $535,000 for 51 grants; range, $50–$115,000.
Assets: $25.9 million
Contact: J.A. Hinson, President
Application information: No application form required
Initial approach: Letter

Copies of proposal: 1
Deadlines: None
Board meeting dates: Semiannually
Final notification: Varies

The South Atlantic Foundation, Inc.
428 Bull Street
Savannah, GA 31401
(912) 238-3288

See full entry under Georgia.

The Wilder Foundation
P.O. Box 99
Key Biscayne, FL 33149

Restrictions: Cultural and educational support funding. Supports general
  purposes, building funds, endowment funds, research, scholarship funds,
  and matching funds.
Focus of giving: Limited primarily to Florida.
$ given: $97,700 for 8 grants; range, $25–$87,000.
Assets: $2.6 million
Contact: Rita or Gary Wilder, President and Vice President
Initial approach: Proposal
Copies of proposal: 1
Deadline: Before September 1st
Board meeting dates: Monthly

GEORGIA

Mary Reynolds Babcock Foundation, Inc.
102 Reynolda Village
Winston-Salem, NC 27106-5123
(919) 748-9222

See full entry under North Carolina.

BellSouth Foundation
c/o BellSouth Corporation
1155 Peachtree Street, N.E., Room 7H08
Atlanta, GA 30367-6000
(404) 249-2396
(404) 249-2429
(404) 249-2428

Restrictions: Program-related investments and seed money for broad-impact educational programs, including programs to recruit and retain faculty and programs for telecommunications research.

Focus of giving: Giving primarily to areas of corporate operations including Alabama, Florida, Georgia, Kentucky, Louisiana, Mississippi, North Carolina, South Carolina, and Tennessee.

$ given: $2.89 million for grants; average range, $6,000–$30,000.

Assets: $39.7 million

Contact: Leslie J. Graitcer, Associate Director, or Wendy L.K. Best, Grants Manager

Application information: No application form required

Initial approach: Brief letter

Copies of proposal: 1

Deadlines: February 1 and August 1

Final notification: April and September

The Coca-Cola Foundation, Inc.

One Coca-Cola Plaza, N.W.
Atlanta, GA 30313
(404) 676-2680
Application address: P.O. Drawer 1734, Atlanta, Georgia 30301

Restrictions: Grants for education, in the forms of annual campaigns, scholarship funds, special projects, endowment funds, and capital campaigns.

$ given: $6.14 million for 164 grants; average range, $10,000–$100,000.

Assets: $15.2 million

Publications: Annual report, application guidelines, and informational brochure

Contact: Donald R. Greene, President

Initial approach: 2-page proposal

Board meeting dates: February, May, July, and November

Final notification: 4 months

Jack Eckerd Corporation Foundation

P.O. Box 4689
Clearwater, FL 34618
(813) 398-8318

See full entry under Florida.

James G. Hanes Memorial Fund/Foundation

c/o NationsBank
One NCNB Plaza, T09-1
Charlotte, NC 28255
(704) 386-8477

See full entry under North Carolina.

The Ray M. and Mary Elizabeth Lee Foundation, Inc.
c/o NationsBank, Trust Department
P.O. Box 4446
Atlanta, GA 30302-4899
(404) 607-4530

Restrictions: Program-related investments and several other forms of
   support for health services, education, cultural programs, and religion.
Focus of giving: Limited to Atlanta, Georgia.
$ given: $429,000 for 67 grants; average award, $6,000.
Assets: $10 million
Contact: Larry B. Hooks, Administrative Manager
Application information: No application form required
Initial approach: Full proposal
Copies of proposal: 1
Deadlines: January 31, April 30, July 31, and October 31
Board meeting dates: February, May, August, and November
Final notification: After board meetings

Metropolitan Atlanta Community Foundation, Inc.
The Hurt Building, Suite 449
Atlanta, GA 30303
(404) 688-5525

Restrictions: Support for social services, arts and culture, education, health,
   and civic causes. Grants for seed money, emergency funds, building
   funds, equipment, land acquisition, technical assistance, program-related
   investments, special projects, publications, capital campaigns, matching
   funds, and renovation projects.
Focus of giving: Limited to Atlanta, Georgia, area.
$ given: $9.4 million for 490 grants; average range, $1,000–$20,000.
Assets: $91.2 million
Publications: Annual report, program policy statement, application guide-
   lines, newsletter, and informational brochure
Contact: Winsome Hawkins, Program Officer
Application information: Application form required
Initial approach: Letter or telephone
Copies of proposal: 1
Deadlines: March 15, July 15, and November 15
Board meeting dates: January, May, and September
Final notification: 6 weeks

Meyer Family Foundation
(formerly The Meyer-Ceco Foundation)
P.O. Box 3098
Oakbrook, IL 60522-3098

See full entry under Illinois.

Norton Company Foundation
New Bond Street
P.O. Box 15008
Worcester, MA 01615-0008
(508) 795-4700

See full entry under Massachusetts.

The South Atlantic Foundation, Inc.
428 Bull Street
Savannah, GA 31401
(912) 238-3288

Restrictions: Program-related investments and several other types of funding for social services, health services, education, and cultural programs.
Focus of giving: Limited primarily to Florida, Georgia, and South Carolina.
$ given: $257,000 for 105 grants.
Assets: $2.38 million
Contact: William W. Byram, Jr., Executive Director
Application information: Application form required
Initial approach: Telephone
Copies of proposal: 1
Deadlines: Before end of each quarter
Board meeting dates: January, April, July, and October

HAWAII

Wallace Alexander Gerbode Foundation
470 Columbus Avenue, Suite 209
San Francisco, CA 94133
(415) 391-0911

See full entry under California.

IDAHO

Northwest Area Foundation
E-1201 First National Bank Building
332 Minnesota Street
St. Paul, MN 55101-1373
(612) 224-9635
FAX: (612) 225-3881

See full entry under Minnesota.

Union Pacific Foundation
Martin Tower
Eighth and Eaton Avenues
Bethlehem, PA 18018
(215) 861-3225

See full entry under Pennsylvania.

ILLINOIS

The Allstate Foundation
Allstate Plaza North
Northbrook, IL 60062
(708) 402-5502

Restrictions: Program-related investments and special project funding for
    organizations encouraging self-help and self-motivation; and for support
    in the fields of education, urban/civic affairs, and health and welfare.
Focus of giving: No geographic limitations.
$ given: $5.7 million for 1673 grants; average range; $5,000–$25,000.
Assets: $2.92 million
Contact: Alan Benedict, Executive Director, Allen Goldhamer, Manager, or
    Dawn Bourgart, Administrative Assistant.
Application information: No application form required
Initial approach: Proposal
Copies of proposal: 1
Deadlines: None
Board meeting dates: March, June, September, and December
Final notification: 30 days–90 days

CBS Foundation, Inc.
51 West 52nd Street
New York, NY 10019
(212) 975-5791

See full entry under New York.

The Chicago Community Trust
22 North LaSalle Street, Suite 1400
Chicago, IL 60601
(312) 372-3356

Restrictions: Program-related investments and several other general and
    project-specific forms of support for health, social services, education,
    civic affairs, and community service.
Focus of giving: Limited primarily to Cook County, Illinois.
$ given: $31.2 million for 622 grants; average range, $10,000–$50,000.

Assets: $339 million
Contact: Ms. Sandy Cheers, Assistant to the Director
Application information: Application form required
Initial approach: Proposal
Copies of proposal: 2
Deadlines: None
Board meeting dates: January, March, June, and September
Final notification: 4 months–6 months

The Coleman Foundation, Inc.
575 West Madison, Suite 4605-11
Chicago, IL 60661
(312) 902-7120

Restrictions: Program-related investments and several other forms of funding for social services and civic concerns, education (including entrepreneurial education), medical research, and programs for the handicapped.
Focus of giving: Primarily limited to metropolitan Chicago area; additional funding to the District of Columbia, Florida, Indiana, Michigan, Minnesota, Missouri, Pennsylvania, and Wisconsin.
$ given: $ 1.5 million for 62 grants; average range, $1,000–$200,000.
Assets: $76 million
Contact: Jean D. Thorne, Executive Director
Application information: No application form required
Initial approach: Brief letter describing program
Copies of proposal: 1
Deadlines: September 30 for solicited proposals
Board meeting dates: January, April, July, and October
Final notification: 3 months for solicited proposals only

Community Foundation of Champaign County
c/o Bank of Illinois in Champaign
100 West University Avenue, P.O. Box 826
Champaign, IL 61824-0826
(217) 351-6607

Restrictions: Building funds, renovation projects, program-related investments, student aid, consulting services and other types of support for social services, education, health services, civic affairs, and the arts and humanities.
Focus of giving: Limited primarily to Champaign, Illinois.
$ given: $107,000 for 35 grants.
Assets: $2 million
Contact: Betty J. Zeedyk, Account Officer
Application information: Application form required
Copies of proposal: 1
Deadlines: February 1
Board meeting dates: February 15
Final notification: March 1

Doris & Victor Day Foundation, Inc.
1705 Second Avenue, Suite 424
Rock Island, IL 61201
(309) 788-2300

Restrictions: Program-related investments and general purpose/capital
   funding for housing, social services, health associations, child welfare, and
   community funds.
Focus of giving: Limited to Quad city area of Rock County, Illinois, and Scott
   County, Iowa.
$ given: $657,780 for 84 grants; average range, $1,000–$25,000.
Assets: $12 million
Contact: Alan Egly, Executive Director
Application information: Application form required
Initial approach: Letter or telephone
Copies of proposal: 1
Deadlines: May 1
Final notification: September

The Field Foundation of Illinois, Inc.
135 South LaSalle Street, Suite 1250
Chicago, IL 60603
(312) 253-3211

Restrictions: Funding for health, welfare, education, cultural activities, and
   civic affairs. Grants focused on youth agencies, race relations, and the
   aged. Support for emergency funds, building funds, equipment, land
   acquisition, technical assistance, and special projects.
Focus of giving: Limited primarily to the Chicago, Illinois area.
$ given: $1.65 million for 66 grants; average range, $10,000–$20,000.
Assets: $28.8 million
Contact: Handy L. Lindsey, Jr., Executive Director
Initial approach: Proposal
Deadlines: None
Board meeting dates: 3 times a year

Hedberg Foundation
P.O. Box 1422
Janesville, WI 53547
(708) 295-7212

See full entry under Wisconsin.

Robert R. McCormick Tribune Foundation
435 North Michigan Avenue, Suite 770
Chicago, IL 60611
(312) 222-3510

Restrictions: Program-related investments and other general-purpose and special-project funding for education, health services and research, cultural programs, conservation and human services.

Focus of giving: Limited primarily to the metropolitan Chicago area.
$ given: $24 million for 549 grants; average range, $2,500–$100,000.
Assets: $550.6 million
Contact: Nicholas Goodban, V.P. of Philanthropy
Application information: No application form required
Initial approach: Letter
Copies of proposal: 1
Deadlines: February 1, May 1, August 1, and November 1
Board meeting dates: March, June, September, and December
Final notification: 2 weeks

Meyer Family Foundation
(formerly Meyer-Ceco Foundation)
P.O. Box 3098
Oakbrook, IL 60522-3098

Restrictions: Continuing support and program-related investments for health, education, civic purpose, religion, the arts, hospitals.
Focus of giving: Limited primarily to Chicago, Illinois; Pinehurst, North Carolina; St. Augustine, Florida.
$ given: $235,265 for 97 grants; average range, $500–$1,000.
Assets: $5.2 million
Contact: Cheryl A. McRoberts, Administrator
Initial approach: Letter or proposal
Deadlines: April 15, July 15, October 15, and December 15
Board meeting dates: 4 times a year

Audrey & Jack Miller Family Charitable Foundation
Seven Bristol Court.
Lincolnshire, IL 60069
Application address: 100 Shelter Road, Lincolnshire, IL, 60069
(708) 634-5711

Restrictions: Funds for Jewish welfare, medical research, the arts, and health associations.
Focus of giving: Illinois.
$ given: $89,602 for 41 grants.
Assets: $2.3 million
Contact: Jack Miller, President
Application information: No application form required
Initial approach: Letter
Deadlines: None

Retirement Research Foundation
8765 West Higgins Road, Suite 401
Chicago, IL 60631
(312) 714-8080
FAX: (312) 714-8089

Restrictions: Program-related investments and several other types of support to improve the quality of life of older persons. Funding for model projects and research concerned with (1) community programs featuring independent living environments, (2) improved nursing home care, (3) volunteer/employment opportunities for the elderly, and (4) solutions to problems associated with aging.
Focus of giving: Limited primarily to the Midwest, including Florida, Illinois, Indiana, Iowa, Kentucky, Michigan, Missouri, and Wisconsin.
$ given: $5.5 million.
Assets: $136 million
Contact: Marilyn Hennessy, Senior Vice President
Application information: No application form required
Initial approach: Letter or proposal
Copies of proposal: 3
Deadlines: Submit January, April, and July
Board meeting dates: February, May, August, and October
Final notification: 4 months–6 months

Union Pacific Foundation
Martin Tower
Eighth and Eaton Avenues
Bethlehem, PA 18018
(215) 861-3225

See full entry under Pennsylvania.

The Wieboldt Foundation
53 West Jackson Boulevard, Room 838
Chicago, IL 60604
(312) 786-9377
FAX: (312) 786-9232

Restrictions: Program-related investments and general purpose funding for community development and urban affairs; priority to multi-issue community organizations working in low-income neighborhoods and encouraging active, vocal participation of local residents. Additional funding to organizations that support such local concerns with training, technical assistance, advocacy, and policy development.
Focus of giving: Limited to metropolitan Chicago and to urban areas of Indiana.
$ given: $590,000 for 76 grants; average award, $7,500.
Contact: Anne C. Hallett, Executive Director
Application information: No application form required
Initial approach: Proposal
Copies of proposal: 1
Deadlines: End of each month (except February, June, and October)
Board meeting dates: Monthly (except April, August, and December)
Final notification: 2 months after receipt

INDIANA

Olive B. Cole Foundation, Inc.
3242 Mallard Cove Lane
Fort Wayne, IN 46804
(212) 436-2182

Restrictions: Support for education, youth agencies, cultural programs, and health. Grants given for seed money, building funds, equipment, land acquisition, matching funds, program-related investments, general purposes, and continuing support.
Focus of giving: Limited to Noble, DeKalb, LaGrange, and Steuben Counties, Indiana.
$ given: $518,000 for 40 grants: average range, $500–$700.
Assets: $19 million
Contact: John E. Hogan, Jr., Executive Vice President
Application information: Application form required
Initial approach: Letter
Copies of proposal: 7
Deadlines: None
Board meeting dates: February, May, August, and November
Final notification: 4 months

The Coleman Foundation, Inc.
575 W. Madison, Suite 4605-11
Chicago, IL 60661
(312) 902-7120

See full entry under Illinois.

Cummins Engine Foundation
500 Jackson Street
Columbus, IN 47201
(812) 377-3114
Mailing Address: Box 3005, MC 60814, Columbus, IN, 47202-3005

Restrictions: Funding primarily for local community needs, youth, civil rights; grants also for national needs that combine equal opportunity and excellence. Support for seed money, emergency funds, special projects, annual campaigns, etc.
Focus of giving: Limited to areas of company operations, particularly the Columbus, Indiana, area.
$ given: $2.54 million for 215 grants; average range, $1,000–$10,000.
Assets: $4 million
Contact: Adele J. Vincent, Associate Director
Initial approach: Letter or proposal
Copies of proposal: 1
Deadlines: None
Board meeting dates: Vary; 3–4 meetings a year
Final notification: 1 months–3 months

Foellinger Foundation, Inc.
520 East Berry Street
Fort Wayne, IN 46802
(219) 422-2900

Restrictions: Operating budgets, building funds, equipment, land acquisition, seed money, and other types of support for cultural organizations, higher education, parks and recreation, social services, youth and the disadvantaged, health, AIDS research, and drug and alcoholism programs.
Focus of giving: Limited to Fort Wayne, Indiana.
$ given: $5.2 million for 210 grants; average range, $10,000–$200,000.
Assets: $116 million
Contact: Harry V. Owen, President
Application information: No application form required
Initial approach: Letter or proposal
Copies of proposal: 1
Deadlines: 90 days before funds needed
Board meeting dates: 3rd Tuesday of month
Final notification: Varies according to request

The Indianapolis Foundation
615 North Alabama Street, Room 119
Indianapolis, IN 46204
(317) 634-7497

Restrictions: Program-related investments and other types of support for research and community planning, education, health and welfare, family and neighborhood services, and civic and cultural programs.
Focus of giving: Limited to Indianapolis and to Marion County, Indiana.
$ given: $3.3 million for 94 grants; average range, $10,000–$50,000.
Assets: $89 million
Contact: Kenneth I. Chapman, Executive Director
Application information: No application form required
Initial approach: Letter or telephone
Copies of proposal: 7
Deadlines: Last day of January, March, May, July, September, and November
Board meeting dates: February, April, June, August, October, and December
Final notification: After board meetings

Irwin-Sweeney-Miller Foundation
420 Third Street
Columbus, IN 47202-0808
(812) 372-0251

Restrictions: Program-related investments and several other types of support for creative programs in social justice, education, the arts, social services, community development, and religion.
Focus of giving: Limited primarily to Columbus, Indiana.
$ given: $705,700 for 53 grants; average range, $500–$5,000.
Assets: $1.63 million

Contact: Sarla Kalsi, Executive Director
Application information: No application form required
Initial approach: Letter and proposal
Copies of proposal: 1
Deadlines: March 1 and September 1
Board meeting dates: April and October
Final notification: 1 month

Journal Gazette Foundation, Inc.

701 South Clinton Street
Fort Wayne, IN 46802
(219) 461-8202

Restrictions: Program-related investments and capital campaign funding for social services, health associations, cultural programs, education, and religion.
Focus of giving: Limited to northeastern Indiana.
$ given: $452,862 for 96 grants; range, $50–$79,700.
Assets: $3.38 million
Contact: Richard G. Inskeep, President
Application information: Application form required
Deadlines: None

Arthur Jordan Foundation

1230 North Delaware Street
Indianapolis, IN 46202
(317) 635-1378

Restrictions: Capital campaigns, operating budgets, building funds, and continuing support for higher education and fine arts.
Focus of giving: Marion County, Indiana.
$ given: $493,000 for 28 grants.
Assets: $11.4 million
Contact: Margaret F. Sallee, Administrative Assistant
Application information: No application form required
Initial approach: Letter
Copies of proposal: 3
Deadlines: May 1 and January 1– submissions April and December
Board meeting dates: May and January
Final notification: 30 days

Lily Endowment, Inc.

2801 North Meridian Street
Indianapolis, IN 46208
(317) 924-5471

Restrictions: Funds for community development projects, higher education, religion, programs that benefit youth, the arts, social services, historic preservation, and public policy. Grants for seed money, technical assis-

tance, scholarships and student aid, general purpose and other types of funding.
Focus of giving: Limited primarily to Indiana, especially Indianapolis.
$ given: $117.4 million for 1856 grants; $725,206 for 91 grants to individuals; $750,000 for 3 program-related investments.
Assets: $2.6 billion
Contact: Gretchen Wolfram, Communications Director
Application information: No application form required
Initial approach: 1–2 page letter
Copies of proposal: 1
Deadlines: None
Board meeting dates: February, April, June, September, and November
Final notification: 3 months–6 months

Retirement Research Foundation
8765 West Higgins Road, Suite 401
Chicago, IL 60631
(312) 714-8080
FAX: (312) 714-8089

See full entry under Illinois.

Wieboldt Foundation
53 West Jackson Boulevard, Room 838
Chicago, IL 60604
(312) 786-9377
FAX: (312) 786-9232

See full entry under Illinois.

IOWA

Doris and Victor Day Foundation, Inc.
1705 Second Avenue, Suite 424
Rock Island, IL 61201
(309) 788-2300

See full entry under Illinois.

The Ralph and Sylvia G. Green Charitable Foundation
601 Locust Street, Suite 933
Des Moines, IA 50309
(515) 245-3766

Restrictions: Support for child development, education, minorities, women, the arts, child welfare, and the disadvantaged. Funds for conferences and seminars, program-related investments, seed money, emergency funds, equipment, renovations projects.

Focus of giving: Limited primarily to Des Moines, Iowa, area.
$ given: $200,000 for 20 grants.
Assets: $5 million
Publications: Program policy statement, informational brochure
Contact: Monroe J. Colston, President
Application information: Application form required
Initial approach: Proposal
Copies of proposal: 1
Deadlines: 60 days prior to board meeting
Board meeting dates: Quarterly

The Hall Foundation, Inc.

115 Third Street, No. 803
Cedar Rapids, IA 52401
(319) 362-9079

Restrictions: Grants for seed money, emergency funds, building funds, equipment, land acquisition, and special projects for the arts, social services, community funds, youth agencies, and health services.
Focus of giving: Limited to Cedar Rapids, Iowa, and immediate trade area only.
$ given: $3.2 million for 44 grants; average, $10,000–$100,000.
Assets: $51.4 million
Contact: John G. Lidvall, Executive Director
Application information: No application form required
Initial approach: Letter
Copies of proposal: 1
Deadlines: None
Board meeting dates: Quarterly
Final notification: 3 months

Peter Kiewit Foundation

Goodman Tower, Suite 900
17th and Farnam Streets
Omaha, NE 68102

See full entry under Nebraska.

Northwest Area Foundation

E-1201 First National Bank Building
332 Minnesota Street
St. Paul, MN 55101-1373
(612) 224-9635
FAX: (612) 225-3881

See full entry under Minnesota.

Retirement Research Foundation
8765 West Higgins Road, Suite 401
Chicago, IL 60631
(312) 714-8080
FAX: (312) 714-8089

See full entry under Illinois.

KANSAS

Beech Aircraft Foundation
9709 East Central Avenue
Wichita, KS 67201
(316) 681-8177

Restrictions: Program-related investments and several other types of support for education, community funds, conservation, cultural activities, health services, the handicapped, the aged, and youth agencies.
Focus of giving: Limited primarily to corporate locations, with emphasis on Kansas.
$ given: $493,390 for 101 grants.
Assets: $6 million
Contact: Larry E. Lawrence, Secretary-Treasurer
Application information: No application form required
Initial approach: Letter
Copies of proposal: 1
Deadlines: March, June, September, and December
Board meeting dates: January, April, July, and October

Garvey Texas Foundation, Inc.
P.O. Box 9600
Fort Worth, TX 76147-0600

See full entry under Texas.

Hall Family Foundations
Charitable & Crown Investment—323
P.O. Box 419580
Kansas City, MO 64141-6580
(816) 274-8516

See full entry under Missouri.

Pearl M. and Julia J. Harmon Foundation
P.O. Box 52568
Tulsa, OK 74152-0568
(918) 743-6191

See full entry under Oklahoma.

De Vore Foundation, Inc.

P.O. Box 118
Wichita, KS 67201
(316) 267-3211

Restrictions: Grants for youth, Protestant giving, arts and cultural programs, higher education, health, social services, and community funds. Money for building funds, capital campaigns, endowment funds, equipment, general purposes, operating budgets, seed money, and continuing support.
Focus of giving: Limited primarily to Wichita, Kansas, area.
$ given: $124,133 for 77 grants.
Assets: $3.03 million
Contact: Richard A. De Vore, President
Application information: No application form required
Initial approach: Letter
Copies of proposal: 1
Deadlines: None

David H. Koch Charitable Foundation

4111 E. 37th St. North
Wichita, KS 67220
(316) 832-5222

Restrictions: Grants for seed money, building funds, annual campaigns, scholarship funds, operating budgets, general purposes, and continuing support. Focus on the arts, education, cultural programs, and economics.
Focus of giving: No geographical restrictions.
$ given: $6.23 million for 44 grants; average, $10,000–$100,000.
Assets: $8.79 million
Contact: Ruth E. Williams
Application information: No application form required
Initial approach: Proposal
Deadlines: None
Board meeting dates: As necessary
Final notification: Varies

The Powell Family Foundation

10990 Roe Avenue
P.O. Box 7270
Shawnee Mission, KS 66207
(913) 345-3000

Restrictions: Support for education, youth agencies, religion and civic concerns. Grants given for program-related investments, operating budgets, emergency funds, equipment, matching funds, special projects, general purposes, and conferences and seminars.
Focus of giving: Limited to Kansas City, Kansas, and the surrounding community.

$ given: $2.27 million for grants.
Assets: $51 million
Publications: Biennial report, application guidelines
Contact: Marjorie P. Allen, President
Initial approach: Proposal of 3 pages–5 pages
Copies of proposal: 2
Deadlines: 30 days prior to board meetings
Board meeting dates: February and October
Final notification: 60 days

Security Benefit Life Insurance Company Charitable Trust

c/o Security Benefit Trust Co.
700 S.W. Harrison Street
Topeka, KS 66636
(913) 295-3000

Restrictions: Program-related investments and several other types of support for arts groups, health, social services, education, youth and women, and the homeless and disadvantaged.
Focus of giving: Limited to the Topeka, Kansas, area.
$ given: $254,460 for 100 grants.
Assets: $519,077
Contact: Howard R. Fricke, Trustee
Application information: No application form required
Initial approach: Letter
Deadlines: None

Union Pacific Foundation

Martin Tower
Eighth and Eaton Avenues
Bethlehem, PA 18018
(215) 861-3225

See full entry under Pennsylvania.

Yellow Freight System Foundation, Inc.

10990 Roe Avenue
Overland Park, KS 66211
(913) 345-3000
Application address: Yellow Freight System, Inc., No. A004, P.O. Box 7270, Overland Park, KS 66207

Restrictions: Program-related investments and several other types of support for arts, theater, family services, cultural programs, social services, and education.

Focus of giving: Limited primarily to the Kansas City, Missouri, area.
$ given: $1.49 million for grants
Assets: $3.07 million
Contact: Mike Kelley, Managing Director
Application information: No application form required
Initial approach: Letter
Copies of proposal: 1
Deadlines: None
Board meeting dates: As needed
Final notification: Within 2 months

KENTUCKY

Bank of Louisville Charities, Inc.
P.O. Box 1101
Louisville, KY 40201
Application address: 500 West Broadway, Louisville, KY 40202
(502) 589-3351

Restrictions: Program-related investments and several other types of support for cultural programs, education, health, housing, civic affairs, and a community fund.
Focus of giving: Limited primarily to Jefferson County, Kentucky.
$ given: $285,580 for 123 grants; range, $25–$52,000.
Assets: $3.56 million
Contact: Beth Paxton Klein, Director
Application information: No application form required
Initial approach: Letter
Deadlines: None
Board meeting dates: Monthly

BellSouth Foundation
c/o BellSouth Corporation
1155 Peachtree Street, N.E., Room 7H08
Atlanta, GA 30367-6000
(404) 249-2396
(404) 249-2429
(404) 249-2428

See full entry under Georgia.

The Henry Vogt Foundation, Inc.
1000 W. Ormsby Avenue
Louisville, KY 40210
Application address: P.O. Box 1918, Louisville, KY 40201-1918

Restrictions: Funds for continuing support, land acquisition, equipment, research, renovation projects for community development, education, youth, computer sciences, and social services.
Focus of giving: Kentucky, with emphasis on Jefferson County and Louisville area.
$ given: $238,850 for 26 grants.
Assets: $2.2 million
Contact: Kent Oyler, Manager
Application information: No application form required
Initial approach: Letter
Copies of proposal: 1
Deadlines: May 1
Board meeting dates: June 30
Final notification: Only notifies successful applicants

Retirement Research Foundation
8765 West Higgins Road, Suite 401
Chicago, IL 60631
(312) 714-8080
FAX: (312) 714-8089

See full entry under Illinois.

LOUISIANA

BellSouth Foundation
c/o BellSouth Corporation
1155 Peachtree Street, N.E., Room 7H08
Atlanta, GA 30367-6000
(404) 249-2396
(404) 249-2429
(404) 249-2428

See full entry under Georgia.

Jack Eckerd Corporation Foundation
P.O. Box 4689
Clearwater, FL 34618
(813) 398-8318

See full entry under Florida.

The Lupin Foundation
3715 Prytania Street, Suite 307
New Orleans, LA 70115
(504) 897-6640
FAX: (504) 894-6640

Restrictions: Support for education, the arts, civic affairs, community development, etc. Grants for equipment, research, scholarship funds, special projects, matching funds, continuing support, general purposes, program-related investments, renovation projects, and seed money.
Focus of giving: Limited primarily to Louisiana.
$ given: $938,687 for 64 grants; range, $170–$60,000.
Assets: $20.2 million
Publications: Application guidelines
Contact: Lori Wesolowski, Coordinator
Application information: Application form required
Initial approach: Brief proposal of not more than 6 pages
Copies of proposal: 1
Deadlines: Before board meetings
Board meeting dates: 9 times annually
Final notification: 2 weeks

MAINE

Dorr Foundation
P.O. Box 281
Bedford, NY 10506
(914) 234-3573
(212)683-1370

See full entry under New York.

The Maine Community Foundation, Inc.
210 Main Street
P.O. Box 148
Ellsworth, ME 04605
(207) 667-9735

Restrictions: Support for education, arts, youth and child welfare, aged, disadvantaged, and health. Grants for seed money, matching funds, general purposes, publications, and conferences.
Focus of giving: Limited primarily to Maine.
$ given: $413,917 for 214 grants; $121,948 for 131 grants to individuals.
Assets: $9.6 million
Contact: Jay Davis, Program Director
Application information: Application form required
Initial approach: Letter
Copies of proposal: 1
Deadlines: January 15, April 1, July 15, and October 1
Board meeting dates: Four times a year
Final notification: 2 months after deadline

The Trust Family Foundation
52 Stiles Road
Salem, NH 03079
(603) 898-6670

See full entry under New Hampshire.

MARYLAND

Peggy & Yale Gordon Charitable Trust
Three Church Lane
Baltimore, MD 21208
(301) 484-6410

Restrictions: Program-related investments and continuing support for
   Jewish associations, cultural programs, and music.
Focus of giving: Limited primarily to Baltimore, Maryland.
$ given: $371,446 for 45 grants; range, $125–$95,000
Assets: $9.6 million
Contact: Sidney S. Sherr, Trustee
Application information: No application form required
Initial approach: Letter
Copies of proposal: 1
Deadlines: None
Board meeting dates: As needed

Marpat Foundation, Inc.
c/o Miller & Chevalier
655 15th Street, N.W., Suite 900
Washington, DC 20005
(202) 626-5832

See full entry under District of Columbia.

The Thomas B. and Elizabeth M. Sheridan Foundation, Inc.
Executive Plaza II, Suite 604
11350 McCormick Road
Hunt Valley, MD 21031
(401) 771-0475

Restrictions: Program-related investments and several other types of
   support for cultural organizations and secondary private schools.
Focus of giving: Limited primarily to Baltimore, Maryland, area.
$ given: $176,656 for 14 grants; range, $500–$53,000.
Assets: $8.6 million
Contact: James L. Sinclair, President
Application information: Application form required

Initial approach: Letter
Copies of proposal: 1
Deadlines: None
Board meeting dates: March, June, September, and December.

MASSACHUSETTS

Dorr Foundation
P.O. Box 281
Bedford, NY 10506
(914) 234-3573
(212) 683-1370

See full entry under New York.

The Paul & Edith Babson Foundation
c/o Nichols & Pratt
50 Congress St.
Boston, MA
(617) 523-6800

Restrictions: Support for music, education, youth, and health.
Focus of giving: Boston, Massachusetts, with few exceptions.
$ given: $259,000 for 44 grants.
Assets: $6.79 million
Publications: Program policy statement, application guidelines
Contact: Elizabeth B. Nichols, Grant Administrator
Application information: No application form required
Initial approach: Letter or telephone
Copies of proposal: 1
Deadlines: April 15 and October 15
Board meeting dates: May and November

Joseph C. and Esther Foster Foundation, Inc.
1088 Park Avenue
New York, NY 10028

See full entry under New York.

Greater Worcester Community Foundation, Inc.
44 Front Street, Suite 530
Worcester, MA 01608-1782
(508) 755-0980

Restrictions: Program-related investments and several other types of
support for health, education, social welfare, civic and cultural needs,
housing, and employment.

Focus of giving: Limited primarily to greater Worcester, Massachusetts, area.
$ given: $1.2 million for 189 grants; $138,350 for 144 grants to individuals; average range, $1,000–$1,500.
Assets: $23.9 million
Contact: Ms. Ann T. Lisi, Executive Director
Application information: Application form required
Initial approach: Letter or telephone
Copies of proposal: 2
Deadlines: January 1, April 1, and September 1 for organizations; March 15 for scholarships.
Board meeting dates: March, June, September, November, and as needed.
Final notification: 3 months

The Hyams Foundation

One Boston Place, 32nd Floor
Boston, MA 02108
(617) 720-2238
FAX: (617) 720-2434

Restrictions: Emphasis on youth agencies and neighborhood centers; support also for other social service and community development purposes, low-income neighborhoods, summer youth programs. Grants given for operating budgets, continuing support, matching funds, special projects, and general purposes.
Focus of giving: Limited primarily to Boston, Cambridge, Chelsea, Lynn, and Somerville.
$ given: $3.25 million for 224 grants; average range $15,000–$25,000.
Assets: $64.6 million
Contact: Elizabeth B. Smith, Executive Director
Initial approach: Proposal
Copies of proposal: 1
Deadlines: None
Board meeting dates: 6 times between September and June
Final notification: 1 to 6 months

Island Foundation, Inc.

589 Mill Street
Marion, MA 02738-1553
(508) 748-2809

Restrictions: Program-related investments and several other types of support for environmental education and research for alternative and appropriate treatment systems of wastewater, land/wildlife conservation, and building capacity in New Bedford, Maine.
Focus of giving: Limited primarily to Northeast; program interest in New Bedford, Maine.
$ given: $720,949 for 80 grants; average range, $3,000–$20,000.
Assets: $24 million
Contact: Jenny D. Russell, Executive Director

Application information: No application form required
Initial approach: Letter or telephone
Copies of proposal: 1
Deadlines: Vary
Board meeting dates: Annual and as needed

The Jebediah Foundation
c/o Bingham, Dana & Gould
150 Federal St.
Boston, MA 02110
(617) 951-8576

Restrictions: Building funds, general-purpose grants and charitable giving
   for performing arts, arts, and higher education.
Focus of giving: Limited primarily to Massachusetts.
$ given: $430,000 for 70 grants.
Assets: $9.2 million
Contact: Colin S. Marshall
Application information: No application form required
Deadlines: None

Norton Company Foundation
New Bond Street
P.O. Box 15008
Worcester, MA 01615-0008
(508) 795-4700

Restrictions: Program-related investments and several other types of
   support for education, social services, youth agencies, community
   development, and cultural programs.
Focus of giving: Limited primarily to the following locations: Huntsville,
   Alabama; Gainesville, Georgia; Worcester and Northboro, Massachusetts;
   Hillsboro and Littleton, and Milford, New Hampshire; Wayne, New Jersey;
   Akron and Stowe, Ohio; Brownsville and Stephenville, Texas.
$ given: $883,920 million for 290 grants.
Assets: $121 million
Contact: Francis J. Doherty, Jr., Secretary and Clerk
Application information: Application form required
Initial approach: Letter
Copies of proposal: 1
Deadlines: None
Board meeting dates: March, June, September, and December
Final notification: 3 weeks

The Theodore Edson Parker Foundation
c/o Grants Management Associates, Inc.
230 Congress Street, 3rd Floor
Boston, MA 02110
(617) 426-7172

Restrictions: Program-related investments and other types of support for social services, housing, community development, the urban environment, the arts, and minority concerns.
Focus of giving: Limited primarily to Lowell, Massachusetts.
$ given: $598,550 for 25 grants; average award $30,000.
Assets: $13 million
Contact: Laura Henze, Administrator; Jean Whitney, Administrator.
Application information: No application form required
Initial approach: Letter, telephone or proposal
Copies of proposal: 1
Deadlines: None
Board meeting dates: Spring and fall
Final notification: 4 months–5 months

Ellis L. Phillips Foundation
29 Commonwealth Ave.
Boston, MA 02116-2349
(617) 424-7607

Restrictions: Seed money and other funding for emerging organizations developing new programs; grants for education on public issues, biodiversity conservation, women's issues, music and the visual arts, and historic preservation.
Focus of giving: Limited primarily to New England.
$ given: $269,210 for 39 grants.
Assets: $5.2 million
Contact: Janet Walsh, Executive Director
Application information: No application form required
Initial approach: Letter of 2 pages–4 pages
Copies of proposal: 1
Deadlines: January 1, April 1, and September 1
Board meeting dates: February, May, and October

State Street Foundation
c/o State Street Bank and Trust Co.
P.O. Box 351
Boston, MA 02101
(617) 654-3381

Restrictions: Program-related investments and several other types of support for organizations working to improve the quality of life in Boston; funds for neighborhood development, job training, cultural programs, education, health and human services, and community funds.
Focus of giving: Limited primarily to the Boston, Massachusetts, area.
$ given: $1.9 for 105 grants; average range, $3000–$20,000.
Assets: $5.64 million
Contact: Madison Thompson, assistant Vice President, State Street Bank & Trust Co.
Application information: No application form required

Initial approach: Proposal
Copies of proposal: 1
Deadlines: None
Board meeting dates: Quarterly
Final notification: 2 weeks after meetings

The Nathaniel and Elizabeth P. Stevens Foundation
P.O. Box 111
North Andover, MA 01845
(508) 688-7211

Restrictions: Support for conservation, housing, social services, historic preservation, and the arts. Grants given for general purposes, program-related investments, seed money, emergency funds, building funds, equipment, land acquisition, matching funds, and special projects.
Focus of giving: Limited to Massachusetts with emphasis on Lawrence area.
$ given: $488,718 for 95 grants.
Assets: $10.7 million
Contact: Elizabeth A. Beland, Administrator
Publications: guidelines, program policy statement
Initial approach: Proposal
Copies of proposal: 1
Deadlines: None
Board meeting dates: Monthly, except July and August
Final notification: 2 months

MICHIGAN

Ann Arbor Area Community Foundation
121 West Washington, Suite 400
Ann Arbor, MI 48104
(313) 663-0401

Restrictions: Support for innovative programs and projects in charities, civic affairs, historic preservation, education, and cultural areas. Grants for seed money, emergency funds, building funds, equipment, special projects, matching funds, publications, research, conferences, seminars, and scholarships.
Focus of giving: Limited to Ann Arbor, Michigan.
$ given: $141,988 for 48 grants; average range, $500–$7,500.
Assets: $6.8 million
Contact: Terry N. Foster, President
Application information: Application form required
Initial approach: Telephone
Copies of proposal: 4
Deadlines: February, May, and October for grants
Board meeting dates: January, March, May, July, September, and November
Final notification: 60 days

The Coleman Foundation, Inc.
575 West Madison, Suite 4605-11
Chicago, IL 60661
(312) 902-7120

See full entry under Illinois.

Consumers Power Foundation
212 West Michigan Avenue
Jackson, MI 49201
(517) 788-0318

Restrictions: Support to organizations that provide solutions to family problems, environmental protection, culture and the arts, public broadcasting, and Michigan community foundations. Grants for operating budgets, building funds, and renovation projects.
Focus of giving: Michigan
$ given: $622,471 for 133 grants.
Assets: $819 million
Contact: Dennis H. Marvin, Secretary-Treasurer
Application information: No application form required
Initial approach: Letter of 1 page–2 pages
Deadlines: None
Board meeting dates: Quarterly

Hudson-Webber Foundation
333 West Fort Street, Suite 1310
Detroit, MI 48226
(313) 963-7777

Restrictions: Concentrates support on physical revitalization of downtown Detroit, reduction of crime in Detroit, growth of Detroit Medical Center, enhancement of Detroit art and culture, and economic development of southeastern Michigan with emphasis on the creation of additional employment opportunities. Grants for renovation projects, seed money, operating budgets, building funds, and equipment.
Focus of giving: Limited primarily to the Detroit metropolitan area.
$ given: $3.9 million for 104 grants; average range, $20,000–$50,000; $49,749 for 40 grants to individuals.
Assets: $97 million
Publications: Biennial report and application guidelines
Contact: Gilbert Hudson, President
Initial approach: Proposal
Copies of proposal: 1
Deadlines: April 15, August 15, and December 15
Board meeting dates: April, July, and December
Final notification: 1 week after meetings

W.K. Kellogg Foundation
One Michigan Avenue East
Battle Creek, MI 49017-4058
(616) 968-1611

Restrictions: Seed money and fellowships to improve human well-being:
youth- and community-based health services, food systems, and ground
water resources. In Michigan, also supports projects for economic
development.
Focus of giving: United States, Latin America, the Caribbean, South Africa,
and international fellowship programs in other countries.
$ given: $9.17 million for grants; average range, $75,000–$250,000.
Assets: $6.45 billion
Contact: Nancy A. Sims, Executive Assistant–Programming
Application information: No application form required
Initial approach: Preproposal letter of 1 page–2 pages
Copies of proposal: 1
Deadlines: None
Board meeting dates: Monthly

The Miller Foundation
310 Wah Wah Tay See Way
Battle Creek, MI 49015
(616) 964-3542

Restrictions: Support for local municipal improvement, cultural programs,
youth, drug abuse, and adult education. Grants for seed money, building
funds, equipment, land acquisition, endowment funds, loans, and
program-related investments.
Focus of giving: Limited primarily to Battle Creek, Michigan, area.
$ given: $590,000 for 25 grants; average range, $300–$101,000.
Assets: $12.5 million
Contact: Arthur W. Angood, Executive Vice President and C.O.O.
Application information: Application form required
Initial approach: Letter
Copies of proposal: 10
Deadlines: March 1, June 1, September 1, and December 1
Board meeting dates: March, June, September, and December
Final notification: 2 months

Charles Stewart Mott Foundation
Office of Proposal Entry
1200 Mott Foundation Building
Flint, MI 48502-1851
(313) 238-5651

Restrictions: Program-related investments and several other types of
support for community improvement, community education, environ-

mental management, vocational education, family services, early childhood education, and minorities.
Focus of giving: No geographic restrictions.
$ given: $41.6 million for 430 grants; average range, $20,000–$200,000.
Assets: $1.16 billion
Contact: Judy Samelson, Vice President, Communications
Application information: No application form required
Initial approach: Proposal
Copies of proposal: 1
Deadlines: None
Board meeting dates: March, June, September, and December
Final notification: 60 days–90 days

Community Foundation for N.E. Michigan
Harborside Mall
150-B North State Avenue
Alpena, MI 49707
(517) 354-6881
Additional address: P.O. Box 282, Alpena, MI 49707

Restrictions: Program-related investments and several other types of support for youth, civic affairs, education, social services, the arts, health, and libraries.
Focus of giving: Limited primarily to Alpena County, Michigan and neighboring counties.
$ given: $79,984 for 46 grants; average range, $200–$9,200.
Assets: $4 million
Contact: Elizabeth L. Connolly, Executive Director
Application information: Application form required
Initial approach: Letter or telephone
Copies of proposal: 1
Deadlines: February 1, May 1, August 1, and November 1
Board meeting dates: Quarterly
Final notification: Days following board meetings

Retirement Research Foundation
8765 West Higgins Road, Suite 401
Chicago, IL 60631
(312) 714-8080
FAX: (312) 714-8089

See full entry under Illinois.

W.B. & Candace Thoman Foundation
222 N. Washington Square, Suite 400
Lansing, MI 48933-1800
(517) 484-5185

Restrictions: Program-related investments and several other types of support for education, the young, literacy, and the disadvantaged.

Focus of giving: Limited primarily to Ingham, Eaton, and Clinton Counties, Michigan.
$ given: $260,320 for 9 grants.
Assets: $2.4 million
Contact: Benjamin O. Schwendener, Jr., President and Secretary
Initial approach: Letter requesting guidelines
Copies of proposal: 6
Deadlines: 2 weeks before board meetings
Board meeting dates: Quarterly

Lula C. Wilson Trust

c/o NBD Bank, N.A.
1116 West Long Lake Road
Bloomfield Hills, MI 48013
(313) 645-7306

Restrictions: Program-related investments and several forms of support for community development; additional funding for social services, health, education, women, youth and child welfare, handicapped, hospitals, and cultural programs.
Focus of giving: Limited to Pontiac and Oakland counties, Michigan.
$ given: $94,000 for 22 grants.
Assets: $2 million
Contact: Wilbur L. Avril, Vice President, NBD Bank, N.A.
Application information: No application form required
Initial approach: Letter
Copies of proposal: 1
Deadlines: None
Board meeting dates: As required
Final notification: 1 month

MINNESOTA

The Blandin Foundation

100 Pokegama Avenue North
Grand Rapids, MN 55744
(218) 326-0523

Restrictions: Local giving for rural community projects and economic development, arts and humanities, environment, and educational opportunities. Support for seed money, matching funds, program-related investments, technical assistance, special projects, and consulting services.
Focus of giving: Limited to Minnesota, with emphasis on rural areas.
$ given: $7.4 million for 192 grants; $362,000 for grants to individuals.
Assets: $184 million
Publications: Annual report, program policy statement, application guidelines, grants list and informational brochure

Contact: Paul M. Olson, President
Initial approach: Letter or visit
Copies of proposal: 1
Deadlines: January 2, May 1, September 1
Board meeting dates: During first two weeks of January, April, and August
Final notification: 2 weeks after board meetings

Otto Bremer Foundation

445 Minnesota Street, Suite 2000
St. Paul, MN 55101-2107
(612) 227-8036
FAX: (612) 227-2522

Restrictions: Program-related investments, loans, operating budgets, seed
money, and several other types of support for programs addressing rural
poverty and racism; additional funding for community affairs, health,
education, social services, and religion.
Focus of giving: Limited to Minnesota, North Dakota, and Wisconsin areas
with Bremer Bank affiliates.
$ given: $5 million for 499 grants; average, $1,200–$25,000.
Assets: $118.6 million
Contact: John Kostishack, Executive Director
Application information: No application form required
Initial approach: Letter or telephone
Copies of proposal: 1
Deadlines: 3 months before funding is required
Board meeting dates: Monthly
Final notification: 3 months

The Coleman Foundation, Inc.

575 West Madison, Suite 4605-11
Chicago, IL 60661
(312) 902-7120

See full entry under Illinois.

Patrick & Aimee Butler Family Foundation

First National Bank Building
332 Minnesota Street, E-1420
St. Paul, MN 55101-1369
(612) 222-2565

Restrictions: Building funds, special projects, continuing support for social
services and family, disadvantaged, drug abuse, women, housing,
humanities, and cultural programs.
Focus of giving: Limited to St. Paul and Minneapolis area.
$ given: $900,000 for 80 grants.
Assets: $10.3 million

Publications: Application guidelines and informational brochure
Contact: Sandra K. Butler, Program Officer
Application information: Application form required
Initial approach: Letter or telephone
Copies of proposal: 1
Deadlines: April 30 for letter of intent, August for proposals
Board meeting dates: June and October
Final notification: November or December

Dayton Hudson Foundation
777 Nicollet Mall
Minneapolis, MN 55402-2055
(612) 370-6555

Restrictions: Support for social action programs for urban affairs, community development, the arts and social services. Funds for operating budgets, continuing support, special projects, general purposes, and publications.
Focus of giving: Limited primarily to areas of company operations including Minnesota, Michigan, California, Florida, Illinois and Texas.
$ given: $9.69 million for 517 grants.
Assets: $19.7 million
Contact: Cynthia Mayeda, Chairperson
Application information: No application form required
Initial approach: Letter with proposal
Copies of proposal: 1
Deadlines: None
Board meeting dates: March, June, and December
Final notification: Usually within 60 days

International Multifoods Charitable Foundation
Multifoods Tower, Box 2942
Minneapolis, MN 55402
(612) 340-3410
(612) 340-3748

Restrictions: Program-related investments and several other types of support for nonprofit organizations serving the needs of local communities, higher education, youth, and the arts.
Focus of giving: Limited to programs and agencies located in or benefiting communities where Multifoods has corporate operations.
$ given: $275,790 for 33 grants; average, $1,000–$3,000.
Assets: $379 million
Contact: Vicki Celski, Vice President of Corporate Communications
Initial approach: Letter
Copies of proposal: 1
Deadlines: None
Board meeting dates: Quarterly
Final notification: 90 days

Marbrook Foundation
400 Baker Building
Minneapolis, MN 55402
(612) 332-2454

Restrictions: Seed money, building funds, equipment, land acquisition, research, and continuing support for education, business education, social services, youth and child welfare, performing arts, health, and conservation.
Focus of giving: Limited primarily to Minneapolis and St. Paul areas.
$ given: $300,000 for 78 grants.
Assets: $7.6 million
Contact: Conley Brooks, Jr., Executive Director
Application information: No application form required
Initial approach: Proposal
Copies of proposal: 1
Deadlines: May 15 and October 15
Board meeting dates: May/June, November/December
Final notification: 4 weeks after meeting

The McNeely Foundation
444 Pine Street
St. Paul, MN 55101
(612) 228-4444

Restrictions: Primarily business, economic education, and community development programs. Provides for matching funds and employee matching gifts.
Focus of giving: Limited primarily to St. Paul-Minneapolis area.
$ given: $201,450 for 34 grants.
Assets: $6.3 million
Contact: Malcolm W. McDonald, Trustee
Application information: No application form required
Initial approach: Letter
Copies of proposal: 1
Deadlines: September or December
Board meeting dates: Varies

The McNight Foundation
600 TCF Tower
121 South Eighth Street
Minneapolis, MN 55402
(612) 333-4220

Restrictions: Emphasis on grantmaking in the areas of human and social services in the seven-county Twin Cities metropolitan area and in Minnesota. Multiyear comprehensive programs in arts, housing, and aid to poor families. Grants for operating budgets, seed money, building funds, equipment, special projects, general support, matching funds, and renovation.

Focus of giving: Limited primarily to Minnesota, especially the 7-county Twin Cities area.
$ given: $41.6 million for 535 grants; average range, $10,000–$250,000.
Assets: $1 billion
Contact: Michael O'Keefe, Executive Vice President
Initial approach: Letter
Copies of proposal: 3
Deadlines: March 1, June 1, September 1, and December 1
Board meeting dates: March, June, September, and December
Final notification: 2¹/₂ months

The Medtronic Foundation
7000 Central Ave., N.E.
Minneapolis, MN 55432
(612) 574-3024

Restrictions: Support for health associations, physical health promotion, education, cultural and arts programs, minorities/race relations, and community funds. Funds for seed money, continuing support, matching funds, and operating budgets.
Focus of giving: Limited primarily to company operations–Phoenix and Tempe, Arizona; Anaheim and San Diego, California; Brooklyn Center, Coon Rapids, Fridley, Milaca, and Minneapolis, Minnesota.
$ given: $1.75 million for 101 grants; average range, $1,000–$20,000.
Assets: $3 million
Contact: Jan Schwarz, Manager
Application information: No application form required
Initial approach: Proposal with letter
Copies of proposal: 1
Deadlines: Submit between August and March
Board meeting dates: April, June, August, October, and December
Final notification: 60 days

Northwest Area Foundation
E-1201 First National Bank Building
332 Minnesota Street
St. Paul, MN 55101-1373
(612) 224-9635
FAX: (612) 225-3881

Restrictions: Grants for health services, community and urban development, regional economic development, basic human needs, natural resource management, and the arts. Support for special projects, program-related investments, seed money, and others.
Focus of giving: Limited to an eight-state region: Idaho, Iowa, Minnesota, Montana, North Dakota, Oregon, South Dakota, and Washington.
$ given: $11.46 million for 193 grants; average range, $50,000–$150,000.
Contact: Terry Tinson Saario, President
Initial approach: Letter

Copies of proposal: 1
Deadlines: None
Board meeting dates: Bimonthly
Final notification: 3 months–4 months

Ordean Foundation

501 Ordean Building
424 West Superior Street
Duluth, MN 55802
(212) 726-4785

Restrictions: Program-related investments, loans, operating budgets and
    several other types of support for community development, social
    services, health services, and youth programs.
Focus of giving: Limited to Duluth and cities in St. Louis counties, Minne-
    sota.
$ given: $867,738 for 46 grants; average range, $100–$166,500.
Assets: $28.2 million
Contact: Antoinette Poupore-Haats, Executive Director
Application information: No application form required
Initial approach: Letter, telephone, or proposal
Copies of proposal: 12
Deadlines: 15th of each month
Board meeting dates: Monthly
Final notification: Within 10 days of board meetings

Rochester Area Foundation

220 South Broadway, Suite 112
Rochester, MN 55904
(507) 282-0203

Restrictions: Program-related investments and several other types of
    support for innovative projects addressing community needs and
    promoting the involvement of local citizens.
Focus of giving: Limited to Olmsted County, Minnesota.
$ given: $137,510 for 20 grants.
Assets: $4.12 million
Contact: Steve Thorton, Executive Director
Application information: Application form required
Initial approach: Letter/application form required
Copies of proposal: 10
Deadlines: January 1, May 1, and September 1
Board meeting dates: February, April, May, August, September, October,
    November, and December
Final notification: 4 months

The Saint Paul Foundation, Inc.
600 Norwest Center
St. Paul, MN 55101-1797
(612) 224-5464

Restrictions: Support for educational, charitable, cultural or benevolent purposes of a public nature, as well as promotion of the well-being of mankind and, preferably, the inhabitants of St. Paul and its vicinity. Grants for seed money, emergency funds, building funds, equipment, matching funds, technical assistance, special projects, matching funds, renovations, and research.
$ given: $9 million for 1,697 grants; $136,146 for 92 grants to individuals.
Assets: $195 million
Contact: Paul A. Verret, President
Initial approach: Letter
Copies of proposal: 1
Deadlines: 4 months before next board meeting
Board meeting dates: April, August, and November
Final notification: 1 month

Wedum Foundation
6860 Flying Cloud Drive
Eden Prairie, MN 55344
(612) 944-5547

Restrictions: Program-related investments, seed money and other forms of support for social services, education, business education, health associations, wildlife, computer sciences, and community/rural development.
Focus of giving: Limited primarily to Alexandria, Minnesota, area.
$ given: $379,465 for 11 grants; $12,280 for 38 grants to individuals.
Assets: $6 million
Contact: Mayo Johnson, President
Application information: Application form required
Copies of proposal: 1
Deadlines: None
Board meeting dates: Fall
Final notification: Late fall

MISSISSIPPI

BellSouth Foundation
c/o BellSouth Corporation
1155 Peachtree Street, N.E., Room 7H08
Atlanta, GA 30367-6000

(404) 249-2396
(404) 249-2429
(404) 249-2428

See full entry under Georgia.

Deposit Guaranty Foundation
One Deposit Guaranty Plaza
P.O. Box 730
Jackson, MS 39205

Restrictions: Program-related investments and other types of support for
    education, community fund, social services, youth, and the arts.
Focus of giving: Limited to Mississippi.
$ given: $477,500 for 82 grants.
Assets: N/A
Contact: William M. Jones, Senior Vice President, Deposit Guaranty National
    Bank
Initial approach: Letter
Copies of proposal: 1
Board meeting dates: Annually

Jack Eckerd Corporation Foundation
P.O. Box 4689
Clearwater, FL 34618
(813) 398-8318

See full entry under Florida.

Phil Hardin Foundation
c/o Citizens National Bank
P.O. Box 911
Meridian, MS 39302
Application address: P.O. Box 3429, Meridian, MS 39302
(601) 483-4282

Restrictions: Support for educational institutions and programs only.
    Primarily schools and museums. Grants for operating budgets, continuing
    support, for seed money, building funds, equipment, endowment funds,
    special projects, matching funds, program-related investments, research,
    conferences, seminars, and publications.
Focus of giving: Limited primarily to Mississippi, but also to out-of-state
    organizations/programs of benefit to the people of Mississippi.
$ given: $815,918 for 52 grants; average range, $1,000–$69,000; $1.2 million
    program-related investments; $7,987 in loans to individuals.
Assets: $22 million
Contact: C. Thompson Wacaster, Vice President
Initial approach: Letter, telephone, or proposal
Copies of proposal: 2

Deadlines: None
Board meeting dates: As required, usually at least every 2 months
Final notification: 3 months

MISSOURI

CBS Foundation, Inc.
51 West 52nd Street
New York, NY 10019
(212) 975-5791

See full entry under New York.

The Coleman Foundation, Inc.
1137 West Jackson Boulevard
Chicago, IL 60607
(312) 243-2700

See full entry under Illinois.

Geraldine & R.A. Barrows Foundation
c/o United Missouri Bank, N.A.
P.O. Box 419692
Kansas City, MO 64141-6692
(816) 860-7711

Restrictions: General purposes support for underprivileged or handicapped children, cancer research, and health associations.
Focus of giving: Kansas City, Missouri.
$ given: $304,325 for 41 grants.
Assets: $6.6 million
Contact: Stephen J. Campbell
Initial approach: Letter
Deadlines: None

Group Health Foundation of Greater St. Louis
3556 Caroline Street
St. Louis, MO 63104
(314) 577-8105

Restrictions: Program-related investments, seed money, research, special projects, and other types of support for health agencies and services which emphasize health promotion and prevention to reduce health care costs.
Focus of giving: Limited to St. Louis, Missouri.
$ given: $231,210 for 15 grants; range, $6,000–$50,000.
Assets: $4 million

Contact: Robert M. Swanson, Ph.D., Secretary
Application information: No application form required
Initial approach: Letter
Copies of proposal: 2
Deadlines: February, May, August, and November
Board meeting dates: February, May, August, and November
Final notification: Following board meetings

Hall Family Foundations
Charitable & Crown Investment–323
P.O. Box 419580
Kansas City, MO 64141-6580
(816) 274-8516

Restrictions: Funding support within four main areas of interest: (1) the performing and visual arts; (2) youth, especially education and programs that promote social welfare, health, and character building; (3) economic development; and (4) the elderly. Grants for program-related investments, seed money, emergency funds, building funds, special projects, and renovation projects.
Focus of giving: Limited to Kansas City, Missouri area, and includes areas within the state of Kansas.
$ given: $6.9 million for 63 grants; average range, $10,000–$300,000.
Assets: $472.5 million
Contact: Wendy Burcham, Peggy Collins, Margaret H. Pence, or John Laney, Program Officers.
Initial approach: Letter
Copies of proposal: 1
Deadlines: 6 weeks before board meetings
Board meeting dates: March, June, September, and December
Final notification: 4 weeks–6 weeks

Hallmark Corporate Foundation
P.O. Box 419580
Mail Drop 323
Kansas City, MO 64141-6580
(816) 274-8515

Restrictions: Program-related investments and several other forms of support for urban affairs, education, social services, the arts, employment, health issues, and youth.
Focus of giving: Limited to Kansas City, Missouri, and other cities with Hallmark facilities.
$ given: $6.1 million for 1000 grants; average range, $5,000–$50,000.

Assets: $19.8 million
Contact: Jeanne Bates, Vice President
Application information: No application form required
Initial approach: Letter describing need, purpose, and general activities of organization.
Copies of proposal: 1
Deadlines: None
Board meeting dates: As needed
Final notification: Within 6 weeks

The McGee Foundation

4900 Main Street, Suite 717
Kansas City, MO 64112-2644
(816) 931-1515

Restrictions: Funding for programs to care for the sick, aged, and helpless, and education to improve the quality of life of same. Support for building funds, equipment, capital campaigns, and continuing support.
Focus of giving: Greater Kansas City, Missouri.
$ given: $299,458 for 41 grants.
Assets: $7.1 million
Contact: Joseph J. McGee, Jr., President
Application information: No application form required
Initial approach: Letter
Copies of proposal: 1
Deadlines: None
Board meeting dates: March, June, September, and December
Final notification: 6 weeks

Retirement Research Foundation

8765 West Higgins Road, Suite 401
Chicago, IL 60631
(312) 714-8080
FAX: (312) 714-8089

See full entry under Illinois.

Union Pacific Foundation

Martin Tower
Eighth and Eaton Avenues
Bethlehem, PA 18018
(215) 861-3225

See full entry under Pennsylvania.

MONTANA

Northwest Area Foundation
E-1201 First National Bank Building
332 Minnesota Street
St. Paul, MN 55101-1373
(612) 224-9635
FAX: (612) 225-3881

See full entry under Minnesota.

Sample Foundation, Inc.
14 North 24th Street
P.O. Box 279
Billings, MT 59103
(406) 256-5667

Restrictions: Support for the disadvantaged, social services, and hospitals.
   Funds for capital outlay, campaign funds, and special projects.
Focus of giving: Montana and Collier County, Florida.
$ given: $211,000 for 47 grants.
Assets: $3.74 million
Contact: Miriam T. Sample, Vice President
Initial approach: Letter
Board meeting dates: October 1st

NEBRASKA

Garvey Texas Foundation, Inc.
P.O. Box 9600
Forth Worth, TX 76147-0600

See full entry under Texas.

Cooper Foundation
304 Cooper Plaza
211 North 12th Street
Lincoln, NE 68508
(402) 476-7571

Restrictions: Seed money, general purposes, and matching funds for the
   arts, social services, and humanities.
Focus of giving: Nebraska, with emphasis on Lancaster and Lincoln County.
$ given: $386,975 for 65 grants.
Assets: $11.3 million

Contact: Art Thompson, President
Application information: Application form required
Initial approach: Telephone
Copies of proposal: 1
Deadlines: 15th day of month
Board meeting dates: Monthly
Final notification: 1 month

Peter Kiewit Foundation

Woodmen Tower, Suite 900
17th and Farnam Streets
Omaha, NE 68102
(402) 344-7890

Restrictions: Challenging or matching grants, land acquisition for the arts, civic affairs, cultural programs, community development, education, health and social services, and youth programs.
Focus of giving: Rancho Mirage, California; western Iowa; Nebraska; and Sheridan, Wyoming.
$ given: $11 million for 95 grants; $650,351 for 128 grants to individuals.
Assets: $240 million
Contact: Lyn Wallin Ziegenbein, Executive Director
Application information: Application form required
Initial approach: Letter or telephone
Deadlines: March 31 for organizations; June 30, September 30, and December 30.
Board meeting dates: March, June, September, and December
Final notification: 30 days following board meetings

Union Pacific Foundation

Martin Tower
Eighth and Eaton Avenues
Bethlehem, PA 18018
(215) 861-3225

See full entry under Pennsylvania.

NEVADA

Union Pacific Foundation

Martin Tower
Eighth and Eaton Avenues
Bethlehem, PA 18018
(215) 861-3225

See full entry under Pennsylvania.

First Interstate Bank of Nevada Foundation

P.O. Box 98588
Las Vegas, NV 89193
(702) 791-6462

Restrictions: Money for community funds, higher education, culture and
    the arts, social services and rural development. Support for equipment,
    capital campaigns, matching funds, and continuing support.
Focus of giving: Nevada.
$ given: $449,378 for 56 grants.
Assets: $64 million
Contact: Karen M. Galatz, Vice President
Application information: Application form required
Initial approach: Letter
Copies of proposal: 1
Deadlines: 10th of each month
Board meeting dates: 3rd Tuesday of each month
Final notification: Immediately after board meetings

NEW HAMPSHIRE

Norwin S. and Elizabeth N. Bean Foundation

c/o New Hampshire Charitable Fund
37 Pleasant St., P.O. Box 1335
Concord, NH 03302-1335
(603) 225-6641

Restrictions: Support for social and human services, including housing
    programs, for education and health, and the arts. Grants for general
    purposes, seed money, emergency funds, building funds, equipment, land
    acquisition, loans, conferences and seminars, program-related invest-
    ments, scholarship funds, special projects, capital campaigns, matching
    funds, and consulting services.
Focus of giving: Limited to Amherst and Manchester, New Hampshire.
$ given: $386,559 for 41 grants.
Assets: $7.5 million
Publications: Application guidelines, annual report and informational
    brochure
Contact: Deborah Cowan, Program Director
Initial approach: Letter or telephone
Copies of proposal: 1
Deadlines: February 1, May 1, August 1, and November 1
Board meeting dates: March, June, September, and December

Dorr Foundation

P.O. Box 281
Bedford, NY 10506
(914) 234-3573
(212) 683-1370

See full entry under New York.

Joseph C. and Esther Foster Foundation, Inc.

1088 Park Avenue
New York, NY 10028

See full entry under New York.

Norton Company Foundation

One New Bond Street
Worcester, MA 01606-2698
(508) 795-5000

See full entry under Massachusetts.

The Trust Family Foundation

52 Stiles Road
Salem, NH 03079
(603) 898-6670

Restrictions: Support for special projects in the arts, humanities, education,
    Jewish giving, and medical sciences.
Focus of giving: New England, primarily Maine and New Hampshire.
$ given: $458,676 for 13 grants.
Assets: $14.17 million
Contact: Carolyn Head Benthien, Director
Application information: No application form required
Initial approach: Summary letter of 1 page–2 pages
Copies of proposal: 1
Board meeting dates: Varies

NEW JERSEY

Campbell Soup Foundation

Campbell Place
Camden, NJ 08103
(609) 342-6431

Restrictions: Seed money, special projects, and research for education, community funds, public interest groups, and health care facilities.
Focus of giving: Limited to areas of company operations and Camden, New Jersey.
$ given: $1.7 million for 50 grants.
Assets: $14.7 million
Contact: Bartram C. Willis, Secretary
Application information: No application form required
Initial approach: Letter
Copies of proposal: 1
Deadlines: None
Board meeting dates: As required
Final notification: 4 weeks–8 weeks

Community Foundation of New Jersey
P.O. Box 317
Knox Hill Road
Morristown, NJ 07963-0317
(201) 267-5533

Restrictions: Program-related investments, seed money, and special project funding for innovative, broad-impact programs and research; includes AIDS, education, health, community development and leadership, social services, family services, and the disadvantaged.
Focus of giving: Limited to New Jersey.
$ given: $695,877 for 216 grants.
Assets: $9.7 million
Contact: Sheila C. Williamson, Executive Director
Application information: Application form required
Initial approach: Telephone
Copies of proposal: 1
Board meeting dates: 4 times a year

Geraldine R. Dodge Foundation, Inc.
163 Madison Avenue, 6th Floor
P.O. Box 1239
Morristown, NJ 07962-1239
(201) 540-8442

Restrictions: Grant-making emphasis in New Jersey on secondary education, performing and visual arts, projects in population, environment, energy, welfare of animals and family planning. Grants for seed money, special projects, conferences and seminars, matching funds, research, continuing support, and publications.
Focus of giving: Primarily in New Jersey.
$ given: $6. million for 344 grants; average, $15,000–$25,000; $250,000 for 50 grants to individuals.
Assets: $182 million
Contact: Scott McVay, Executive Director

Initial approach: Letter or proposal of 6 pages
Copies of proposal: 1
Deadlines: Submit proposal in March, June, September, or December; deadlines December 15 for education, September 15 for public issues, March 15 for arts, June 15 for welfare of animals and special projects.
Board meeting dates: March, June, September, and December
Final notification: End of the months in which board meets

Jack Eckerd Corporation Foundation
P.O. Box 4689
Clearwater, FL 34618
(813) 398-8318

See full entry under Florida.

The Robert Wood Johnson Foundation
P.O. Box 2316
Princeton, NJ 08543-2316
(609) 452-8701

Restrictions: Program-related investments, seed money, research, and special-projects funding to improve health and health care of Americans through services; prevention of AIDS and drug abuse; also for minorities, the aged, and mental health.
Focus of giving: Provided throughout the United States.
$ given: $103 million for 763 grants; $6.5 million for program-related investments.
Assets: $2.9 billion
Contact: Edward H. Robbins, Proposal Manager
Application information: No application form required
Initial approach: Letter
Copies of proposal: 1
Deadlines: None
Board meeting dates: quarterly
Final notification: 6 months–12 months

Norton Company Foundation
One New Bond Street
Worcester, MA 01606-2698
(508) 795-5000

See full entry under Massachusetts.

The Harold B. and Dorothy A. Snyder Foundation
P.O. Box 671
Moorestown, NJ 08057-0671
(609) 273-9745

Restrictions: Program-related investments and other types of support for

local programs, for BSN programs, and scholarships for local residents and for Protestant ministries.
Focus of giving: Limited primarily to the Union County, New Jersey, area.
$ given: $155,193 for 34 grants; $26,305 for 17 grants to individuals.
Assets: $8 million
Contact: Audrey Snyder, Executive Director
Application information: No application form required except for scholarship program
Initial approach: Letter or telephone
Copies of proposal: 5
Deadlines: None
Board meeting dates: Bimonthly or quarterly
Final notification: August

NEW MEXICO

Carlsbad Foundation, Inc.
116 South Canyon Street
Carlsbad, NM 88220
(505) 887-1131

Restrictions: Focus on education, mental and medical health, and community development. Grants and loans for operating budgets, seed money, emergency funds, building funds, equipment, land acquisition, consulting services, technical assistance, special projects, and program-related investments.
Focus of giving: Limited to South Eddy County, New Mexico.
$ given: $380,877 for grants.
Assets: $5.8 million
Publications: Annual report, newsletter and application guidelines
Contact: John Mills, Executive Director
Application information: No application form required
Initial approach: Letter
Copies of proposal: 1
Deadlines: 1 week before board meeting
Board meeting dates: Monthly

Pearl M. and Julia J. Harmon Foundation
P.O. Box 52568
Tulsa, OK 74152-0568
(918) 743-6191

See full entry under Oklahoma.

NEW YORK

The Achelis Foundation
c/o Morris and McVeigh
767 Third Avenue
New York, NY 10017
(212) 418-0588

Restrictions: Giving for social service—youth & child welfare, AIDS, elderly, drug abuse, handicapped—literacy programs, and the arts. Support for building funds, land acquisition, general purposes, and renovation projects.
Focus of giving: New York area.
$ given: $960,000 for 56 grants; average, $10,000–$30,000.
Assets: $23 million
Publications: Biennial report
Contact: Mary Caslin Ross, Secretary and Executive Director
Application information: No application form required
Initial approach: Letter and proposal
Copies of proposal: 1
Deadlines: None
Board meeting dates: May, September, and December

Carnegie Corporation of New York
437 Madison Avenue
New York, NY 10022
(212) 371-3200

Restrictions: Program-related investments and other types of support for: (1) child development and education and health of children and youth; (2) strengthening human resources in developing countries; and (3) cooperative international security and international development.
Focus of giving: No geographic restrictions.
$ given: $43.8 million for grants.
Assets: $1 billion
Contact: Dorothy W. Knapp, Secretary
Application information: No application form required
Initial approach: Letter
Deadlines: None
Board meeting dates: January, April, June, and October
Final notification: 6 months

Mary Flagler Cary Charitable Trust
350 Fifth Avenue, Room 6622
New York, NY 10118
(212) 563-6860

Restrictions: Funding in three areas: (1) music in New York City; (2) urban environmental programs in New York City; and (3) programs for the conservation of natural resources on the Atlantic coastline. Grants for operating budgets, continuing support, program-related investments, land acquisition, special projects, and matching funds.
Focus of giving: Primarily in the New York City area; conservation funding to eastern coastal states.
$ given: $4.3 million for 122 grants; average range, $15,000–$25,000.
Assets: $110 million
Contact: Edward A. Ames, Trust
Initial approach: Letter with brief proposal
Copies of proposal: 1
Deadlines: None
Board meeting dates: Monthly
Final notification: 2 months

CBS Foundation, Inc.
51 West 52nd Street
New York, NY 10019
(212) 975-5791

Restrictions: Funds for operating budgets, continuing support, research, and general purposes. Support given for higher education, performing and fine arts, civic affairs, and journalism.
Focus of giving: Limited to areas of company operation–Los Angeles, California; Miami, Florida; Chicago, Illinois; St. Louis, Missouri; New York, New York; and Philadelphia, Pennsylvania.
$ given: $1.62 million for 197 grants.
Assets: $7.5 million
Contact: Kathryn Edmundson, President
Application information: No application form required
Initial approach: Letter
Copies of proposal: 1
Deadlines: None
Board meeting dates: Quarterly and as needed
Final notification: 4 months–6 months

Dorr Foundation
P.O. Box 281
Bedford, NY 10506
(914) 234-3573
(212) 683-1370 (during business hours)

Restrictions: Program-related investments and other types of support for science programs, especially educational projects relating science to the environment.
Focus of giving: Limited primarily to the Northeast.
$ given: $133,000 for 8 grants; average range, $5,000–$30,000.
Assets: $3.5 million

Contact: Hugh McMillan, Chairperson
Application information: No application form required
Initial approach: Brief proposal summary of 1 page–2 pages
Copies of proposal: 7
Deadlines: None
Board meeting dates: April and December
Final notification: 1 month

East Hill Foundation
Main Street
Akron, NY 14001
(716) 542-3494

Restrictions: Program-related investments, seed money, and special project
  support for child welfare, historic preservation, and social services.
Focus of giving: Limited to Clarence and Newstead, New York.
$ given: $29,523 for 5 grants; $66,270 for program-related investments.
Assets: $1.23 million
Contact: Peter Greatbatch, President
Application information: Application form required
Initial approach: Letter or telephone
Copies of proposal: 1
Deadlines: None
Board meeting dates: Quarterly

The Ford Foundation
320 East 43rd Street
New York, NY 10017
(212) 573-5000

Restrictions: Program-related investments and several other types of
  support for demonstration and development efforts in the following
  areas: (1) urban poverty; (2) rural poverty and resources; (3) rights and
  social justice; (4) governance and public policy; (5) education and culture;
  (6) international affairs; and (7) reproductive health and population. Also
  for women, music, youth, and AIDS.
Focus of giving: Provided on worldwide basis.
$ given: $259 million for 1482 grants; average range, $15,000–$1.5 million;
  $3.65 million for 248 grants to individuals; $16 million for program-related
  investments.
Assets: $6.47 billion
Contact: Barron M. Tenny, Secretary
Application information: No application form required
Initial approach: Letter, telephone, or proposal
Copies of proposal: 1
Deadlines: None
Board meeting dates: March, June, September, and December
Final notification: Usually within 1 month

Joseph C. and Esther Foster Foundation, Inc.
1088 Park Avenue
New York, NY 10028

Restrictions: Program-related investments and annual campaign support for education and research, fine arts, Jewish welfare, cultural programs, health services, minorities, and race relations.
Focus of giving: Limited primarily to New York and New England.
$ given: $36,350 for 33 grants; average range, $250–$15,000.
Assets: $2.3 million
Contact: Jacqueline Foster, President
Application information: No application form required
Initial approach: Letter; no telephone calls
Deadlines: Prior to December 31
Board meeting dates: December 31

Gebbie Foundation, Inc.
Hotel Jamestown Building, Room 308
P.O. Box 1277
Jamestown, NY 14702-1277
(716) 487-1062

Restrictions: Grants primarily for local organizations—hospitals, libraries, community funds, and theater. Also for medical and scientific research to alleviate human suffering and ills related to metabolic diseases of the bone. Interested in programs to detect deafness in children and education of the deaf. Funding for seed money, building funds, equipment, annual campaigns, general purposes, loans, and continuing support.
Focus of giving: Limited primarily to Chautauqua County and Western New York; giving in other areas only when the project is consonant with program objectives that cannot be developed locally.
$ given: $3.7 million for 86 grants; average range, $1,000–$400,000.
Assets: $63 million
Contact: John D. Hamilton, President
Initial approach: Letter
Copies of proposal: 12
Deadlines: January 1, May 1, and September 1
Board meeting dates: March, July, and November
Final notification: 1 month–4 months

The John A. Hartford Foundation, Inc.
55 East 59th Street
New York, NY 10022
(212) 832-7788
FAX: (212) 593-4913

Restrictions: Program-related investments and several other types of support provided through aging and health programs, and health care quality and cost programs.

Focus of giving: No geographic restrictions.
$ given: $9.4 million for 78 grants; average range, $50,000–$300,000; $650,000 for 1 program-related investment.
Assets: $304 million
Contact: Richard S. Sharpe, Program Director
Application information: No application form required
Initial approach: Letter or proposal
Copies of proposal: 1
Deadlines: Make inquiry at least 6 months before funding is required
Board meeting dates: March, May, September, and December
Final notification: 6 weeks

International Paper Company Foundation
Two Manhattanville Road
Purchase, NY 10577
(914) 397-1503

Restrictions: Program-related investments and several other types of funding for model, broad-impact projects in company communities, with emphasis on primary/secondary education and programs for minorities and women. Also sciences, health and welfare, and community and cultural affairs.
Focus of giving: Limited primarily to communities where the company has plants and mills, and to Memphis, Tennessee.
$ given: $1.04 million for 543 grants; average range, $2,500–$10,000.
Assets: $39.9 million.
Contact: Sandra Wilson, Vice President
Application information: Application form required
Initial approach: Letter, telephone, or proposal to local facility
Copies of proposal: 1
Deadlines: March 1st for current year funding
Board meeting dates: June
Final notification: July

Abe and Frances Lastfogel Foundation
c/o Wallin, Simon, Black and Co.
1350 Avenue of the Americas
New York, NY 10019
(212) 586-5100

Restrictions: Program-related investments, annual campaigns, research and special project funding for cultural programs, film, performing arts, Jewish welfare, child welfare, and health.
Focus of giving: Limited primarily to Los Angeles, California, and New York, New York.
$ given: $637,655 for 248 grants.
Assets: $4.2 million
Contact: Bruce Baker, Vice President

Metropolitan Life Foundation
One Madison Avenue
New York, NY 10010-3690
(212) 578-6272

Restrictions: Program-related investments and several other types of
    support for education, health, civic concerns, social services, cultural
    programs, urban development, music, dance, and theater.
Focus of giving: No geographic restrictions.
$ given: $7.2 million for 406 grants; average range, $1,000–$150,000; 4
    program-related investments for $3 million.
Assets: $102 million
Contact: Sibyl C. Jacobson, President and Chief Executive Officer
Application information: Application form required for some programs
Initial approach: Letter
Copies of proposal: 1
Deadlines: Varies for competitive awards, but none for grants
Board meeting dates: 6 times annually
Final notification: 4 weeks–6 weeks

The New World Foundation
100 East 85th Street
New York, NY 10028
(212) 249-1023

Restrictions: Program-related investments, seed money, loans, and special
    project funding for programs addressing equal rights, public education,
    public health, rural and urban initiatives, and peace.
Focus of giving: No geographic restrictions
$ given: $1.33 million for 122 grants; average range, $1,000–$25,000.
Assets: $21.6 million
Contact: Colin Greer, President
Application information: No application form required
Initial approach: Letter
Copies of proposal: 1
Deadlines: None
Board meeting dates: 3 times annually
Final notification: 3 months

New York Foundation
350 Fifth Avenue, Room 2901
New York, NY 10118
(212) 594-8009

Restrictions: Giving for projects that will improve the quality of life for the
    disadvantaged, handicapped, and minority populations; emphasis on
    youth and the elderly; strong support for projects with a firm community
    base. Funding for seed money, operating budgets, special projects,
    technical assistance, and general purposes.

Focus of giving: Limited primarily to the New York City metropolitan area.
$ given: $2.7 million for 96 grants; average range, $25,000–$40,000; $345,000 for 2 program-related investments.
Assets: $56 million
Contact: Madeline Lee, Executive Director
Initial approach: Letter
Copies of proposal: 1
Deadlines: March 1, July 1, and November 1
Board meeting dates: February, June, and October
Final notification: 3 months–6 months

A. Lindsay and Olive B. O'Connor Foundation
P.O. Box D
Hobart, NY 13788
(607) 538-9248

Restrictions: Funding emphasis on local giving, community centers, hospital, child development, and historic restoration. Grants are awarded for general purposes, continuing support, seed money, emergency funds, building funds, equipment, land acquisition, special projects, publications, conferences and seminars, research, renovation projects, and program-related investments.
Focus of giving: Limited primarily to Delaware County, New York, and contiguous rural counties in upstate New York.
$ given: $1.76 million for 133 grants; average range, $1,000–$800,000; $320,000 for 1 program-related investment.
Assets: $35 million
Contact: Donald F. Bishop II, Executive Director
Initial approach: Letter
Copies of proposal: 1
Deadlines: April 1 and September 1
Board meeting dates: May or June, and September or October; committee meets monthly to consider grants under $5,000
Final notification: 7–10 days after semi-annual meeting

The Carl and Lily Pforzheimer Foundation, Inc.
650 Madison Avenue, 23rd Floor
New York, NY 10022
(212) 223-6500

Restrictions: Program-related investments, seed money special projects, and professorships for education, cultural programs, and health care.
Focus of giving: No geographical restrictions.
$ given: $1.47 million for 31 grants; average range, $10,000–$50,000.
Assets: $37 million
Contact: Carl H. Pforzheimer, Jr., President
Initial approach: Letter or proposal
Copies of proposal: 1

Deadlines: None
Board meeting dates: April, June, October, and December
Final notification: Immediately following board meetings

Reader's Digest Foundation
Reader's Digest Road
Pleasantville, NY 10570
(914) 241-5370

Restrictions: Scholarship funds, employee matching gifts, and general
   purpose funding for journalism education, youth services, and literacy.
Focus of giving: No geographic restrictions.
$ given: $902,000 for 264 grants; average range, $10,000–$60,000.
Assets: $28.5 million
Contact: Claudia Edwards-Watts, Director
Application information: No application form required
Initial approach: Letter
Copies of proposal: 1
Deadlines: 60 days prior to board meetings
Board meeting dates: February, June, and October
Final notification: 90 days

The Rockefeller Foundation
1133 Avenue of the Americas
New York, NY 10036
(212) 869-8500

Restrictions: Program-related investments, fellowships, research, special
   projects, grants to individuals, and several other types of support for (1)
   science-based, international development in the areas of agriculture,
   health, population sciences; (2) arts and humanities; and (3) equal
   opportunity.
Focus of giving: No geographic restrictions.
$ given: $78.7 million for 1,115 grants; $8.1 million for 463 grants to
   individuals.
Assets: $2 billion
Contact: Lynda Mullen, Secretary
Application information: No application form required
Initial approach: Letter or proposal
Copies of proposal: 1
Deadlines: Varies by program
Board meeting dates: March, June, September, and December

Helena Rubinstein Foundation, Inc.
405 Lexington Avenue
New York, NY 10174
(212) 986-0806

Restrictions: Seed money, operating budgets, continuing support, general-

purpose funding for projects that benefit women and children, youth, education, social services, health, and the arts.
Focus of giving: Limited primarily to New York, New York.
$ given: $4 million for 208 grants; average range, $5,000–$25,000.
Assets: $33 million
Contact: Diane Moss, President and Chief Executive Officer
Application information: No application form required
Initial approach: Letter
Copies of proposal: 1
Deadlines: None
Board meeting dates: November and May
Final notification: 1 month–3 months

The Scherman Foundation, Inc.

315 West 57th Street, Suite 204
New York, NY 10019
(212) 489-7143

Restrictions: Grants for conservation, peace and disarmament, family planning, human rights and liberties, the arts, and social welfare. Specifically, social welfare funding is given to New York City organizations working for social justice, housing, and community affairs. Grants given for operating budgets, continuing support, seed money, emergency funds, matching funds, program-related investments, special projects, technical assistance, and general purposes.
Focus of giving: Priority given to New York City organizations in the arts and social welfare fields.
$ given: $4 million for 139 grants; average range, $5,000–$25,000.
Assets: $71 million
Contact: Sandra Silverman, Executive Director
Initial approach: Letter
Copies of proposal: 1
Deadlines: None
Board meeting dates: Quarterly
Final notification: 3 months

Schlumberger Foundation, Inc.

277 Park Avenue
New York, NY 10172
(212) 350-9455

Restrictions: Program-related investments, general purposes, scholarship funds, special projects, and other types of support for educational institutions; small number of awards to medical and humanitarian programs.
Focus of giving: Limited to North America.
$ given: $675,000 for 68 grants; average range, $3,000–$20,000.
Assets: $15.3 million
Contact: Arthur W. Alexander, Executive Secretary-Treasurer

Application information: No application form required
Initial approach: Letter
Deadlines: None
Board meeting dates: February/March
Final notification: Within 3 weeks

The John Ben Snow Foundation, Inc.

P.O. Box 376
Pulaski, NY 13142
(315) 298-6401

Restrictions: Grants for education, community development, handicapped, and minority programs. Funding for special projects, equipment, building funds, matching funds, fellowships, and scholarships.
Focus of giving: Limited to central New York; emphasis on Oswego County.
$ given: $198,625 for 26 grants; average range, $10,000–$15,000.
Assets: $4.9 million
Contact: Allen R. Malcolm, President
Application information: Application form required
Initial approach: Letter
Copies of proposal: 1
Deadlines: March 15
Board meeting dates: June
Final notification: July 1

The Statler Foundation

107 Delaware Avenue, Suite 508
Buffalo, NY 14202
(716) 852-1104

Restrictions: Program-related investments, building funds, equipment, and other types of support for education and research relating to the hotel industry.
Focus of giving: Limited primarily to upstate New York.
$ given: $964,745 for 20 grants.
Assets: $25.8 million
Contact: Arthur J. Musarra, Chairman
Application information: Application form required for scholarship in the hospitality field.
Initial approach: Letter
Copies of proposal: 3
Deadlines: April 15 for scholarships
Board meeting dates: Monthly
Final notification: December 1

The Sulzberger Foundation, Inc.

229 West 43rd Street
New York, NY 10036
(212) 556-1750

Restrictions: Program-related investments, building funds, seed money, special projects, equipment, annual campaigns, and several other types of support for education, cultural programs, conservation, hospitals, welfare, and community funds.
Focus of giving: Limited primarily to New York and Chattanooga, Tennessee.
$ given: $1 million for 231 grants.
Assets: $21.5 million
Contact: Marian S. Heiskell, President
Initial approach: Telephone
Deadlines: None
Board meeting dates: January and as required

United States Trust Company of New York Foundation
c/o U.S. Trust Co. of New York
114 West 47th Street
New York, NY 10036
(212) 852-1000

Restrictions: Program-related investments, seed money, endowment funds, operating budgets, and equipment for cultural programs, health, arts, education, and urban affairs and development, including programs for housing, employment, and improved quality of life for the disadvantaged.
Focus of giving: Limited primarily to New York, New York, metropolitan area.
$ given: $394,000 for 66 grants; average range, $3,000–$5,000.
Assets: $164 million
Contact: Carol A. Strickland, Vice President
Application information: No application form required
Initial approach: Letter or proposal
Copies of proposal: 1
Deadlines: April 1
Board meeting dates: March, May, and October
Final notification: 2 months–6 months

Uris Brothers Foundation, Inc.
300 Park Avenue
New York, NY 10022
(212) 355-7080

Restrictions: Program-related investments and several other types of support for services/housing for homeless families, social services for youth, cultural institutions, employment, and community development, particularly the Bronx.
Focus of giving: Limited primarily to New York, New York.
$ given: $1.45 million for 78 grants; average range, $5,000–$25,000.
Assets: $25.9 million
Contact: Alice Paul, Executive Director
Application information: No application form required
Initial approach: Letter or brief proposal

Copies of proposal: 1
Deadlines: None
Board meeting dates: Quarterly

The John L. Weinberg Foundation
c/o Goldman Sachs & Co.
85 Broad Street, 22nd Floor
New York, NY 10004

Restrictions: Program-related investments and several other types of support for Jewish welfare, hospitals, medical research, and education.
Focus of giving: Limited primarily to New York, New York, and Greenwich, Connecticut.
$ given: $1.39 million for 125 grants.
Assets: $20.7 million
Contact: John L. Weinberg, Trustee
Application information: No application form required
Initial approach: Letter
Copies of proposal: 1

Westchester Health Fund
3010 Westchester Avenue
Purchase, NY 10577-2524
(914) 694-6428

Restrictions: Program-related investments, consulting services, and special project funding for efforts to provide high-quality, low-cost health care.
Focus of giving: Limited primarily to Westchester County, New York.
$ given: $197,011 for 3 grants.
Assets: $2 million
Contact: Ross H. Weale, Chairman
Initial approach: Letter or proposal
Copies of proposal: 1
Deadlines: None

NORTH CAROLINA

Mary Reynolds Babcock Foundation, Inc.
102 Reynolda Village
Winston-Salem, NC 27106-5123
(919) 748-9222

Restrictions: Grants primarily for social services, grassroots organizing, women, youth, child development, and the arts; includes community development, rural issues, the environment, and citizen participation in the development of public policy. Grants for operating budgets, seed money, emergency funds, special projects, and program-related investments.

Focus of giving: Limited primarily to North Carolina and the southeastern United States and national organizations.
$ given: $4.6 million for grants; average range, $5,000–$35,000.
Assets: $62.9 million
Publications: Annual report, program policy statement, application guidelines
Contact: Gayle W. Dorman, Executive Director
Application information: Application form required
Initial approach: Proposal
Copies of proposal: 1
Deadlines: March 1 and September 1
Board meeting dates: May and November
Final notification: First week of the month following a board meeting

BellSouth Foundation

c/o BellSouth Corporation
1155 Peachtree Street, N.E., Room 7H08
Atlanta, GA 30367-6000
(404) 249-2396
(404) 249-2429
(404) 249-2428

See full entry under Georgia.

Broyhill Family Foundation, Inc.

P.O. Box 500, Golfview Park
Lenoir, NC 28645
(704) 758-6120

Restrictions: Scholarship funds, special projects for child development and child welfare, and the free enterprise system.
Focus of giving: Limited primarily to North Carolina.
$ given: $1.3 million for grants.
Assets: $31.9 million
Contact: Paul H. Broyhill, President, or Mrs. Lee E. Pritchard, Assistance. Secretary-Treasurer.
Initial approach: Letter
Deadlines: June 15 and December 15
Board meeting dates: Quarterly
Final notification: Within calendar year

Kathleen Price and Joseph M. Bryan Family Foundation

One North Pointe, Suite 170
3101 North Elm Street
Greensboro, NC 27408
(919) 288-5455

Restrictions: Grants for community projects, AIDS, education, arts, health and human services, and youth. Support for seed money, building funds, renovation projects, special projects, and program-related investments.

Focus of giving: Limited primarily to North Carolina; focus on Greensboro and Guilford counties and rural areas.
$ given: $2.3 million for 124 grants; average range, $5,000–$100,000.
Assets: $39.9 million
Contact: Robert K. Hampton, Executive Director
Initial approach: Letter or telephone
Copies of proposal: 1
Deadlines: March 1 and September 1
Board meeting dates: May and November
Final notification: 2 weeks after board meeting

Camp Foundation
P.O. Box 813
Franklin, VA 23851
(804) 562-3439

See full entry under Virginia.

Jack Eckerd Corporation Foundation
P.O. Box 4689
Clearwater, FL 34618
(813) 398-8318

See full entry under Florida.

James G. Hanes Memorial Fund/Foundation
c/o NationsBank
One NCNB Plaza, T09-1
Charlotte, NC 28255
(704) 386-8477

Restrictions: Support for community development programs as well as for conservation, health, and cultural programs. Funds for seed money, annual campaigns, equipment, land acquisition, building funds, and special projects.
Focus of giving: Limited primarily to North Carolina and the Southeast.
$ given: $497,000 for 21 grants; average range, $1,000–$25,000.
Assets: $1.5 million
Contact: Manager, Foundations/Endowments
Application information: Application form required
Initial approach: Proposal
Copies of proposal: 1
Deadlines: March 15, June 15, September 15, and December 15
Board meeting dates: January, April, July, and October
Final notification: 10 days

Meyer Family Foundation
(formerly The Meyer-Ceco Foundation)
P.O. Box 3098
Oakbrook, IL 60522-3098

See full entry under Illinois.

NORTH DAKOTA

Otto Bremer Foundation
445 Minnesota Street, Suite 2000
St. Paul, MN 55101-2107
(612) 227-8036
FAX: (612) 227-2522

See full entry under Minnesota.

Fargo-Moorhead Area Foundation
609-1/2 First Avenue North, No. 205
Fargo, ND 58102
(701) 234-0756

Restrictions: Seed money, equipment, renovation projects, capital campaigns, and other support for the arts, youth, health, social services, education, and civic affairs.
Focus of giving: Counties of Cass, Nevada and Clay, Minnesota.
$ given: $698,975 for 126 grants.
Assets: $8.6 million
Contact: Susan M. Hunke, Executive Director
Application information: Application form required
Initial approach: Letter
Copies of proposal: 10
Deadlines: June 30 and December 31
Board meeting dates: Quarterly
Final notification: October 31 and May 31

North Dakota Community Foundation
P.O. Box 387
Bismarck, ND 58502-0387
(701) 222-8349

Restrictions: Support for aid to the elderly, disadvantaged, youth, the arts, and community development. Funds for operating budgets, continuing support, seed money, equipment, building funds, and other types of support.

Focus of giving: North Dakota.
$ given: $475,690 for 313 grants.
Assets: $4.1 million
Contact: Richard H. Timmins, President
Application information: Application form required
Initial approach: Letter
Copies of proposal: 1
Deadlines: August 31
Board meeting dates: Annual, in 2nd quarter of year

Northwest Area Foundation
E-1201 First National Bank Building
332 Minnesota Street
St. Paul, Minnesota 55101-1373
(612) 224-9635
FAX: (612) 225-3881

See full entry under Minnesota.

OHIO

The William Bingham Foundation
1250 Leader Building
Cleveland, OH 44114
(216) 781-3275

Restrictions: Funding for environmental concerns. Grants for general
  purposes, equipment, matching funds, technical assistance, and continu-
  ing support.
Focus of giving: Limited primarily to the eastern United States with some
  emphasis on the Cleveland, Ohio, area.
$ given: $1.3 million for 46 grants; average range, $10,000–$50,000.
Assets: $23.8 million
Publications: Annual report and application guidelines
Contact: Laura C. Hitchcox, Director
Initial approach: Letter of two pages or less
Copies of proposal: 1
Deadlines: Submit letter any time
Board meeting dates: Usually May and October
Final notification: 3 months–6 months

The Cleveland Foundation
1422 Euclid Avenue, Suite 1400
Cleveland, OH 44115-2001
(216) 861-3810
FAX: (216) 861-1729

Restrictions: Grants only to private tax-exempt and governmental agencies/

programs serving the greater Cleveland area in the following areas: civic and cultural affairs, education and economic development, health, and social services. Priorities include economic development; neighborhood development; downtown revitalization; lakefront enhancement; the young, the aged, and special constituencies; health care for the medically indigent and for under-served populations; and performing and visual arts. Grants serve mainly as seed money for innovative projects or for developing institutions or services addressing unmet community needs. Support also for special projects, renovation projects, and program-related investments.

Focus of giving: Limited primarily to the greater Cleveland area, with emphasis on Cleveland, Cuyahoga, Geauga, and Lake counties, Ohio.

$ given: $32.7 million 1498 grants; average range, $1,000–$150,000; $3 million for 5 program-related investments.

Assets: $710 million

Contact: Steven A. Minter, Executive Director

Initial approach: Letter

Copies of proposal: 2

Deadlines: March 31, June 30, September 15, and December 31

Board meeting dates: March, June, September, and December

Final notification: 1 month

Community Foundation of Greater Lorain County

1865 North Ridge Road East, Suite A
Lorain, OH 44055
(216) 277-0142
(216) 323-4445

Restrictions: Grants for social services, health, education, civic affairs, and cultural programs. Seed money, matching funds, and general support provided.

Focus of giving: Limited primarily to Lorain County, Ohio, and vicinity.

$ given: $1.1 million for 83 grants; average range, $1,500–$10,000; $42,181 for grants to individuals.

Assets: $22.6 million

Contact: Carol G. Simonetti, Executive Director

Initial approach: Letter, telephone, or proposal

Deadlines: None

Board meeting dates: November and May

Final notification: 1 week–2 weeks after board meetings

Charles H. Dater Foundation, Inc.

508 Atlas Bank Building
Cincinnati, OH 45202
(513) 241-1234

Restrictions: Program-related investments, seed money, building funds, equipment, continuing support, and several other types of funds for social services (emphasis on children), health, education, fine arts, and museums.

Focus of giving: Limited primarily to the greater Cincinnati, Ohio, area.
$ given: $222,000 for 42 grants; average range, $500–$20,000.
Assets: $8.9 million
Contact: Bruce A. Krone, Secretary
Application information: Application form required
Initial approach: Letter requesting application
Copies of proposal: 4
Deadlines: None
Board meeting dates: Monthly
Final notification: 2 months

The Greater Cincinnati Foundation
425 Walnut Street, Suite 1110
Cincinnati, OH 45202-3915
(513) 241-2880

Restrictions: Program-related investments, seed money, capital campaigns, building funds, loans, and several other types of support for economic development, civic affairs, social services, education, health, and community development.
Focus of giving: Limited primarily to the greater Cincinnati, Ohio, area.
$ given: $8.3 million for grants.
Assets: $112 million
Contact: Ruth A. Cronenberg, Program Officer
Application information: Application form required
Initial approach: Letter or telephone; interview with staff
Copies of proposal: 15
Deadlines: 90 days prior to board meetings
Board meeting dates: February, May, August, and November
Final notification: Immediately after board meetings

The George Gund Foundation
1845 Guildhall Building
45 Prospect Avenue West
Cleveland, OH 44115
(216) 241-3114
FAX: (216) 241-6560

Restrictions: Program-related investments and several other types of support for women, youth, AIDS, childhood development, social services, ecology, arts, race relations, and support for education projects; programs for economic revitalization and job creation; neighborhood development projects; low-income housing projects, etc.
Focus of giving: Limited primarily to northeastern Ohio.
$ given: $18.3 million for grants; $975,000 for 4 program-related investments.
Assets: $505 million
Contact: David Bergholz, Executive Director
Application information: No application form required

Initial approach: Proposal
Copies of proposal: 1
Deadlines: January 15, March 30, June 30, and September 30
Board meeting dates: March, June, September, and December
Final notification: 8 weeks

The Huffy Foundation, Inc.
P.O. Box 1204
Dayton, OH 45401
(513) 866-6251

Restrictions: Support for museums, theaters, fine arts, human services, welfare for women and children, recreation, drug abuse and alcoholism, and civic affairs. Grants for operating budgets, seed money, continuing support, building funds, and more.
Focus of giving: Limited primarily to company operations in Ohio, Colorado, California, Pennsylvania, and Wisconsin.
$ given: $323,107 for 143 grants.
Assets: $665 million
Contact: Robert R. Wieland, Secretary
Application information: No application form required
Initial approach: Letter or proposal
Copies of proposal: 1
Deadlines: None
Board meeting dates: April, August, and December
Final notification: 2 weeks after board meeting

The Meyer Family Foundation
P.O. Box 3098
Oakbrook, IL 60522-3098

See full entry under Illinois.

The Nord Family Foundation
347 Midway Boulevard, Suite 312
Elyria, OH 44035
(216) 324-2822
(216) 233-8401

Restrictions: Program-related investments, continuing support, and special projects funding for projects assisting the disadvantaged and minorities, and for family services and child development. Additional funding for projects encouraging local social and economic progress.
Focus of giving: Limited primarily to Cuyahoga and Lorain counties, Ohio.
$ given: $3 million for grants; average range, $5,000–$50,000.
Assets: $66.9 million
Contact: Sandra L. Pyer, Executive Director
Application information: No application form required
Initial approach: Proposal

Copies of proposal: 1
Deadlines: April 1, August 1, and December 1
Board meeting dates: February, June, and October
Final notification: 1 month–3 months

Norton Company Foundation
One New Bond Street, P.O. Box 15008
Worcester, MA 01615-0008
(508) 795-4700

See full entry under Massachusetts.

The Reynolds and Reynolds Company Foundation
P.O. Box 2608
Dayton, OH 45401
(513) 449-4375

Restrictions: Program-related investments, annual campaigns, special projects, and operating budgets for programs with positive impact on local community; includes community development, education, health, culture, and the arts.
Focus of giving: Areas of company operations, especially Dayton, Ohio.
$ given: $831,000 for 64 grants; range, $100–$254,000.
Assets: $45 million
Contact: Susan Webster, Administrator
Application information: No application form required
Initial approach: Proposal
Copies of proposal: 1
Board meeting dates: Quarterly
Final notification: 3 months

The Springfield Foundation
4 West Main Street, Suite 828
Springfield, OH 45502
(513) 324-8773

Restrictions: Program-related investments, equipment, operating budgets, building funds, and other types of support for the arts, social services, civic affairs, and education.
Focus of giving: Limited to City of Springfield and Clark County, Ohio.
$ given: $249,000 for 49 grants.
Assets: $5.9 million
Contact: Lori M. Kuhn, Executive Director
Application information: Application form required
Initial approach: Letter
Copies of proposal: 2
Deadlines: March 1
Board meeting dates: February, June, and October
Final notification: July 15

The Troy Foundation

c/o Star Bank, N.A., Troy
910 West Main Street
Troy, OH 45373
(513) 335-8351

Restrictions: Program-related investments, seed money, building funds, and equipment for community development, conservation, cultural programs, recreation, health services, education, welfare, and youth.
Focus of giving: Limited primarily to the Troy City, Ohio, school district and its vicinity.
$ given: $1 million for 54 grants.
Assets: $14.6 million
Contact: Richard J. Fraas, Secretary
Application information: No application form required
Initial approach: Proposal
Copies of proposal: 5
Deadlines: None
Board meeting dates: As needed
Final notification: 1 month–2 months

The Leo Yassenoff Foundation

16 East Broad Street, Suite 403
Columbus, OH 43215
(614) 221-4315

Restrictions: Funding for social services, the disadvantaged, youth agencies, civic affairs, education, culture, and minorities. Grants awarded for seed money, emergency funds, equipment, matching funds, special projects, renovation projects and building funds.
Focus of giving: Limited to Franklin County, Ohio.
$ given: $592,000 for 117 grants; average range, $1,000–$20,000.
Assets: $4.8 million
Contact: Cynthia Cecil Lazarus, Executive Director
Initial approach: Letter or telephone
Copies of proposal: 1
Deadlines: January 1, April 1, July 1, and October 1
Board meeting dates: March, June, September, and December
Final notification: 3 months

OKLAHOMA

Ken W. Davis Foundation

P.O. Box 3419
Fort Worth, TX 76113
(817) 332-4081

See full entry under Texas.

Jack Eckerd Corporation Foundation
P.O. Box 4689
Clearwater, FL 34618
(813) 398-8318

See full entry under Florida.

Garvey Texas Foundation, Inc.
P.O. Box 9600
Forth Worth, TX 76147-0600

See full entry under Texas.

Pearl M. and Julia J. Harmon Foundation
P.O. Box 52568
Tulsa, OK 74152-0568
(918) 743-6191

Restrictions: Program-related investments and standard loans to charitable
   organizations.
Focus of giving: Limited to Arkansas, Kansas, New Mexico, Oklahoma, and
   Texas, with emphasis on northeastern Oklahoma.
$ given: $404,188 for grants; average range, $80–$12,000.
Assets: $20.6 million
Contact: George L. Hangs, Jr., Secretary-Treasurer
Application information: Application form required
Initial approach: Letter or telephone
Copies of proposal: 1
Deadlines: None
Board meeting dates: Monthly

Phillips Petroleum Foundation, Inc.
16 C4 Phillips Building
Bartlesville, OK 74004
(918) 661-6248

Restrictions: Funding for social services, education, civic organizations,
   cultural programs, and health agencies. Grants given for operating
   budgets, seed money, building funds, equipment, land acquisition,
   conferences and seminars, continuing support, renovation projects, and
   research.
Focus of giving: Limited primarily to areas of company operations, including
   Colorado, Oklahoma, Texas, and other southern and southwestern states.
$ given: $3.8 million for 545 grants; average range, $1,000–$25,000.
Contact: John C. West, Executive Manager
Initial approach: Letter, telephone or proposal
Copies of proposal: 1
Deadlines: None

Board meeting dates: March and as required
Final notification: 8 to 12 weeks

Union Pacific Foundation
Martin Tower
Eighth and Eaton Avenues
Bethlehem, PA 18018
(215) 861-3225

See full entry under Pennsylvania.

OREGON

Blue Mountain Area Foundation
11 South Second
P.O. Box 603
Walla Walla, WA 99362
(509) 529-4371

See full entry under Washington.

The Collins Foundation
1618 S.W. First Avenue, Suite 305
Portland, OR 97201
(503) 227-7171

Restrictions: Funding for education, youth, hospices, social services, art, health services, and cultural programs. Grants are awarded for building funds, equipment, matching funds, program-related investments, special projects, and research.
Focus of giving: Limited to Oregon, with emphasis on Portland.
$ given: $4.6 million for 168 grants; average range, $5,000–$200,000.
Assets: $103 million
Contact: William C. Pine, Executive Vice President
Initial approach: Letter
Copies of proposal: 1
Deadlines: None
Board meeting dates: Approximately 6 times a year
Final notification: 4 weeks–8 weeks

The Jackson Foundation
c/o U.S. Bank, Trust Department
P.O. Box 3168
Portland, OR 97208
(503) 275-5718

Restrictions: Funding to social service agencies to aid the poor and youth; also for community and civic organizations. Support for program-related investments, one-time special projects, continuing support, and research.
Focus of giving: Limited to Oregon.
$ given: $509,477 for 116 grants; average range, $1,000–$25,000.
Assets: $9.1 million
Contact: Frank E. Staich, Assistant Vice President, U.S. Bank
Application information: Application form required
Initial approach: Letter requesting application
Deadlines: March 25, August 25, and November 25
Board meeting dates: April, September, December, and as needed
Final notification: 3 weeks–4 weeks

Meyer Memorial Trust

1515 Southwest Fifth Avenue, Suite 500
Portland, OR 97201
(503) 228-5512

Restrictions: Funding provided for arts, education, humanities, health and social services, welfare, and small grants programs. Grants for seed money, building funds, equipment, matching funds, technical assistance, program-related investments, special projects, research, and renovation projects.
Focus of giving: Limited primarily to Oregon.
$ given: $15.4 million in total grant giving; range of Small Grants Program awards, $500 to $8,000.
Assets: $295 million
Contact: Charles S. Rooks, Executive Director
Application information: Application form required
Initial approach: Proposal
Copies of proposal: 1
Deadlines: Varies by program
Board meeting dates: Monthly
Final notification: 3 months–5 months for proposals that pass first screening; 1 month–2 months for those that do not

Northwest Area Foundation

E-1201 First National Bank Building
332 Minnesota Street
St. Paul, MN 55101-1373
(612) 224-9635
FAX: (612) 225-3881

See full entry under Minnesota.

Union Pacific Foundation
Martin Tower
Eighth and Eaton Avenues
Bethlehem, PA 18018
(215) 861-3225

See full entry under Pennsylvania.

PENNSYLVANIA

The Annenberg Foundation
St. Davids Center
150 Radnor-Chester Road, Suite A-200
St. Davids, PA 19087

Restrictions: Seed money and special project funding for programs designed to improve the communication of ideas and knowledge; support for early childhood and K-12 education and cultural programs.
Focus of giving: No geographic restrictions.
$ given: $53.3 million for 319 grants; average range, $25,000–$250,000.
Assets: $1.4 billion
Contact: Gail C. Levin, Sr., Program Officer
Initial approach: Letter
Copies of proposal: 1
Board meeting dates: April and November
Final notification: 6 months

Barra Foundation, Inc.
8200 Flourtown Avenue, Suite 12
Wyndmoor, PA 19118
(215) 233-5115

Restrictions: Matching funds and special projects funding for arts, education, health and social services.
Focus of giving: Limited primarily to Philadelphia, Pennsylvania, area.
$ given: $1.8 million for 284 grants; average range, $1,000–$10,000.
Assets: $28 million
Contact: Robert L. McNeil, Jr., President
Application information: Application form required
Initial approach: Letter of 1 page–2 pages
Copies of proposal: 3
Deadlines: None
Board meeting dates: December and as needed
Final notification: 3 months–6 months

Claude Worthington Benedum Foundation
1400 Benedum-Trees Building
Pittsburgh, PA 15222
(414) 288-0360

Restrictions: Funds for organizations in areas of education, health, human
   services, community development, and the arts. Grants awarded for
   matching funds, consulting services, building funds, operating budgets,
   technical assistance, special projects, program-related investments,
   research, and seed money.
Focus of giving: West Virginia and southwestern Pennsylvania.
$ given: $6.83 million for 133 grants; average range, $20,000–$50,000.
Assets: $199 million
Publications: Multi-year report and application guidelines
Contact: Paul R. Jenkins, President
Initial approach: Letter or telephone
Copies of proposal: 1
Deadlines: None
Board meeting dates: March, June, September, and December
Final notification: 6 months

Allen H. & Selma W. Berkman Charitable Trust
1500 Oliver Building
Pittsburgh, PA 15232
(412) 355-8640
Application address: 5000 Fifth Avenue, Apt. 207, Pittsburgh, PA 15232

Restrictions: Program-related investments, building funds, continuing
   support and special projects funding for education, social services, health,
   the arts, family planning, historic preservation, and for community and
   urban development.
Focus of giving: Limited primarily to the Pittsburgh, Pennsylvania, area.
$ given: $573,334 for 18 grants; average award, $1,500.
Assets: $1.8 million
Contact: Allen H. Berkman, Trustee
Application information: No application form required
Initial approach: Letter
Copies of proposal: 1
Deadlines: September 1

CBS Foundation, Inc.
51 West 52nd Street
New York, NY 10019
(212) 975-5791

See full entry under New York.

The Coleman Foundation, Inc.
575 West Madison, Suite 4605-11
Chicago, IL 60661
(312) 902-7120

See full entry under Illinois.

Grable Foundation
650 Smithfield Street, Suite 240
Pittsburgh, PA 15222
(412) 471-4550

Restrictions: Program-related investments, building funds, and continuing
    support for health, social services, family services, education, and youth.
Focus of giving: Limited primarily to the vicinities of Pittsburgh, Pennsylva-
    nia, and Orlando, Florida.
$ given: $229,700 for 25 grants.
Assets: $6.6 million
Contact: Charles R. Burke, Chairperson
Application information: No application form required
Initial approach: Proposal
Copies of proposal: 1
Deadlines: None
Board meeting dates: Vary

Howard Heinz Endowment
30 CNG Tower
625 Liberty Avenue
Pittsburgh, PA 15222-3115
(412) 281-5777

Restrictions: One time, nonrenewable grants, seed money, and capital-
    projects funding for new programs in music, education, the arts, health,
    child development, and urban affairs.
Focus of giving: Limited to Pennsylvania; emphasis on Pittsburgh and on
    Allegheny County.
$ given: $22 million for 199 grants; average range, $50,000–$500,000.
Assets: $679 million
Contact: Franklin Tugwell, Executive Director
Application information: Application form required
Initial approach: Letter or proposal
Copies of proposal: 1
Deadlines: 90 days before board meeting
Board meeting dates: May and November
Final notification: Within several days of board meeting

Kohn Foundation
1101 Market Street
2400 One Reading Center
Philadelphia, PA 19107-2996
(215) 238-1700

Restrictions: Seed money, annual campaigns, and scholarship funds for the
   aged, higher education, Jewish giving, hospitals, and theater.
Focus of giving: Philadelphia, Pennsylvania, and Israel.
$ given: $234,353 for 38 grants.
Assets: $976 million
Contact: Harold E. Kohn, Treasurer
Application information: No application form required
Initial approach: Letter
Copies of proposal: 1
Deadlines: None

Richard King Mellon Foundation
One Mellon Bank Center
500 Grant Street, 41st Floor
Pittsburgh, PA 15219-2502
(412) 392-2800
Mailing address: P.O. Box 2930, Pittsburgh, PA 15230-2930

Restrictions: Grant programs for medical research, education, social
   services, civic affairs, health care, and conservation; also interested in
   conservation of natural areas and wildlife preservation in other areas of
   the United States. Grants awarded for seed money, building funds,
   equipment, land acquisition, research, matching funds, general purposes,
   continuing support, and renovation projects.
Focus of giving: Limited primarily to Pittsburgh and western Pennsylvania;
   all areas of United States for conservation.
$ given: $30 million for 169 grants; range, $25,000–$200,000; $12 million for
   program-related investments.
Assets: $987 million
Contact: George H. Taber, Vice President
Initial approach: Proposal
Copies of proposal: 1
Deadlines: April 1 and October 1; submit proposal between January and
   March, July, and September.
Board meeting dates: June and December
Final notification: 1 month–6 months

The Pew Charitable Trusts
One Commerce Square
2005 Market St., Suite 1700
Philadelphia, PA 19102-7017
(215) 568-3330

Restrictions: Seed money, matching funds, continuing support, and program-related investments for conservation and the environment, the arts, culture, education, religion, and public policy.
Focus of giving: No geographic restrictions.
$ given: $143 million for grants; average range, $50,000–$200,000.
Assets: $3.3 billion
Contact: Rebecca W. Rimel, Executive Director
Application information: Application form required
Initial approach: Letter of inquiry of 2 pages
Copies of proposal: 1
Deadlines: Vary according to type of program
Board meeting dates: March, June, September, and December
Final notification: 3 weeks after board meetings

The Pittsburgh Foundation
One PPG Place, 30th Floor
Pittsburgh, PA 15222-5401
(412) 391-5122

Restrictions: One-time funding for programs to support special projects of regularly established agencies, capital and equipment needs, research of a nontechnical nature, and demonstration projects. Funds for urban affairs, human services, health, education, and the arts.
Focus of giving: Limited to Pittsburgh and Allegheny County, Pennsylvania.
$ given: $7.37 million for 363 grants; average range, $500–$70,000; $378,000 for program-related investments.
Assets: $210 million
Publications: Program policy statement, application guidelines
Contact: Alfred W. Wishart, Jr., President and Executive Director
Initial approach: Letter or proposal
Copies of proposal: 1
Deadlines: January 1, March 15, July 1, and September 15.
Board meeting dates: March, June, September, and December
Final notification: 4 weeks–6 weeks

Union Pacific Foundation
Martin Tower
Eighth and Eaton Avenues
Bethlehem, PA 18018
(215) 861-3225

Restrictions: Program-related investments and several other types of support for education, health, social services, and culture; preference for funding organizations not supported by taxes.
Focus of giving: Limited primarily to areas of company operations including Arkansas, California, Colorado, Idaho, Illinois, Kansas, Louisiana, Missouri, Nebraska, Nevada, Oklahoma, Oregon, Pennsylvania, Texas, Utah, Washington, and Wyoming.

$ given: $7.16 million for 800 grants; average range, $1,000–$10,000.
Assets: $1.8 million
Contact: Mrs. Judy L. Swantak, President
Application information: Application form required
Initial approach: Letter
Copies of proposal: 1
Deadlines: August 15
Board meeting dates: Late January
Final notification: February through May

PUERTO RICO

Puerto Rico Community Foundation
Royal Bank Center Building, Suite 1417
Hato Rey, PR 00917
(809) 751-3822
(809) 751-3885

Restrictions: Program-related investments, continuing support, renovation
   projects, research, and other types of support for economic development,
   community development, education, science and technology, health,
   culture, AIDS, fine arts, and agriculture.
Focus of giving: Limited to Puerto Rico.
$ given: $1.09 million for 45 grants.
Assets: $13.8 million
Contact: Elivth M. Alvarez, Administrator
Application information: Application form required
Initial approach: Letter
Deadlines: None
Board meeting dates: March, June, September, and December
Final notification: 2 weeks after board meetings

RHODE ISLAND

Dorr Foundation
P.O. Box 281
Bedford, NY 10506
(914) 234-3573
(212) 683-1370

See full entry under New York.

Joseph C. and Esther Foster Foundation, Inc.
1088 Park Avenue
New York, NY 10028

See full entry under New York.

Hasbro Industries Charitable Trust, Inc.

c/o Hasbro, Inc.
1027 Newport Avenue
Pawtucket, RI 02861
(401) 727-5429

Restrictions: Program-related investments and capital campaign funding for education, health, family services, child development and welfare, social services, and youth organizations.
Focus of giving: Limited primarily to Rhode Island and areas of corporate operations.
$ given: $895,610 for 71 grants; average range, $500–$5,000.
Assets: $3.5 million
Contact: Mary Louise Fazzano
Application information: No application form required
Initial approach: Letter
Copies of proposal: 1
Deadlines: July 1
Board meeting dates: Throughout spring and summer

Horace A. Kimball & S. Ella Kimball Foundation

c/o The Washington Trust Co.
23 Broad Street
Westerly, RI 02891
Application address: 130 Woodville Road, Hope Valley, RI 02832
(401) 364-3565

Restrictions: Seed money, matching funds, general purposes money for health services, disadvantaged, youth, community funds, cultural programs, and education.
Focus of giving: Rhode Island.
$ given: $152,000 for 22 grants.
Assets: $3.9 million
Contact: Thomas F. Black III, President
Application information: Application form required
Copies of proposal: 3
Deadlines: None
Board meeting dates: Varies

The Rhode Island Foundation/The Rhode Island Community Foundation

70 Elm Street
Providence, RI 02903
(401) 274-4564

Restrictions: To improve living conditions and well-being of Rhode Island inhabitants through support for education, the arts, social services, child welfare, AIDS, health, and the environment. Grants for seed money, operating budgets, capital campaigns, land acquisitions, building funds, and equipment.

Focus of giving: Rhode Island.
$ given: $6.6 million for grants.
Assets: $175.9 million
Contact: Robert D. Rosendale, Vice President, Finance and Administration
Application information: No application form required
Initial approach: Letter–priority to first 25 applicants received prior to board meeting
Copies of proposal: 5
Deadlines: None
Board meeting dates: January, March, May, July, September, and November
Final notification: 3 months–6 months

Fred M. Roddy Foundation, Inc.
c/o The Rhode Island Hospital Trust National Bank
One Hospital Trust Plaza
Providence, RI 02903
(401) 278-8700

Restrictions: Grants for higher education and medical research, also for hospitals.
Focus of giving: Rhode Island and Maine.
$ given: $497,350 for 27 grants.
Assets: $9.8 million
Application information: Application form required
Initial approach: Letter
Copies of proposal: 1
Deadlines: None

SOUTH CAROLINA

Mary Reynolds Babcock Foundation, Inc.
102 Reynolda Village
Winston-Salem, NC 27106-5123
(919) 748-9222

See full entry under North Carolina.

BellSouth Foundation
c/o BellSouth Corporation
1155 Peachtree Street, N.E., Room 7H08
Atlanta, GA 30367-6000
(404) 249-2396
(404) 249-2429
(404) 249-2428

See full entry under Georgia.

Jack Eckerd Corporation Foundation
P.O. Box 4689
Clearwater, FL 34618
(813) 398-8318

See full entry under Florida.

James G. Hanes Memorial Fund/Foundation
c/o NationsBank
One NCNB Plaza, T09-1
Charlotte, NC 28255
(704) 386-8477

See full entry under North Carolina.

The Meyer Family Foundation
P.O. Box 3098
Oakbrook, IL 60522-3098

See full entry under Illinois.

Post and Courier Foundation
134 Columbus Street
Charleston, SC 29403-4800
(803) 577-7111

Restrictions: Program-related investments, building funds, capital campaigns, continuing support, and other forms of funding for community development, conservation, law enforcement, health services, and cultural programs.
Focus of giving: Limited primarily to Charleston, South Carolina.
$ given: $623,722 for grants.
Assets: $3.38 million
Contact: J.F. Smoak, Foundation Manager
Application information: No application form required
Initial approach: Proposal
Deadlines: None

The South Atlantic Foundation, Inc.
428 Bull Street
Savannah, GA 31401
(912) 238-3288

See full entry under Georgia.

Trident Community Foundation
456 King Street
Charleston, SC 29403-6230
(803) 723-3635
(803) 723-2124
FAX: (803) 577-3671

Restrictions: Program-related investments, renovation projects, seed money, special projects, and other types of support for social services, education, the arts, health, housing, child development, humanities, community development, and the environment.
Focus of giving: Limited primarily to Berkeley, Charleston, and Dorchester counties, South Carolina.
$ given: $666,290 for 329 grants; average range, $10,000–$36,000; $17,500 for 3 program-related investments.
Assets: $6.6 million
Contact: Ruth Heffron, Executive Director
Application information: Application form required
Initial approach: Letter of intent by July 15
Copies of proposal: 5
Board meeting dates: 2nd Tuesday of month
Final notification: 3 months

SOUTH DAKOTA

Larson Foundation
2333 East Brook Drive
Brookings, SD 57006

Restrictions: Grants for cultural programs, community funds and development, education, child welfare, and health associations.
Focus of giving: South Dakota.
$ given: $236,298 for grants.
Assets: $314 million
Contact: Bernard Remer, Secretary
Application information: No application form required
Deadlines: None

Northwest Area Foundation
E-1201 First National Bank Building
332 MN Street
St. Paul, Minnesota 55101-1373
(612) 224-9635
FAX: (612) 225-3881

See full entry under Minnesota.

TENNESSEE

Mary Reynolds Babcock Foundation, Inc.
102 Reynolda Village
Winston-Salem, NC 27106-5123
(919) 748-9222

See full entry under North Carolina.

BellSouth Foundation

c/o BellSouth Corporation
1155 Peachtree Street, N.E., Room 7H08
Atlanta, GA 30367-6000
(404) 249-2396
(404) 249-2429
(404) 249-2428

See full entry under Georgia.

H.W. Durham Foundation

5050 Poplar Avenue, Suite 1522
Memphis, TN 38157
(901) 683-3583

Restrictions: Program-related investments, seed money, special projects, and fellowships for issues related to aging, mental health, cultural programs, adult education, health, recreation, and employment.
Focus of giving: Limited primarily to Memphis, Tennessee, and midsouth region of United States.
$ given: $216,215 for grants; average range, $1,500–$64,000.
Assets: $10.9 million
Contact: Jenks McCrory, Program Director
Application information: Application form required
Initial approach: Letter
Copies of proposal: 5
Deadlines: January 1, April 1, and August 1
Board meeting dates: February, May, and September
Final notification: Immediately after board meetings

Jack Eckerd Corporation Foundation

P.O. Box 4689
Clearwater, FL 34618
(813) 398-8218

See full entry under Florida.

James G. Hanes Memorial Fund/Foundation

c/o NationsBank
One NCNB Plaza, T09-1
Charlotte, NC 28255
(704) 386-8477

See full entry under North Carolina.

Lyndhurst Foundation

Tallan Building, Suite 701
100 West Martin Luther King Boulevard
Chattanooga, TN 37402-2561
(615) 756-0767
FAX: (615) 756-0770

Restrictions: Emphasis on the arts, education, and environmental improvement in the Southeast. Support for general purposes, seed money, matching funds, operating budgets, and special projects.
Focus of giving: Grants generally limited to Chattanooga, Tennessee, and southeastern states.
$ given: $7 million for 65 grants; average range, $10,000–$100,000; $805,000 for 22 grants to individuals; $300,000 for 1 loan.
Assets: $132 million
Contact: Jack E. Murrah, President
Application information: No application form required
Initial approach: Letter, no more than 3 pages
Copies of proposal: 1
Deadlines: January 1, March 30, June 30, and September 30
Board meeting dates: February, May, August, November, and December
Final notification: 3 months

The Meyer Family Foundation

P.O. Box 3098
Oakbrook, IL 60522-3098

See full entry under Illinois.

The Sulzberger Foundation, Inc.

229 West 43rd Street
New York, NY 10036
(212) 556-1750

See full entry under New York.

TEXAS

The Clayton Fund, Inc.

c/o First City, Texas-Houston
P.O. Box 809
Houston, TX 77001

Restrictions: Program-related investments, continuing support, operating budgets, and other types of support for education, youth, social services, and family planning.
Focus of giving: Limited primarily to Texas.
$ given: $829,570 for 39 grants; average range, $5,000–$25,000.
Assets: $28.9 million
Contact: Joe Patane, Trust Officer, First City, Texas-Houston
Application information: No application form required
Copies of proposal: 1

Communities Foundation of Texas, Inc.
4605 Live Oak Street
Dallas, TX 75204
(214) 826-5231

Restrictions: Funding for social services, health, education, hospitals, youth, and cultural programs. Support for seed money, emergency funds, building funds, equipment, land acquisition, matching funds, technical assistance, and special projects.
Focus of giving: Limited primarily to the Dallas, Texas, area.
$ given: $26.2 million for grants; average range, $500–$25,000.
Assets: $219.6 million
Contact: J. Cook, Grants Administrator
Application information: No application form required
Initial approach: Letter requesting guidelines
Copies of proposal: 1
Deadlines: February 1, July 1, and October 1
Board meeting dates: March, August, and November
Final notification: 1 week after distribution committee meeting

Ken W. Davis Foundation
P.O. Box 3419
Fort Worth, TX 76113
(817) 332-4081

Restrictions: Program-related investments and general purpose funding for community development, civic affairs, health, welfare, culture, and the arts.
Focus of giving: Limited primarily to Fort Worth and Midland, Texas, and Tulsa, Oklahoma.
$ given: $133,000 for 31 grants.
Assets: $3.4 million
Contact: Kay Davis, Vice President
Application information: No application form required
Initial approach: Proposal
Copies of proposal: 1
Deadlines: None–fiscal year ends October 31
Board meeting dates: Varies

M.S. Doss Foundation, Inc.
P.O. Box 1677
Seminole, TX 79360-1677
(915) 758-2770

Restrictions: Student aid, operating budgets, building and renovation funding for youth organizations, social services, and scholarships for higher education.
Focus of giving: Limited primarily to western Texas.

$ given: $890,395 for 26 grants; average range, $15,000–$40,000; $31,133 for 8 grants to individuals.
Assets: $35.9 million
Contact: Joe K. McGill, President
Application information: Application form required
Initial approach: Letter
Copies of proposal: 1
Deadlines: January 31, May 31, and September 30
Board meeting dates: February and as required
Final notification: Following board meetings

Jack Eckerd Corporation Foundation
P.O. Box 4689
Clearwater, FL 34618
(813) 398-8218

See full entry under Florida.

El Paso Community Foundation
Texas Commerce Bank Building, Suite 1616
El Paso, TX 79901
(915) 533-4020
FAX: (915) 532-0716

Restrictions: Program-related investments, matching funds, special projects, seed money, and other types of support for community development, the environment, social services, health, education, the arts, and the disabled.
Focus of giving: Limited to the El Paso, Texas, area.
$ given: $1.98 million for grants; $2,459 for 1 individual grant; $5,000 for 1 program-related investment.
Assets: $33 million
Contact: Janice W. Windle, President
Application information: No application form required
Initial approach: Letter requesting guidelines
Copies of proposal: 1
Deadlines: None
Board meeting dates: February, May, September, and November
Final notification: Following board meetings

The Fondren Foundation
7 TCT 37
P.O. Box 2558
Houston, TX 77252-8037
(713) 236-4403

Restrictions: Funds for higher and secondary education, social services, health services, cultural programs, and youth.
Focus of giving: Texas, with emphasis on Houston and the southwest.

$ given: $4.87 million for 75 grants; average range, $10,000–$60,000.
Assets: $105 million
Contact: Melanie A. Boone, Assistant Secretary
Application information: No application form required
Initial approach: Letter
Copies of proposal: 1
Deadlines: None
Board meeting dates: Quarterly

Garvey Texas Foundation, Inc.

P.O. Box 9600
Forth Worth, TX 76147-0600

Restrictions: Program-related investments and capital campaign funding for youth agencies, education, child welfare, health services, cultural programs, and museums.
Focus of giving: Limited primarily to Colorado, Kansas, Nebraska, Oklahoma, and Texas.
$ given: $262,000 for 91 grants.
Assets: $6.8 million
Contact: Shirley F. Garvey, President
Application information: Application form required
Initial approach: Letter
Copies of proposal: 1
Deadlines: None

Pearl M. and Julia J. Harmon Foundation

P.O. Box 52568
Tulsa, OK 74152
(918) 743-6191

See full entry under Oklahoma.

Irene Cafcalas Hofheinz Foundation

c/o NCNB Texas National Bank Houston
Trust Department
P.O. Box 298502
Houston, TX 77298-0502
(713) 787-4553

Restrictions: Program-related investments and conventional loans to civic affairs, social services, education, and the arts.
Focus of giving: Limited primarily to Houston, Texas.
$ given: $74,000 for 27 grants; range, $20–$25,000.
Assets: $2.2 million
Contact: Fred Hofheinz, Trustee
Application information: No application form required
Initial approach: Letter
Deadlines: None

Kimberly-Clark Foundation, Inc.
P.O. Box 619100
Dallas, TX 75261-9100
(214) 830-1200

Restrictions: Program-related investments, seed money, annual campaigns, building funds and equipment for homeless, youth, health, cancer, drug abuse, museums, performing arts, conservation, higher education, cultural programs, community development funds, and social services.
Focus of giving: Limited to communities where the company has operations.
$ given: $2.36 million for 42 grants; average range, $5,000–$20,000.
Assets: $161.9 million
Contact: Colleen B. Berman, Vice President
Application information: No application form required
Initial approach: Proposal
Copies of proposal: 1
Deadlines: None
Board meeting dates: April
Final notification: By year-end

The Edward and Betty Marcus Foundation
One Preston Center
8222 Douglas, Suite 360
Dallas, TX 75225
(214) 361-4681

Restrictions: Program-related investments and special project funding for innovative programs in visual arts education for youth and adults.
$ given: $184,000 for 9 grants.
Assets: $7.6 million
Contact: M'Lou Bancroft, Executive Director
Application information: No application form required
Initial approach: Proposal
Copies of proposal: 1
Deadlines: March 1 and September 1
Board meeting dates: 1st Tuesday in February, May, and November

Meadows Foundation, Inc.
Wilson Historic Block
3003 Swiss Avenue
Dallas, TX 75204-6090
(214) 826-9431

Restrictions: Funding for historic preservation, social services, the arts, education, health, and civic concerns. Support for operating budgets, continuing support, seed money, emergency funds, deficit financing, building funds, equipment, land acquisition, matching funds, special projects, publication, conferences and seminars, program-related investments, technical assistance, consulting services, research, and renovation projects.

Focus of giving: Limited to Texas.

$ given: $17.4 million for 226 grants; average range, $30,000–$60,000; $6.2 million for 2 program-related investments.

Assets: $579 million

Contact: Bruce Esterline, Vice President, Grants

Initial approach: Proposal

Copies of proposal: 1

Deadlines: None

Board meeting dates: Grants review committee meets monthly; full board considers major grants 2–3 times per year

Final notification: 3 months–4 months

Norton Company Foundation

New Bond Street, P.O. Box 15008
Worcester, MA 01615-0008
(508) 795-4700

See full entry under Massachusetts.

Phillips Petroleum Foundation, Inc.

16 C4 Phillips Building
Bartlesville, OK 74004
(918) 661-6248

See full entry under Oklahoma.

The Sonat Foundation, Inc.

1900 Fifth Avenue, North
P.O. Box 2563
Birmingham, AL 35202
(205) 325-7460

See full entry under Alabama.

Union Pacific Foundation

Martin Tower
Eighth and Eaton Avenues
Bethlehem, PA 18018
(215) 861-3225

See full entry under Pennsylvania.

Rachael & Ben Vaughan Foundation

P.O. Box 1579
Corpus Christi, TX 78403
(512) 241-2890

Restrictions: Program-related investments, annual campaigns, building funds, seed money and other types of support for community development, as well as development in the areas of education, culture, environment, religion, and the needy and disadvantaged.
Focus of giving: Limited to southern and central Texas.
$ given: $131,732 for 47 grants.
Assets: $2.6 million
Contact: William R. Ward, Jr., Assistant Secretary-Treasurer
Application information: No application form required
Initial approach: Letter
Copies of proposal: 1
Deadlines: September 1
Board meeting dates: November
Final notification: Early December

Crystelle Waggoner Charitable Trust
c/o NationsBank of Texas, N.A.
P.O. Box 1317
Fort Worth, TX 76101
(817) 390-6114

Restrictions: Funding for women, health organizations, child welfare, homeless, cultural programs, and social services. Support for general purposes, annual campaigns, building funds, emergency funds, endowment funds, equipment, operating budgets, publications, research, seed money, special projects, and renovation projects.
Focus of giving: Limited to Texas, especially Decatur and Fort Worth.
$ given: $163,064 for 34 grants; average range, $2,000–$4,000.
Assets: $4.95 million
Contact: Darlene Mann, Vice President, NationsBank of Texas, N.A.
Initial approach: Letter
Copies of proposal: 1
Deadlines: June 30 and December 31
Board meeting dates: January, April, July, and October
Final notification: 6 months

UTAH

The George S. and Dolores Dore Eccles Foundation
Deseret Building
79 South Main Street, 12th Floor
Salt Lake City, UT 84111
(801) 350-5336

Restrictions: Program-related investments, building funds, capital campaigns, equipment and other types of support for education, medical research, social services, performing and fine arts, youth, child welfare, and economics.

Focus of giving: Limited primarily to the inter-mountain area, with emphasis on Utah.

$ given: $6.3 million for 118 grants; average range, $10,000–$100,000.

Assets: $207 million

Contact: David P. Gardener, Chairperson; or Lisa Eccles

Application information: Application form required

Initial approach: Letter

Copies of proposal: 3

Deadlines: 2 weeks prior to board meetings

Board meeting dates: Quarterly

Final notification: Following board meetings

Union Pacific Foundation

Martin Tower
Eighth and Eaton Avenues
Bethlehem, PA 18018
(215) 861-3225

See full entry under Pennsylvania.

VERMONT

Dorr Foundation

P.O. Box 281
Bedford, NY 10506
(914) 234-3573
(212) 683-1370

See full entry under New York.

Joseph C. and Esther Foster Foundation, Inc.

1088 Park Avenue
New York, NY 10028

See full entry under New York.

Ellis L. Phillips Foundation

29 Commonwealth Avenue
Boston, MA 02116-2349
(617) 424-7609

See full entry under Massachusetts.

The Vermont Community Foundation
P.O. Box 30
Middlebury, VT 05753
(802) 462-3355

Restrictions: Program-related investments, seed money, special projects,
    and other types of support for the arts, humanities, community develop-
    ment, public affairs, social services, and education; emphasis on citizens'
    commitment to community needs.
Focus of giving: Limited to Vermont.
$ given: $716,219 for 273 grants.
Assets: $7.1 million
Contact: Charlotte M. Stetson, Assistant Director
Application information: No application form required
Initial approach: Letter
Copies of proposal: 3
Deadlines: April 1 and October 1
Board meeting dates: 8 times per year
Final notification: 2 months

VIRGINIA

Mary Reynolds Babcock Foundation, Inc.
102 Reynolda Village
Winston-Salem, NC 27106-5123
(919) 748-9222

See full entry under North Carolina.

Camp Foundation
P.O. Box 813
Franklin, VA 23851
(804) 562-3439

Restrictions: Support for libraries, hospitals, health services, aged, youth,
    civic affairs, and cultural programs to aid Franklin, Virginia, community;
    also for playgrounds and recreational facilities. Grants for annual cam-
    paigns, seed money, building funds, student aid, and research.
Focus of giving: Isle of Wight and Franklin, Southampton, counties; Tidewa-
    ter, Virginia; northeastern North Carolina.
$ given: $620,170 for 65 grants; $74,500 for grants to individuals.
Assets: $12.8 million
Contact: Harold S. Atkinson, Executive Director
Application information: No application form required
Initial approach: Proposal

Copies of proposal: 7
Deadlines: Between June and August
Board meeting dates: May and November
Final notification: 3 months

James G. Hanes Memorial Fund/Foundation
c/o NationsBank
One NCNB Plaza, T09-1
Charlotte, NC 28255
(704) 388-8477

See full entry under North Carolina.

Marpat Foundation, Inc
c/o Miller & Chevalier
655 15th Street, NW, Suite 900
Washington, DC 20005
(202) 626-5832

See full entry under District of Columbia.

The Meyer Family Foundation
P.O. Box 3098
Oakbrook, IL 60522-3098

See full entry under Illinois.

Portsmouth General Hospital Foundation
P.O. Box 1053
Portsmouth, VA 23705
(804) 398-4661

Restrictions: Program-related investments, seed money, equipment, and
general-purpose funding for innovative and established health programs.
Focus of giving: Limited to Portsmouth, Virginia.
$ given: $494,000 for 34 grants; $10,000 for in-kind gifts.
Assets: $10.2 million
Contact: Alan E. Gollihue, Executive Director
Application information: No application form required
Initial approach: Letter
Copies of proposal: 1
Deadlines: January 31, April 30, July 31, and October 31
Board meeting dates: 1st Wednesday of March, June, September, and
December

WASHINGTON

Norman Archibald Charitable Foundation
c/o First Interstate Bank of Washington, N.A.
P.O. Box 21927
Seattle, WA 98111
(206) 292-3543

Restrictions: Program-related investments, general purposes, seed money, building funds, land acquisition, and other types of support for youth/ child development programs, AIDS and medical research, the arts, conservation, housing programs, and animal welfare.
Focus of giving: Limited primarily to Puget Sound region of Washington.
$ given: $325,700 for 113 grants; range, $500–$15,000.
Assets: $7.3 million
Contact: Lawrence E. Miller, Vice President and Trust Officer, First Interstate Bank of Washington, N.A.
Application information: No application form required
Initial approach: Letter or telephone
Copies of proposal: 3
Deadlines: None
Board meeting dates: 5 times–6 times a year

Blue Mountain Area Foundation
11 South Second
P.O. Box 603
Walla Walla, WA 99362
(509) 529-4371

Restrictions: Program-related investments, seed money, special projects, and equipment for community projects as well as for programs promoting welfare, education, social services, family services, the aged, animal welfare, historic preservation, and the arts.
Focus of giving: Limited to Walla Walla, Columbia, Garfield, Benton, and Franklin counties, Washington, and Umatilla County, Oregon.
$ given: $161,000 for grants; $29,820 for 66 grants to individuals.
Assets: $3.9 million
Contact: Eleanor S. Kane, Administrator
Application information: No application form required
Initial approach: Letter
Copies of proposal: 1
Deadlines: July 1
Final notification: October

Comstock Foundation
819 Washington Trust Financial Center
West 717 Sprague Avenue
Spokane, WA 99204
(509) 747-1527

Restrictions: Support for recreational facilities and other community development projects, social services, youth agencies, the arts, hospitals, child welfare, Native Americans, hunger programs, and drug abuse programs. Grants for building funds, equipment, land acquisition, research, scholarship funds, general purposes, and capital funds.
Focus of giving: Washington, with emphasis on Spokane and Inland Empire areas.
$ given: $887,159 for 50 grants; average range, $300–$35,000.
Assets: $13.5 million
Contact: Horton Herman, Trustee
Application information: Application form required
Initial approach: Proposal
Copies of proposal: 1
Deadlines: None
Board meeting dates: Weekly
Final notification: 10 days

Northwest Area Foundation
E-1201 First National Bank Building
332 Minnesota Street
St. Paul, MN 55101-1373
(612) 224-9635
FAX: (612) 225-3881

See full entry under Minnesota.

Union Pacific Foundation
Martin Tower
Eighth and Eaton Avenues
Bethlehem, PA 18018
(215) 861-3225

See full entry under Pennsylvania.

WEST VIRGINIA

Claude Worthington Benedum Foundation
1400 Benedum-Trees Building
Pittsburgh, PA 15222
(412) 288-0360

See full entry under Pennsylvania.

WISCONSIN

Judd S. Alexander Foundation, Inc.
500 Third Street, Suite 509
P.O. Box 2137
Wausau, WI 54402-2137
(715) 845-4556

Restrictions: Support for community development, social services, youth,
    civic affairs, education, and programs for minorities. Grants for seed
    money, emergency funds, building funds, equipment, land acquisition,
    matching funds, technical assistance, and program-related investments.
Focus of giving: Limited primarily to Wisconsin; emphasis on Marathon
    County.
$ given: $964,084 for 75 grants; average range, $3,000–$8,000; $88,000 for 2
    program-related investments.
Assets: $32 million
Contact: Stanley F. Staples, Jr., President
Initial approach: Letter, telephone or proposal
Copies of proposal: 1
Deadlines: None
Board meeting dates: Monthly
Final notification: 60 days

Walter Alexander Foundation, Inc.
500 Third Street, Suite 509
P.O. Box 2137
Wausau, WI 54402-2137
(715) 845-4556

Restrictions: Program-related investments, seed money, land acquisition,
    building funds, capital campaigns, and other types of support for
    education, social services, and cultural programs.
Focus of giving: Primarily to Marathon County, Wisconsin.
$ given: $124,105 for 25 grants; average range, $1,000–$5,000.
Assets: $2.6 million
Contact: Stanley F. Staples, Jr., Secretary
Application information: No application form required
Initial approach: Letter
Copies of proposal: 1
Deadlines: Preferably before June
Board meeting dates: 3 times annually
Final notification: 4 months

Banc One Wisconsin Foundation
111 East Wisconsin Avenue
Milwaukee, WI 53202
(414) 765-2625

Restrictions: Support for cultural programs, higher education, youth, and community funds. Grants for general purposes, seed money, emergency funds, equipment, building funds, and continuing support.
Focus of giving: Wisconsin.
$ given: $863,744 for 450 grants.
Assets: $513 million
Contact: Frances G. Smyth, Secretary
Application information: No application form required
Initial approach: Proposal
Copies of proposal: 1
Deadlines: 15 days before board meetings
Board meeting dates: January, May, August, and December
Final notification: 2 months–3 months

Otto Bremer Foundation
445 Minnesota Street, Suite 2000
St. Paul, MN 55101-2107
(612) 227-8036
FAX: (612) 227-2522

See full entry under Minnesota.

The Coleman Foundation, Inc.
575 West Madison, Suite 4605-11
Chicago, IL 60661
(312) 902-7120

See full entry under Illinois.

Hedberg Foundation
P.O. Box 1422
Janesville, WI 53547
(708) 295-7212
Application address: 1115 West Deerpath, Lake Forest, IL 60045

Restrictions: Funds for higher education, wildlife, conservation, health associations and community funds.
Focus of giving: Wisconsin and Illinois.
$ given: $285,300 for 61 grants.
Assets: $415 million
Contact: Carla H. Westcott, Secretary-Treasurer
Application information: No application form required
Deadlines: None

Kohler Foundation, Inc.
104 Orchard Road
Kohler, WI 53044
(414) 458-1972

Restrictions: Program-related investments, seed money, building funds, equipment, special projects, and other types of support for education and the arts.
Focus of giving: Limited to Wisconsin.
$ given: $351,455 for grants.
Assets: $29.9 million
Contact: Eleanor A. Jung, Executive Director
Application information: No application form required
Initial approach: Letter
Copies of proposal: 1
Deadlines: May 1 and November 1
Board meeting dates: June, December, and as needed
Final notification: 1 week after meetings

La Crosse Community Foundation
P.O. Box 578
La Crosse, WI 54602-0578
(608) 782-3223

Restrictions: Local giving for civic affairs, education, social services, the arts, youth, family services, and child development. Grants for operating budgets, continuing support, seed money, equipment, renovation funds, special projects, and general purposes.
Focus of giving: Limited to La Crosse County, Wisconsin.
$ given: $269,906 for 45 grants; range, $300–$57,000.
Assets: $7.8 million
Contact: Sheila Garrity, Executive Director
Application information: Application form required
Initial approach: Letter
Copies of proposal: 9
Deadlines: February 15, May 15, August 15, and November 15
Board meeting dates: March, June, September, and December
Final notification: Within 1 month of meeting

The Meyer Family Foundation
P.O. Box 3098
Oakbrook, IL 60522-3098

See full entry under Illinois.

Retirement Research Foundation
8765 West Higgins Road, Suite 401
Chicago, IL 60631
(312) 714-8080
FAX: (312) 714-8089

See full entry under Illinois.

Ziemann Foundation, Inc.

P.O. Box 86
Waukesha, WI 53187-0086

Restrictions: Support for community-based social service agencies to benefit child welfare and handicapped/developmentally disabled people. Also, funds for early childhood and literacy education and family services. Grants for building funds, equipment, seed money, special projects, continuing support, and renovation projects.
Focus of giving: Wisconsin.
$ given: $96,000 for 18 grants.
Assets: $2 million
Contact: Cindy Linnan, Vice President
Application information: No application form required
Initial approach: Letter
Copies of proposal: 1
Deadlines: January 1 through September 30
Board meeting dates: May and October
Final notification: December

WYOMING

Union Pacific Foundation

Martin Tower
Eighth and Eaton Avenues
Bethlehem, PA 18018
(215) 861-3225

See full entry under Pennsylvania.

2

Program-Related Investments by Type of Business

AGRICULTURE

The Rockefeller Foundation
1133 Avenue of the Americas
New York, NY 10036
(212) 869-8500

Restrictions: Program-related investments, fellowships, research, special
    projects, grants to individuals and several other types of support for (1)
    science-based, international development in the areas of agriculture,
    health and population sciences; (2) humanities and the arts; and (3) equal
    opportunity.
Focus of giving: No geographic restrictions.
$ given: $78.7 million for 1,115 grants; $8.1 million for 463 grants to
    individuals.
Assets: $2 billion
Contact: Lynda Mullen, Secretary
Application information: No application form required
Initial approach: Letter or proposal

Copies of proposal: 1
Deadlines: Varies by program
Board meeting dates: March, June, September, and December

CONSERVATION

Norman Archibald Charitable Foundation
c/o First Interstate Bank of Washington, N.A.
P.O. Box 21927
Seattle, WA 98111
(206) 292-3543

Restrictions: Program-related investments, general purposes, seed money, building funds, land acquisition, and other types of support for youth/ child development programs, AIDS and medical research, the arts, conservation, housing programs, and animal welfare.
Focus of giving: Limited primarily to Puget Sound region of Washington.
$ given: $325,700 for 113 grants; range, $500–$15,000.
Assets: $7.3 million
Contact: Lawrence E. Miller, Vice President and Trust Officer, First Interstate Bank of Washington, N.A.
Application information: No application form required
Initial approach: Letter or telephone
Copies of proposal: 3
Deadlines: None
Board meeting dates: 5 times–6 times a year

Arizona Community Foundation
2122 East Highland Avenue, Suite 400
Phoenix, AZ 85016
(602) 381-1400

Restrictions: Program-related investments and other forms of support for health programs, human services programs (including services for the handicapped), conservation, and community-based economic development.
Focus of giving: Limited to Arizona.
$ given: $1.7 million for grants; average range, $1,000–$10,000.
Assets: $33 million
Contact: Stephen D. Mittenthal, President
Application information: Application form required
Initial approach: Letter
Copies of proposal: 15
Deadlines: February 1, June 1, and October 1
Board meeting dates: Semiannually
Final notification: 60 days

Beech Aircraft Foundation
9709 East Central Avenue
Wichita, KS 67201
(316) 681-8177

Restrictions: Program-related investments and several other types of
support for education, community funds, conservation, cultural activities,
health services, the handicapped, the aged, and youth agencies.
Focus of giving: Limited primarily to corporate locations, with emphasis on
Kansas.
$ given: $493,390 for 101 grants.
Assets: $6 million
Contact: Larry E. Lawrence, Secretary-Treasurer
Application information: No application form required
Initial approach: Letter
Copies of proposal: 1
Deadlines: March, June, September, and December
Board meeting dates: January, April, July, and October

Kimberly-Clark Foundation, Inc.
P.O. Box 619100
Dallas, TX 75261-9100
(214) 830-1200

Restrictions: Program-related investments, seed money, annual campaigns,
building funds, and equipment for homeless, youth, health, cancer, drug
abuse, museums, performing arts, conservation, higher education,
cultural programs, community development funds, and social services.
Focus of giving: Limited to communities where the company has opera-
tions.
$ given: $2.36 million for 42 grants; average range, $5,000–$20,000.
Assets: $161.9 million
Contact: Colleen B. Berman, Vice President
Application information: No application form required
Initial approach: Proposal
Copies of proposal: 1
Deadlines: None
Board meeting dates: April
Final notification: By year-end

The James G. Hanes Memorial Fund/Foundation
c/o NationsBank
One NCNB Plaza, T09-1
Charlotte, NC 28255
(704) 386-8477

Restrictions: Support for community development programs as well as for
conservation, health, and cultural programs. Funds for seed money,

annual campaigns, equipment, land acquisition, building funds, and special projects.
Focus of giving: Limited primarily to North Carolina and the Southeast.
$ given: $497,000 for 21 grants; average range, $1,000–$25,000.
Assets: $1.5 million
Contact: Manager, Foundations/Endowments
Application information: Application form required
Initial approach: Proposal
Copies of proposal: 1
Deadlines: March 15, June 15, September 15, and December 15
Board meeting dates: January, April, July, and October
Final notification: 10 days

Hedberg Foundation

P.O. Box 1422
Janesville, WI 53547
(708) 295-7212
Application address: 1115 West Deerpath, Lake Forest, IL 60045

Restrictions: Funds for higher education, wildlife, conservation, health associations, and community funds.
Focus of giving: Wisconsin and Illinois.
$ given: $285,300 for 61 grants.
Assets: $415 million
Contact: Carla H. Westcott, Secretary-Treasurer
Application information: No application form required
Deadlines: None

Island Foundation, Inc.

589 Mill Street
Marion, MA 02738-1553
(508) 748-2809

Restrictions: Program-related investments and several other types of support for environmental education and research for alternative and appropriate treatment systems of wastewater, land/wildlife conservation, and building capacity in New Bedford, Maine.
Focus of giving: Limited primarily to Northeast; program interest in New Bedford, Maine.
$ given: $720,949 for 80 grants; average range, $3,000–$20,000.
Assets: $24 million
Contact: Jenny D. Russell, Executive Director
Application information: No application form required
Initial approach: Letter or telephone
Copies of proposal: 1
Deadlines: Vary
Board meeting dates: Annual and as needed

Marbrook Foundation
400 Baker Bldg.
Minneapolis, MN 55402
(612) 332-2454

Restrictions: Seed money, building funds, equipment, land acquisition, research, and continuing support for education, business education, social services, youth and child welfare, performing arts, health, and conservation.
Focus of giving: Limited primarily to Minneapolis and St. Paul areas.
$ given: $300,000 for 78 grants.
Assets: $7.6 million
Contact: Conley Brooks, Jr., Executive Director
Application information: No application form required
Initial approach: Proposal
Copies of proposal: 1
Deadlines: May 15 and October 15
Board meeting dates: May/June, November/December
Final notification: 4 weeks after meeting

Robert R. McCormick Tribune Foundation
435 North Michigan Avenue, Suite 770
Chicago, IL 60611
(312) 222-3510

Restrictions: Program-related investments and other general purpose and special project funding for education, health services and research, cultural programs, conservation, and human services.
Focus of giving: Limited primarily to the metropolitan Chicago area.
$ given: $24 million for 549 grants; average range, $2,500–$100,000.
Assets: $550.6 million
Contact: Nicholas Goodban, Vice President of Philanthropy
Application information: No application form required
Initial approach: Letter
Copies of proposal: 1
Deadlines: February 1, May 1, August 1, and November 1
Board meeting dates: March, June, September, and December
Final notification: 2 weeks

Community Foundation of New Jersey
P.O. Box 317
Knox Hill Road
Morristown, NJ 07963-0317
(201) 267-5533

Restrictions: Program-related investments, seed money, and special project funding for innovative, broad-impact programs and research; includes

AIDS, education, health, community development and leadership, social services, family services, and the disadvantaged.

Focus of giving: Limited to New Jersey.
$ given: $695,877 for 216 grants.
Assets: $9.7 million
Contact: Sheila C. Williamson, Executive Director
Application information: Application form required
Initial approach: Telephone
Copies of proposal: 1
Board meeting dates: 4 times a year

The David and Lucille Packard Foundation

300 Second Street, Suite 200
Los Altos, CA 94022
(415) 948-7658

Restrictions: Program-related investments and several other forms of funding-locally, for educational, cultural, and community development concerns; on a national and international basis, for conservation, population studies, film preservation, and ancient studies.
Focus of giving: Local funding in the San Francisco and Monterey Bay areas of California, with additional funding in the Pueblo area of Colorado; national funding has no geographic restrictions.
$ given: $29.2 million for 365 grants; average range, $5,000–$500,000.
Assets: $718.1 million
Contact: Colburn S. Wilbur, Executive Director
Application information: No application form required
Initial approach: Full proposal
Copies of proposal: 1
Deadlines: March 15, June 15, September 15, and December 15
Board meeting dates: March, June, September, and December
Final notification: Immediately following board meetings

The Pew Charitable Trusts

One Commerce Square
2005 Market St., Suite 1700
Philadelphia, PA 19102-7017
(215) 568-3330

Restrictions: Seed money, matching funds, continuing support, and program-related investments for conservation and the environment, the arts, culture, education, religion, and public policy.
Focus of giving: No geographic restrictions
$ given: $143 million for grants; average range, $50,000–$200,000.
Assets: $3.3 billion
Contact: Rebecca W. Rimel, Executive Director
Application information: Application form required
Initial approach: Letter of inquiry of 2 pages
Copies of proposal: 1

Deadlines: Vary according to type of program
Board meeting dates: March, June, September, and December
Final notification: 3 weeks after board meetings

Post and Courier Foundation
134 Columbus Street
Charleston, SC 29403-4800
(803) 577-7111

Restrictions: Program-related investments, building funds, capital cam-
   paigns, continuing support, and other forms of funding for community
   development, conservation, law enforcement, health services, and cultural
   programs.
Focus of giving: Limited primarily to Charleston, South Carolina.
$ given: $623,722 for grants.
Assets: $3.38 million
Contact: J.F. Smoak, Foundation Manager
Application information: No application form required
Initial approach: Proposal
Deadlines: None

The Sulzberger Foundation, Inc.
229 West 43rd Street
New York, NY 10036
(212) 556-1750

Restrictions: Program-related investments, seed money, building funds,
   special projects, equipment, annual campaigns, and several other types
   of support for education, cultural programs, conservation, hospitals,
   welfare, and community funds.
Focus of giving: Limited primarily to New York and Chattanooga, Tennessee.
$ given: $1 million for 231 grants.
Assets: $21.5 million
Contact: Marian S. Heiskell, President
Initial approach: Telephone
Deadlines: None
Board meeting dates: January and as required

The Troy Foundation
c/o Star Bank, N.A., Troy
910 West Main Street
Troy, OH 45373
(513) 335-8351

Restrictions: Program-related investments, seed money, building funds, and
   equipment for community development, conservation, cultural programs,
   recreation, health services, education, welfare, and youth.
Focus of giving: Limited primarily to the Troy City, Ohio, school district and
   its vicinity.

$ given: $1 million for 54 grants.
Assets: $14.6 million
Contact: Richard J. Fraas, Secretary
Application information: No application form required
Initial approach: Proposal
Copies of proposal: 5
Deadlines: None
Board meeting dates: As needed
Final notification: 1 month–2 months

ENERGY

Geraldine R. Dodge Foundation, Inc.
163 Madison Avenue, 6th Floor
P.O. Box 1239
Morristown, NJ 07962-1239
(201) 540-8442

Restrictions: Grant-making emphasis in New Jersey on secondary education, performing and visual arts, projects in population, environment, energy, welfare of animals, and family planning. Grants for seed money, special projects, conferences and seminars, matching funds, research, continuing support, and publications.
Focus of giving: Primarily in New Jersey.
$ given: $6 million for 344 grants; average, $15,000–$25,000; $250,000 for 50 grants to individuals.
Assets: $182 million
Contact: Scott McVay, Executive Director
Initial approach: Letter or 6-page proposal
Copies of proposal: 1
Deadlines: Submit proposal in March, June, September, or December; deadlines December 15 for education, September 15 for public issues, March 15 for arts, June 15 for welfare of animals and special projects
Board meeting dates: March, June, September, and December
Final notification: End of the months in which board meets

ENGINEERING

International Paper Company Foundation
Two Manhattanville Road
Purchase, NY 10577
(914) 397-1503

Restrictions: Program-related investments and several other types of funding for model, broad-impact projects in company communities, with emphasis on primary/secondary education, and programs for minorities

and women. Also sciences, health and welfare, and community and
cultural affairs.
Focus of giving: Limited primarily to communities where the company has
plants and mills, and Memphis, Tennessee.
$ given: $1.04 million for 543 grants; average, $2,500–$10,000.
Assets: $39.9 million
Contact: Sandra Wilson, Vice President
Application information: Application form required
Initial approach: Letter, telephone or proposal to local facility
Copies of proposal: 1
Deadlines: March 1st for current year funding
Board meeting dates: June
Final notification: July

ENVIRONMENT

Consumers Power Foundation
212 West Michigan Avenue
Jackson, MI 49201
(517) 788-0318

Restrictions: Support to organizations that provide solutions to family
problems, environmental protection, arts and culture, public broadcasting,
and Michigan community foundations. Grants for operating budgets,
building funds, and renovation projects.
Focus of giving: Michigan.
$ given: $622,471 for 133 grants.
Assets: $819 million
Contact: Dennis H. Marvin, Secretary-Treasurer
Application information: No application form required
Initial approach: Letter, 1 to 2 pages
Deadlines: None
Board meeting dates: Quarterly

Dorr Foundation
P.O. Box 281
Bedford, NY 10506
(914) 234-3573
(212) 683-1370 (during business hours)

Restrictions: Program-related investments and other types of support for
science programs, especially educational projects relating science to the
environment.
Focus of giving: Limited primarily to the Northeast.
$ given: $133,000 for 8 grants; average, $5,000–$30,000.
Assets: $3.5 million
Contact: Hugh McMillan, Chairperson

Application information: No application form required
Initial approach: Brief proposal with 1–2 page summary
Copies of proposal: 7
Deadlines: None
Board meeting dates: April and December
Final notification: 1 month

El Paso Community Foundation
Texas Commerce Bank Building, Suite 1616
El Paso, TX 79901
(915) 533-4020
FAX: (915) 532-0716

Restrictions: Program-related investments, matching funds, special projects, seed money, and other types of support for community development, the environment, social services, health, education, the arts, and the disabled.
Focus of giving: Limited to the El Paso, Texas, area.
$ given: $1.98 million for grants; $2,459 for 1 individual grant; $5,000 for 1 program-related investment.
Assets: $33 million
Contact: Janice W. Windle, President
Application information: No application form required
Initial approach: Letter requesting guidelines
Copies of proposal: 1
Deadlines: None
Board meeting dates: February, May, September, and November
Final notification: Following board meetings

Geraldine R. Dodge Foundation, Inc.
163 Madison Avenue, 6th Floor
P.O. Box 1239
Morristown, NJ 07962-1239
(201) 540-8442

See full entry under Energy in this section.

Lyndhurst Foundation
Tallan Building, Suite 701
100 West Martin Luther King Boulevard
Chattanooga, TN 37402-2561
(615) 756-0767
FAX: (615) 756-0770

Restrictions: Emphasis on the arts, education, and environmental improvement in the Southeast. Support for general purposes, seed money, matching funds, operating budgets, and special projects.
Focus of giving: Grants generally limited to Chattanooga, Tennessee and southeastern states.

$ given: $7 million for 65 grants; average range, $10,000–$100,000; $805,000 for 22 grants to individuals; $300,000 for 1 loan.
Assets: $132 million
Contact: Jack E. Murrah, President
Application information: No application form required
Initial approach: Letter, no more than 3 pages
Copies of proposal: 1
Deadlines: January 1, March 30, June 30, and September 30
Board meeting dates: February, May, August, November, and December
Final notification: 3 months

Marin Community Foundation

17 East Sir Francis Drake Boulevard, Suite 200
Larkspur, CA 94939
(415) 461-3333

Restrictions: Program-related investments and several other forms of funding support for programs in humanities and the arts, education, environment, housing and community development, human needs, religion, and integrative approaches.
Focus of giving: Limited to Marin County, California.
$ given: $29.8 million for grants.
Assets: $548.9 million
Contact: Pamela Lynch, Corporate Secretary
Application information: Application form required
Initial approach: Written request for guidelines
Copies of proposal: 2
Deadlines: November 15 for environment, arts and humanities, and housing and community development; December 14 for education; January 15 for human needs; February 15 for religion
Board meeting dates: Monthly
Final notification: 3 months

Charles Stewart Mott Foundation

Office of Proposal Entry
1200 Mott Foundation Building
Flint, MI 48502-1851
(313) 238-5651

Restrictions: Program-related investments and several other types of support for community improvement, community education, environmental management, vocational education, family services, early childhood education, and minorities.
Focus of giving: No geographic restrictions.
$ given: $41.6 million for 430 grants; average range, $20,000–$200,000.
Assets: $1.16 billion
Contact: Judy Samelson, Vice President, Communications
Application information: No application form required
Initial approach: Proposal

Copies of proposal: 1
Deadlines: None
Board meeting dates: March, June, September, and December
Final notification: 60 days–90 days

The Pew Charitable Trusts
Three Parkway, Suite 501
Philadelphia, PA 19102-1305
(215) 568-3330

See full entry under Conservation in this section.

Trident Community Foundation
456 King Street
Charleston, SC 29403-6230
(803) 723-3635
(803) 723-2124
FAX: (803) 577-3671

Restrictions: Program-related investments, renovation projects, seed money, special projects, and other types of support for social services, education, the arts, health, housing, child development, humanities, community development, and the environment.
Focus of giving: Limited primarily to Berkeley, Charleston, and Dorchester counties, South Carolina.
$ given: $666,290 for 329 grants; average range, $10,000–$36,000; $17,500 for 3 program-related investments.
Assets: $6.6 million
Contact: Ruth Heffron, Executive Director
Application information: Application form required
Initial approach: Letter of intent by July 15
Copies of proposal: 5
Board meeting dates: 2nd Tuesday of month
Final notification: 3 months

Rachael & Ben Vaughan Foundation
P.O. Box 1579
Corpus Christi, TX 78403
(512) 241-2890

Restrictions: Program-related investments, annual campaigns, building funds, seed money, and other types of support for community development, as well as development in the areas of education, culture, environment, religion, the needy, and the disadvantaged.
Focus of giving: Limited to southern and central Texas.
$ given: $131,732 for 47 grants.
Assets: $2.6 million
Contact: William R. Ward, Jr., Assistant Secretary-Treasurer
Application information: No application form required

Initial approach: Letter
Copies of proposal: 1
Deadlines: September 1
Board meeting dates: November
Final notification: Early December

FILM

Abe and Frances Lastfogel Foundation
c/o Wallin, Simon, Black and Co.
1350 Avenue of the Americas
New York, NY 10019
(212) 586-5100
Restrictions: Program-related investments, annual campaigns, research and
  special project funding for cultural programs, film, performing arts, Jewish
  welfare, child welfare, and health.
Focus of giving: Limited primarily to Los Angeles, California, and New York,
  New York.
$ given: $637,655 for 248 grants.
Assets: $4.2 million
Contact: Bruce Baker, Vice President
The David and Lucille Packard Foundation
300 Second Street, Suite 200
Los Altos, CA 94022
(415) 948-7658

See full entry under Conservation in this section.

HEALTH

The John A. Hartford Foundation, Inc.
55 East 59th Street
New York, NY 10022
(212) 832-7788
FAX: (212) 593-4913

Restrictions: Program-related investments and several other types of
  support provided through aging and health programs, and health care
  quality and cost programs.
Focus of giving: No geographic restrictions.
$ given: $9.4 million for 78 grants; average range, $50,000–$300,000;
  $650,000 for 1 program-related investment.
Assets: $304 million
Contact: Richard S. Sharpe, Program Director
Application information: No application form required
Initial approach: Letter or proposal

Copies of proposal: 1
Deadlines: Make inquiry at least 6 months before funding is required
Board meeting dates: March, May, September, and December
Final notification: 6 weeks

The Robert Wood Johnson Foundation
P.O. Box 2316
Princeton, NJ 08543-2316
(609) 452-8701

Restrictions: Program-related investments, seed money, research and special-projects funding to improve health and health care of Americans through services, prevention of AIDS, drug abuse; also for minorities, the aged, and mental health.
Focus of giving: Provided throughout the United States.
$ given: $103 million for 763 grants; $6.5 million for program-related investments.
Assets: $2.9 billion
Contact: Edward H. Robbins, Proposal Manager
Application information: No application form required
Initial approach: Letter
Copies of proposal: 1
Deadlines: None

HISTORIC PRESERVATION

Allen H. & Selma W. Berkman Charitable Trust
1500 Oliver Building
Pittsburgh, PA 15232
(412) 355-8640
Application address: 5000 Fifth Avenue, Apt. 207, Pittsburgh, PA 15232

Restrictions: Program-related investments, building funds, continuing support, and special projects funding for education, social services, health, the arts, family planning, historic preservation, and for community and urban development.
Focus of giving: Limited primarily to the Pittsburgh, Pennsylvania, area.
$ given: $573,334 for 18 grants; average award, $1,500.
Assets: $1.8 million
Contact: Allen H. Berkman, Trustee
Application information: No application form required
Initial approach: Letter
Copies of proposal: 1
Deadlines: September 1

Blue Mountain Area Foundation
11 South Second
P.O. Box 603
Walla Walla, WA 99362
(509) 529-4371

Restrictions: Program-related investments, seed money, special projects, and equipment for community projects as well as for programs promoting welfare, education, social services, family services, the aged, animal welfare, historic preservation, and the arts.
Focus of giving: Limited to Walla Walla, Columbia, Garfield, Benton, and Franklin counties, Washington, and Umatilla County, Oregon.
$ given: $161,000 for grants; $29,820 for 66 grants to individuals.
Assets: $3.9 million
Contact: Eleanor S. Kane, Administrator
Application information: No application form required
Initial approach: Letter
Copies of proposal: 1
Deadlines: July 1
Final notification: October

East Hill Foundation
Main Street
Akron, NY 14001
(716) 542-3494

Restrictions: Program-related investments, seed money, and special project support for child welfare, historic preservation, and social services.
Focus of giving: Limited to Clarence and Newstead, New York.
$ given: $29,523 for 5 grants; $66,270 for program-related investments.
Assets: $1.23 million
Contact: Peter Greatbatch, President
Application information: Application form required
Initial approach: Letter or telephone
Copies of proposal: 1
Deadlines: None
Board meeting dates: Quarterly

Meadows Foundation, Inc.
Wilson Historic Block
3003 Swiss Avenue
Dallas, TX 75204-6090
(214) 826-9431

Restrictions: Funding for historic preservation, social services, arts, education, health, and civic concerns. Support for operating budgets, continuing support, seed money, emergency funds, deficit financing, building funds, equipment, land acquisition, matching funds, special projects, publication, conferences and seminars, program-related investments, technical assistance, consulting services, research, and renovation projects.

Focus of giving: Limited to Texas.

$ given: $17.4 million for 226 grants; average range, $30,000–$60,000; $6.2 million for 2 program-related investments.

Assets: $579 million

Contact: Bruce Esterline, Vice President, Grants

Initial approach: Proposal

Copies of proposal: 1

Deadlines: None

Board meeting dates: Grants review committee meets monthly; full board considers major grants 2 times–3 times per year.

Final notification: 3 months–4 months

HOTEL INDUSTRY

The Statler Foundation
107 Delaware Avenue, Suite 508
Buffalo, NY 14202
(716) 852-1104

Restrictions: Program-related investments, building funds, equipment, and other types of support for education and research relating to the hotel industry.

Focus of giving: Limited primarily to upstate New York.

$ given: $964,745 for 20 grants.

Assets: $25.8 million

Contact: Arthur J. Musarra, Chairman

Application information: Application form required for scholarship in hospitality field.

Initial approach: Letter

Copies of proposal: 3

Deadlines: April 15 for scholarships

Board meeting dates: December 1

HOUSING

Norman Archibald Charitable Foundation
c/o First Interstate Bank of Washington, N.A.
P.O. Box 21927
Seattle, WA 98111
(206) 292-3543

See full entry under Conservation in this section.

Bank of Louisville Charities, Inc.
P.O. Box 1101
Louisville, KY 40201
Application address: 500 West Broadway, Louisville, KY 40202
(502) 589-3351

Restrictions: Program-related investments and several other types of
support for cultural programs, education, health, housing, civic affairs,
and a community fund.
Focus of giving: Limited primarily to Jefferson County, Kentucky.
$ given: $285,580 for 123 grants; range, $25–$52,000.
Assets: $3.56 million
Contact: Beth Paxton Klein, Director
Application information: No application form required
Initial approach: Letter
Deadlines: None
Board meeting dates: Monthly

Doris & Victor Day Foundation, Inc.
1705 Second Avenue, Suite 424
Rock Island, IL 61201
(309) 788-2300

Restrictions: Program-related investments and general-purpose/capital
funding for housing, social services, health associations, child welfare, and
community funds.
Focus of giving: Limited to Quad city area of Rock County, Illinois, and Scott
County, Iowa.
$ given: $657,780 for 84 grants; average range, $1,000–$25,000.
Assets: $12 million
Contact: Alan Egly, Executive Director
Application information: Application information required.
Initial approach: Letter or telephone.
Copies of proposal: 1
Deadlines: May 1
Final notification: September

Greater Worcester Community Foundation, Inc.
44 Front Street, Suite 530
Worcester, MA 01608-1782
(508) 755-0980

Restrictions: Program-related investments and several other types of
support for health, education, social welfare, civic and cultural needs,
housing, and employment.
Focus of giving: Limited primarily to greater Worcester, Massachusetts, area.
$ given: $1.2 million for 189 grants; $138,350 for 144 grants to individuals;
average range, $1,000–$1,500.
Assets: $23.9 million

Contact: Ms. Ann T. Lisi, Executive Director
Application information: Application form required
Initial approach: Letter or telephone
Copies of proposal: 2
Deadlines: January 1, April 1, and September 1 for organizations; March 15 for scholarships.
Board meeting dates: March, June, September, November, and as needed.
Final notification: 3 months

The George Gund Foundation
1845 Guildhall Building
45 Prospect Avenue West
Cleveland, OH 44115
(216) 241-3114
FAX: (216) 241-6560

Restrictions: Program-related investments and several other types of support for women, youth, AIDS, childhood development, social services, ecology, the arts, race relations, and support for education projects; programs for economic revitalization and job creation; neighborhood development projects; low-income housing projects etc.
Focus of giving: Limited primarily to northeastern Ohio.
$ given: $18.3 million for grants; $975,000 for 4 program-related investments.
Assets: $505 million
Contact: David Bergholz, Executive Director
Application information: No application form required
Initial approach: Proposal
Copies of proposal: 1
Deadlines: January 15, March 30, June 30, and September 30
Board meeting dates: March, June, September, and December
Final notification: 8 weeks

The Theodore Edson Parker Foundation
c/o Grants Management Associates, Inc.
230 Congress Street, 3rd Floor
Boston, MA 02110
(617) 426-7172

Restrictions: Program-related investments and other types of support for social services, housing, community development, the urban environment, the arts, and minority concerns.
Focus of giving: Limited primarily to Lowell, Massachusetts.
$ given: $598,550 for 25 grants; average award $30,000.
Assets: $13 million
Contact: Laura Henze, Administrator; Jean Whitney, Administrator

Application information: No application form required
Initial approach: Letter, telephone, or proposal
Copies of proposal: 1
Deadlines: None
Board meeting dates: Spring and fall
Final notification: 4 months–5 months

United States Trust Company of New York Foundation

c/o U.S. Trust Co. of New York
114 West 47th Street
New York, NY 10036
(212) 852-1000

Restrictions: Program-related investments, seed money, endowment funds,
    operating budgets, and equipment for cultural programs, health, the arts,
    education, and urban affairs and development (including programs for
    housing, employment, and improved quality of life for the disadvantaged).
Focus of giving: Limited primarily to New York, New York, metropolitan area.
$ given: $394,000 for 66 grants; average range, $3,000–$5,000.
Assets: $164 million
Contact: Carol A. Strickland, Vice President
Application information: No application form required
Initial approach: Letter or proposal
Copies of proposal: 1
Deadlines: April 1
Board meeting dates: March, May, and October
Final notification: 2 months–6 months

Uris Brothers Foundation, Inc.

300 Park Avenue
New York, NY 10022
(212) 355-7080

Restrictions: Program-related investments and several other types of
    support for services/housing for homeless families, social services for
    youth, cultural institutions, employment, and community development,
    particularly the Bronx.
Focus of giving: Limited primarily to New York, New York.
$ given: $1.45 million for 78 grants; average range, $5,000–$25,000.
Assets: $25.9 million
Contact: Alice Paul, Executive Director
Application information: No application form required
Initial approach: Letter or brief proposal
Copies of proposal: 1
Deadlines: None
Board meeting dates: Quarterly

MEDICAL RESEARCH

The Trust Family Foundation
52 Stiles Road
Salem, NH 03079
(603) 898-6670
Restrictions: Support for special projects in the arts, humanities, education, Jewish giving, and medical sciences.
Focus of giving: New England, primarily Maine and New Hampshire.
$ given: $458,676 for 13 grants.
Assets: $14.17 million
Contact: Carolyn Head Benthien, Director
Application information: No application form required
Initial approach: Summary letter of 1 page–2 pages
Copies of proposal: 1
Board meeting dates: Varies

Norman Archibald Charitable Foundation
c/o First Interstate Bank of Washington, N.A.
P.O. Box 21927
Seattle, WA 98111
(206) 292-3543

See full entry under Conservation in this section.

The Coleman Foundation, Inc.
575 West Madison, Suite 4605-11
Chicago, IL 60661
(312) 902-7120

Restrictions: Program-related investments and several other forms of funding for social services and civic concerns, education (including entrepreneurial education), medical research, and programs for the handicapped.
Focus of giving: Primarily limited to metropolitan Chicago area; additional funding to the District of Columbia, Florida, Indiana, Michigan, Minnesota, Missouri, Pennsylvania, and Wisconsin.
$ given: $ 1.5 million for 62 grants; average range, $1,000–$200,000.
Assets: $76 million
Contact: Jean D. Thorne, Executive Director
Application information: No application form required.
Initial approach: Brief letter describing program
Copies of proposal: 1
Deadlines: September 30 for solicited proposals
Board meeting dates: January, April, July, and October
Final notification: 3 months for solicited proposals only

The George S. and Dolores Dore Eccles Foundation
Deseret Building
79 South Main Street, 12th Floor
Salt Lake City, UT 84111
(801) 350-5336

Restrictions: Program-related investments, building funds, capital cam- paigns, equipment, and other types of support for education, medical research, social services, performing and fine arts, youth, child welfare, and economics.
Focus of giving: Limited primarily to the inter-mountain area, with emphasis on Utah.
$ given: $6.3 million for 118 grants; average range, $10,000–$100,000.
Assets: $207 million
Contact: David P. Gardener, Chairperson; or Lisa Eccles
Application information: Application form required
Initial approach: Letter
Copies of proposal: 3
Deadlines: 2 weeks prior to board meetings
Board meeting dates: Quarterly
Final notification: Following board meetings

Fred M. Roddy Foundation, Inc.
c/o The Rhode Island Hospital Trust National Bank
One Hospital Trust Plaza
Providence, RI 02903
(401) 278-8700

Restrictions: Grants for higher education and medical research, also for hospitals.
Focus of giving: Rhode Island and Maine.
$ given: $497,350 for 27 grants.
Assets: $9.8 million
Application information: Application form required
Initial approach: Letter
Copies of proposal: 1
Deadlines: None

The John L. Weinberg Foundation
c/o Goldman Sachs & Co.
85 Broad Street, 22nd Floor
New York, NY 10004

Restrictions: Program-related investments and several other types of support for Jewish welfare, hospitals, medical research, and education.
Focus of giving: Limited primarily to New York, New York, and Greenwich, Connecticut.

$ given: $1.39 million for 125 grants.
Assets: $20.7 million
Contact: John L. Weinberg, Trustee
Application information: No application form required
Initial approach: Letter
Copies of proposal: 1

POPULATION STUDIES

The Ford Foundation
320 East 43rd Street
New York, NY 10017
(212) 573-5000

Restrictions: Program-related investments and several other types of
support for demonstration and development efforts in the following
areas: (1) urban poverty; (2) rural poverty and resources; (3) rights and
social justice; (4) governance and public policy; (5) education and culture;
(6) international affairs; and (7) reproductive health and population. Also
for women, music, youth, and AIDS.
Focus of giving: Provided on worldwide basis.
$ given: $259 million for 1482 grants; average range, $15,000–$1.5 million;
$3.65 million for 248 grants to individuals; $16 million for program-related
investments.
Assets: $6.47 billion
Contact: Barron M. Tenny, Secretary
Application information: No application form required
Initial approach: Letter, telephone, or proposal
Copies of proposal: 1
Deadlines: None
Board meeting dates: March, June, September, and December
Final notification: Usually within 1 month

The David & Lucille Packard Foundation
300 Second Street, Suite 200
Los Altos, CA 94022
(415) 948-7658

See full entry under Conservation in this section.

The Rockefeller Foundation
1133 Avenue of the Americas
New York, NY 10036
(212) 869-8500

See full entry under Agriculture in this section.

SCIENCE AND TECHNOLOGY

The Henry Vogt Foundation, Inc.
1000 W. Ormsby Avenue
Louisville, KY 40210
Application address: P.O. Box 1918, Louisville, KY 40201-1918

Restrictions: Funds for continuing support, land acquisition, equipment, research, renovation projects for community development, education, youth, computer sciences, and social services.
Focus of giving: Kentucky, with emphasis on Jefferson County and Louisville area.
$ given: $238,850 for 26 grants.
Assets: $2.2 million
Contact: Kent Oyler, Manager
Application information: No application form required
Initial approach: Letter
Copies of proposal: 1
Deadlines: May 1
Board meeting dates: June 30
Final notification: Only notifies successful applicants

The Xerox Foundation
P.O. Box 1600
Stamford, CT 06904
(203) 968-3306
Restrictions: Program-related investments and several other types of funding for science and technology, higher education, social, civic, and cultural organizations, the encouragement of public policy debates, and social responsibility.
Focus of giving: Limited primarily to areas of corporate operations.
$ given: $14.7 million for 1,526 grants; average range, $2,000–$20,000.
Assets: $777,500
Contact: Robert H. Gudger, Vice President
Application information: No application form required
Initial approach: Brief proposal
Copies of proposal: 1
Deadlines: None
Board meeting dates: December, and as needed
Final notification: 3 months

TELECOMMUNICATIONS

BellSouth Foundation
c/o BellSouth Corporation
1155 Peachtree Street, N.E., Room 7H08
Atlanta, GA 30367-6000
(404) 249-2396
(404) 249-2429
(404) 249-2428

Restrictions: Program-related investments and seed money for broad-impact educational programs, including programs to recruit and retain faculty and programs for telecommunications research.
Focus of giving: Giving primarily to areas of corporate operations including Alabama, Florida, Georgia, Kentucky, Louisiana, Mississippi, North Carolina, South Carolina, and Tennessee.
$ given: $2.89 million for grants; average range, $6,000–$30,000.
Assets: $39.7 million
Contact: Leslie J. Graitcer, Associate Director, or Wendy L.K. Best, Grants Manager
Application information: No application form required
Initial approach: Brief letter
Copies of proposal: 1
Deadlines: February 1 and August 1
Final notification: April and September

Section **II**

Flow-Through Funding

The grants in this section consist of cash awards, consulting services, and technical assistance. Loan information is also contained within this section. Most of these foundations will not fund individuals or businesses directly, but instead will only give money to enterprises that are designated as charitable under section 501(c)(3) of the Internal Revenue Code. However, you, as an individual or business, can work through a nonprofit organization that will act as your sponsor or parent organization. The monies given to you are paid directly to the nonprofit organization, which in turn pays you. Usually the nonprofit organization receives a fee of between three and seven percent of monies raised. There is NO upfront fee paid to the sponsor or parent organization; the three to seven percent fee is customary, it is not an obligation.

How do you go about finding a nonprofit conduit? Check any local directory of nonprofit organizations available (your local library will usually have such directories in its collection, perhaps in a community service section). Contact local citywide consortium-styled associations that operate in your area of interest, such as the United Way, arts councils, health and welfare planning bodies, federations, and so on. Speak to their directors or public information officers and elicit their suggestions for possible sponsors. Also check national organizational reference books, such as the Encyclopedia of Associations, for other potential candidates.

This section also provides information on donated services. Technical assistance, consulting services, and other donated services can be an invaluable help to new or existing businesses. I have also included in this section community foundations that serve a wide variety of local needs.

3

Flow-Through Funding by State

ALABAMA

The Ben May Charitable Trust
AmSouth Bank, N.A.
P.O. Drawer 1628
Mobile, AL 36629
Application address: P.O. Box 123, Mobile, AL 36601

Restrictions: Grants for higher education, cancer, and community development.
Focus of giving: Alabama.
$ given: $440,000 for 9 grants.
Assets: $8.4 million
Contact: Mr. Vivian G. Johnston, Jr., Chairperson, Distribution Committee
Application information: No application form required
Deadlines: None

ALASKA

ARCO Foundation
515 South Flower Street
Los Angeles, CA 90071
(213) 486-3342

See full entry under California.

ARIZONA

Phelps Dodge Foundation
2600 North Central Avenue, Tax Dept.
Phoenix, AZ 85004-3014
(602) 234-8100

Restrictions: Support for higher education, community funds, health,
welfare, cultural programs, and the arts. Grants for continuing support,
endowment funds, employee matching gifts, scholarship funds, and
fellowships.
Focus of giving: Limited primarily to areas of company operations.
$ given: $822,454 for 139 grants.
Assets: $12.8 million
Contact: William C. Tubman, President
Application information: No application form required
Initial approach: Letter or proposal
Copies of proposal: 1
Deadlines: None
Board meeting dates: April
Final notification: 3 months–4 months

First Interstate Bank of Arizona, N.A. Charitable Foundation
P.O. Box 29743
Phoenix, AZ 85038-9743
(602) 229-4544

Restrictions: Funding for the arts, community development, AIDS, homeless,
the aged, social services, health, and education. Money for annual
campaigns, building funds, emergency funds, equipment, general
purposes, land acquisition, research, seed money, renovation projects, and
special projects.
Focus of giving: Limited to Arizona-based organizations and national
organizations that fund programs in Arizona.
$ given: $1.1 million for 270 grants.
Assets: $2.6 million
Contact: Dianne Kossnar, Secretary
Application information: Application form required
Initial approach: Letter
Copies of proposal: 1
Deadlines: Proposals accepted January through October
Board meeting dates: Once a month
Final notification: 2 months

The Marshall Fund of Arizona
4000 North Scottsdale Road, Suite 203
Scottsdale, AZ 85251
(602) 941-5249

Restrictions: Funding for cultural and artistic programs, civil liberties, human and social problems, environmental protection and conservation, and promotion of world peace and understanding. Grants provided for matching funds, special projects, seed money, and exchange programs.
Focus of giving: Arizona.
$ given: $177,278 for 16 grants.
Assets: $2.9 million
Contact: Maxine Marshall, Vice President
Application information: No application form required
Initial approach: Letter
Copies of proposal: 6
Deadlines: March 1, August 1, and November 1
Board meeting dates: 3 times a year
Final notification: 4 months–6 months

ARKANSAS

The Ross Foundation
1039 Henderson Street
Arkadelphia, AR 71923
(501) 246-9881
Application address: P.O. Box 335, Arkadelphia, AK 71923

Restrictions: Support for community improvement programs, conservation of natural resources, public education, youth agencies, and mental retardation programs. Money for emergency funds, seed money, building funds, equipment funds, matching funds, research, general purposes, and special projects.
Focus of giving: Limited to Arkadelphia and Clark County, Arkansas.
$ given: $335,730 for 38 grants; average range, $1,000–$10,000.
Assets: $24.7 million
Contact: Ross M. Whipple, President
Application information: Application form required
Initial approach: Letter or telephone
Copies of proposal: 5
Deadlines: September 30
Board meeting dates: August, November, February, and May
Final notification: 30 days

CALIFORNIA

ARCO Foundation
515 South Flower Street
Los Angeles, CA 90071
(213) 486-3342

Restrictions: Grants for education, higher education, engineering, business, social services, the aged, the arts, public policy, and the environment. "Programs that address causes of educational, social and cultural disparity in American life." Money for technical assistance, seed money, equipment, land acquisition, operating budgets, matching funds, and special projects.
Focus of giving: Areas of company operations: Anchorage, Alaska; Los Angeles, California; Dallas, Texas.
$ given: $70,000 for 2 grants.
Assets: $2 million
Contact: Eugene R. Wilson, President
Application information: No application form required
Initial approach: Proposal of 2 pages
Copies of proposal: 1
Deadlines: None
Board meeting dates: June and December
Final notification: 4 months–6 months

BankAmerica Foundation

Bank of America Center
Department 3246, P.O. Box 37000
San Francisco, CA 94137
(415) 953-3175

Restrictions: Grants and loans in health, human resources, community and economic development, education, and culture and the arts. **Focus of giving:** Limited to areas of major company operations, including California communities, metropolitan areas nationwide and foreign countries.
$ given: $7 million for 515 grants; average range, $1,000–$20,000.
Assets: $731 million
Contact: Caroline O. Boitano, President and Executive Director
Initial approach: Letter
Copies of proposal: 1
Deadlines: July 31 for capital/major campaigns; none for all others.
Board meeting dates: annually and as needed
Final notification: Varies

Columbia Foundation

One Lombard Street, Suite 305
San Francisco, CA 94111
(415) 986-5179

Restrictions: Seed money and special project funding for programs that make a significant positive impact in environmental preservation and conservation, urban community life/culture, intercultural relations, arms control, and protection of human rights.
Focus of giving: Funding focused primarily in San Francisco Bay area.
$ given: $2.19 million for 180 grants; average range, $1,000–$50,000.
Assets: $44.6 million

Contact: Susan Clark Silk, Executive Director
Application information: Application form required
Initial approach: Letter
Copies of proposal: 1
Deadlines: February 1 and August 1
Board meeting dates: Twice a year
Final notification: 2 months–3 months

Community Foundation of Santa Clara County
960 West Hedding, Suite 220
San Jose, CA 95126-1215
(408) 241-2666

Restrictions: Funding for education, health and social services, women and minorities, youth and child welfare, employment and housing, welfare, the arts, community development, and urban affairs. Grants for seed money, emergency funds, matching funds, consulting services, technical assistance, loans, and special projects.
Focus of giving: Limited primarily to Santa Clara County, California.
$ given: $2.3 million for 481 grants; average range, $1,000–$10,000.
Assets: $27 million
Publications: Annual report, newsletter, financial statement, application guidelines and informational brochure
Contact: Winnie Chu, Program Officer
Application information: No application form required
Initial approach: Letter or telephone
Copies of proposal: 1
Deadlines: 12 weeks prior to board meetings
Board meeting dates: January 1, July 1, and October 1
Final notification: Within 2 weeks of meetings

Dayton Hudson Foundation
777 Nicollet Mall
Minneapolis, MN 55402-2055
(612) 370-6553

See full entry under Minnesota.

Fannie Mae Foundation
3900 Wisconsin Avenue, NW
Washington, DC 20016
(202) 752-6500

See full entry under District of Columbia.

Evelyn and Walter Haas, Jr. Fund
One Lombard Street, Suite 305
San Francisco, CA 94111
(415) 398-3744
FAX: (415) 986-4779

Restrictions: Support for corporate social responsibility and business ethics, alternatives to institutional care of the elderly, programs for hunger, community development, education, the Hispanic community, and the homeless. Grants for seed money, special projects, technical assistance, and general purposes.
Focus of giving: Limited primarily to San Francisco and Alameda counties, California.
$ given: $4.1 million for 171 grants; average range, $5,000–$50,000.
Assets: $208 million
Publications: Annual report and application guidelines
Contact: Ira Hirschfield, President
Initial approach: Letter of 1 page–2 pages
Copies of proposal: 1
Deadlines: None
Board meeting dates: 3 times annually
Final notification: Within 90 days

The Brotman Foundation of California
16830 Ventura Boulevard, No.#236
Encino, CA 91436

Restrictions: Grants for children, health and medical research, some support for the arts, education, and environmental organizations.
Focus of giving: Southern California.
$ given: $296,925 for 44 grants.
Assets: $8 million
Contact: c/o Robert D. Hartford
Application information: No application form required
Initial approach: Letter
Copies of proposal: 1
Deadlines: None
Board meeting dates: 3rd Friday of each month

Peninsula Community Foundation
1700 South El Camino Real, No.#300
San Mateo, CA 94402-3049
(415) 358-9369
FAX: (415) 358-9817

Restrictions: Funding for youth, the environment, the elderly, the disabled, civic concerns, and recreation; counseling services for local fund seekers. Support for operating budgets, continuing support, seed money, emergency funds, equipment, matching funds, consulting services, technical assistance, special projects, publications, conferences and seminars, general purposes, student aid, and renovation projects.
Focus of giving: Limited to San Mateo County and northern Santa Clara County, California.
$ given: $3 million for 542 grants; $70,947 for 137 grants to individuals.
Assets: $59.2 million

Publications: Annual report, informational brochure, grants list, newsletter, and application guidelines
Contact: Sterling K. Speirn, Executive Director
Initial approach: Letter
Copies of proposal: 1
Deadlines: None
Board meeting dates: Distribution committee meets in January, March, May, July, September, and November
Final notification: 2 months–3 months

The Prudential Foundation
Prudential Plaza
751 Broad Street
Newark, NJ 07102-3777
(201) 802-7354

See full entry under New Jersey.

San Diego Community Foundation
Wells Fargo Bank Building
101 West Broadway, Suite 1120
San Diego, CA 92101
(619) 239-8815
FAX: (619) 239-1710

Restrictions: Funding for civic affairs, education, cultural programs, health; social service agencies with emphasis on children, youth, families, and recreational activities. Support for seed money, equipment, matching funds, technical assistance, building funds, special projects, and renovation projects.
Focus of giving: Limited to San Diego County, California.
$ given: $319 million for 523 grants; average range, $2,000–$15,000.
Assets: $69 million
Publications: Annual report, newsletter, informational brochure, and application guidelines
Contact: John Ramsey, Executive Director
Application information: Application form required
Initial approach: Telephone
Copies of proposal: 1
Deadlines: Quarterly, call for details
Board meeting dates: Bimonthly, beginning in January
Final notification: 3 months

George H. Sandy Foundation
P.O. Box 591717
San Francisco, CA 94159-1717

Restrictions: Grants for charitable and educational purposes, aid to the

handicapped, underprivileged, and disadvantaged. Money for operating budgets, continuing support, and equipment.
Focus of giving: San Francisco Bay area, California.
$ given: $657,000 for 85 grants; average range, $3,000.
Assets: $13.6 million
Contact: Chester R. MacPhee, Jr., Trustee
Application information: No application form required
Initial approach: Letter
Copies of proposal: 1
Board meeting dates: Semiannually
Final notification: 6 months

L.J. Skaggs and Mary C. Skaggs Foundation

1221 Broadway, 21st Floor
Oakland, CA 94612-1837
(510) 451-3300

Restrictions: Funding for ecology programs, historic preservation, and the performing arts specifically, theater. Grants for special projects, general purposes, and continuing support.
Focus of giving: Limited to northern California for everything except historic preservation projects which are funded nationally.
$ given: $1.9 million for 140 grants; average range, $10,000–$30,000.
Assets: $4.4 million
Publications: Annual report, grants list, informational brochure, and application guidelines.
Contact: Philip M. Jelley, Secretary or David G. Knight, Program Director and Office Manager
Initial approach: Letter
Copies of proposal: 1
Deadlines: June 1 for letter of intent, September 1 for solicited proposals
Board meeting dates: November
Final notification: 2 weeks–3 weeks after board meeting

COLORADO

E.L. & Oma Bacon Foundation, Inc.

355 Main Street
Grand Junction, CO 81501
(303) 243-1611

Restrictions: General-purpose grants for health services, social services, religion, cultural programs and community development.
Focus of giving: Mesa County, Colorado.
$ given: $124,250 for 17 grants.
Assets: $3.2 million
Contact: Herbert L. Bacon, President

Application information: No application form required
Initial approach: Letter requesting guidelines
Copies of proposal: 2
Deadlines: None
Board meeting dates: As needed
Final notification: Within 30 days of approval

The Aspen Foundation
400 East Main Street
Aspen, CO 81611
(303) 925-9300

Restrictions: Support for the arts, education, youth, welfare-indigent
   individuals, and social services. Grants for seed money, technical assis-
   tance, special projects, matching funds, continuing support, and general
   purposes.
Focus of giving: Pitkin, Garfield, and Eagle counties, Colorado.
$ given: $969,064 for 90 grants.
Assets: $2.2 million
Publications: annual report with guidelines
Contact: Lynn Russell, Executive Director
Application information: Application form required
Initial approach: Proposal
Copies of proposal: 1
Deadlines: March 1 and October 15
Board meeting dates: Varies
Final notification: Mid-April and early December

The JFM Foundation
c/o Gloria Higgins
P.O. Box 5083
Denver, CO 80217
(303) 832-3131

Restrictions: Seed money and special project funding for transportation,
   legal systems, community service projects, innovative social service
   projects with focus on children and youth, and archaeological programs.
Focus of giving: Limited to Colorado for community projects.
$ given: $609,961 for 40 grants.
Contact: Loretta Roulier
Initial approach: Letter and concept paper of 2 pages
Copies of proposal: 3
Deadlines: None

The Needmor Fund
1730 15th Street
Boulder, CO 80302
(303) 449-5801

Restrictions: Seed money, technical assistance, general purposes, and operating budgets for projects designed to empower traditionally disadvantaged populations. Emphasis on grassroots, member-controlled organizations with realistic strategies and goals. Funding interest includes the environment, agriculture, rural development, housing, community development, and minority populations.
Focus of giving: Limited to the United States.
$ given: $2.17 million for 243 grants; average range, $5,000–$25,000.
Assets: $17 million
Contact: Lynn Gisi, Coordinator
Application information: Application form required
Initial approach: Letter or telephone
Copies of proposal: 1
Deadlines: January 10 and July 10; call to confirm
Board meeting dates: May and November
Final notification: 2 weeks after board meetings

StorageTek Foundation
2270 South 88th Street
Louisville, CO 80028-4310

Restrictions: Grants for higher education, social services, mathematics, science, and technology.
Focus of giving: Colorado.
$ given: $790,603 for 58 grants.
Assets: $281.7 million
Publications: corporate report
Contact: Ms. Arlyce Lewis, Vice President
Application information: No application form required
Deadlines: None

CONNECTICUT

Aetna Foundation, Inc.
151 Farmington Avenue
Hartford, CT 06156-3180
(203) 273-1932

Restrictions: Funding emphasis on immunization and health care for children, and minority education. Support for matching funds, employee matching gifts, and other types of funding.
Focus of giving: Limited to organizations in the United States.
$ given: $7.3 million for 200 grants; average range, $5,000–$25,000.
Assets: $30.2 million
Publications: Program policy statement, application guidelines, informational brochure, and corporate giving report
Contact: Diana Kinosh, Management Information Supervisor

Initial approach: Letter with proposal summary
Copies of proposal: 1
Deadlines: None
Board meeting dates: March, July, September, and November
Final notification: 2 months

The Greater Bridgeport Area Foundation, Inc.
280 State Street
Bridgeport, CT 06604
(203) 334-7511
FAX: (203) 333-4652

Restrictions: Support for community projects, civic concerns, housing, the environment, health, education, cultural programs, drug abuse, AIDS, and the homeless. Grants for continuing support, seed money, emergency funds, consulting services, technical assistance, conferences and seminars, special projects, general purposes, and scholarship funds.
Focus of giving: Limited primarily to communities of Bridgeport, Easton, Fairfield, Milford, Monroe, Shelton, Stratford, Trumbull, and Westport, Connecticut.
$ given: $877,298 for 380 grants; average range, $3,000–$5,000.
Assets: $12.19 million
Publications: Annual report, newsletter, financial statement, informational brochure, and application guidelines
Contact: Richard O. Dietrich, President and Chief Executive Officer
Application information: Application form required
Initial approach: Letter
Copies of proposal: 2
Deadlines: February 15, May 15, and September 15
Board meeting dates: March, July, and November; distribution committee meets in March, June, and October
Final notification: November

Hartford Foundation for Public Giving
85 Gillett Street
Hartford, CT 06105
(203) 548-1888

Restrictions: Giving emphasis on community advancement, with funding for demonstration programs and capital projects, cultural and civic endeavors, educational institutions, youth groups, and social services. Grants for seed money, emergency funds, building funds, equipment, land acquisition, technical assistance, capital campaigns, matching funds, renovations, and loans.
Focus of giving: Limited to the greater Hartford, Connecticut, area.
$ given: $11.7 million for 481 grants; average range, $45,000–$55,000; loans totaling $78,254.
Assets: $228.9 million

Publications: Program policy statement, annual report, newsletter, informa-
tional brochure, and application guidelines
Contact: Michael R. Bangser, Executive Director
Application information: Application form required
Initial approach: Telephone
Copies of proposal: 3
Deadlines: Varies by program
Board meeting dates: Monthly, except August
Final notification: 60 days–90 days

DELAWARE

Fair Play Foundation
350 Delaware Trust Building
Wilmington, DE 19801
(302) 658-6771

Restrictions: Renovation projects, equipment and land acquisition for
historic preservation, museums, environment, and wildlife.
Focus of giving: Washington, DC, Delaware, and Maryland.
$ given: $492,722 for 32 grants; average range, $20,000–$30,000.
Assets: $8 million
Contact: Blaine T. Phillips, President
Initial approach: Brief letter
Deadlines: October 1
Board meeting dates: December

DISTRICT OF COLUMBIA

Walter A. Bloedorn Foundation
c/o Reasoner, Davis & Fox
888 17th Street, NW, Suite 800
Washington, DC 20006
(202) 463-8282

Restrictions: Support for higher education, medical education, youth,
hospitals, medical research, civic affairs, and conservation. Grants for
continuing support, annual campaigns, endowments, and professorships.
Focus of giving: Washington, DC area.
$ given: $211,500 for 29 grants; average range, $1,000–$4,000.
Assets: $5.8 million
Contact: Phillip J. Sweeny, Attorney
Application information: No application form required
Initial approach: Proposal
Copies of proposal: 1

Deadlines: January and February; March for consideration at April meeting.
Board meeting dates: April
Final notification: 30 days later

Fannie Mae Foundation
3900 Wisconsin Avenue, NW
Washington, DC 20016
(202) 752-6500

Restrictions: Seed money and general-purpose funding for housing and community development programs, as well as the arts, health, AIDS, media and communications, youth, public policy, and social concerns.
Focus of giving: Limited primarily to the Washington, DC area and to cities with regional corporate offices, including Pasadena, California; Atlanta, Georgia; Chicago, Illinois; Philadelphia, Pennsylvania: and Dallas, Texas.
$ given: $6.38 million for 554 grants; average range, $1,000–$10,000.
Assets: $17.5 million
Contact: Harriet M. Ivey, Executive Director
Application information: No application form required
Initial approach: Proposal
Copies of proposal: 1
Deadlines: None
Board meeting dates: Twice annually

FLORIDA

Dade Community Foundation
200 South Biscayne Boulevard, Suite 4770
Miami, FL 33131-2343
(305) 371-2711

Restrictions: Seed money, land acquisition, and several other types of support for innovative projects addressing recognized community needs: AIDS, health services, social services, family planning, housing, education, religion, animal welfare, and the arts.
Focus of giving: Limited primarily to Dade County, Florida.
$ given: $2.48 million for 320 grants; $141,995 for 159 grants to individuals; $8,175 for 4 loans.
Assets: $29 million
Contact: Ruth Shack, President
Application information: No application form required
Initial approach: Letter
Copies of proposal: 1
Deadlines: November 30
Board meeting dates: February, May, September, and November
Final notification: 1st quarter of the year

Dayton Hudson Foundation
777 Nicollet Mall
Minneapolis, MN 55402-2055
(612) 370-6553

See full entry under Minnesota.

The Prudential Foundation
Prudential Plaza
751 Broad Street
Newark, NJ 07102-3777
(201) 802-7354
See full entry under New Jersey.

GEORGIA

AnnCox Foundation, Inc.
c/o Dow Lohnes & Albertson
One Ravina Drive, Suite 1600
Atlanta, GA 30346
Application address: 426 West Paces Ferry Road, Atlanta, GA 30305

Restrictions: Giving for higher education, museums, cultural programs,
  wildlife, conservation, medical research, and health.
Focus of giving: Limited primarily to Georgia and greater metropolitan New
  York, New York, area.
$ given: $375,473 for 40 grants.
Assets: $20 million
Contact: Anne C. Chambers, President
Initial approach: Letter
Deadlines: None

Fannie Mae Foundation
3900 Wisconsin Avenue, NW
Washington, DC 20016
(202) 752-6500

See full entry under District of Columbia.

Trust Company of Georgia Foundation
c/o Trust Co. Bank, Atlanta
P.O. Box 4418; MC 041
Atlanta, GA 30302
(404) 588-8250

Restrictions: Special project funding, building funds, renovation projects,
  equipment and employee matching gifts for local community develop-

ment, welfare, social services, education, cultural programs, the arts, and youth agencies.

Focus of giving: Limited primarily to metropolitan Atlanta, Georgia.

$ given: $1.29 million for grants.

Assets: $13.9 million

Contact: Victor A. Gregory, Secretary

Application information: Application form required

Initial approach: Letter or telephone

Copies of proposal: 1

Deadlines: March 1, June 1, September 1, and December 1

Board meeting dates: January, April, July, and October

HAWAII

The Hawaii Community Foundation
222 Merchant Street, 2nd Floor
Honolulu, HI 96813
(808) 537-6333
FAX: (808) 521-6286

Restrictions: Funding for families in crisis, youth problems, environmental concerns, historic preservation, community-based economic development and family services. Grants for operating budgets, seed money, equipment, technical assistance, research, special projects, renovation projects, student aid, scholarship funds, consulting services, conferences, and seminars.

Focus of giving: Limited to Hawaii.

$ given: $8.5 million for 1261 grants; average range, $500–$50,000; $586,453 for 575 grants to individuals.

Assets: $166 million

Publications: Program policy statement, application guidelines, informational brochure, newsletter, and annual report

Contact: Jane Renfro Smith, Chief Executive Officer

Application information: No application form required

Initial approach: Letter requesting guidelines

Copies of proposal: 1

Deadlines: 2 months prior to board meetings

Board meeting dates: Monthly, except April and September

Final notification: 2 weeks after meetings

IDAHO

Harry W. Morrison Foundation, Inc.
3505 Crescent Rim Drive
Boise, ID 83706

Restrictions: General purpose, scholarship funds, conferences and seminars, and building/renovation funding for education and Christian religion.
Focus of giving: Limited primarily to Boise, Idaho.
$ given: $272,836 for 43 grants.
Assets: $8.2 million
Contact: Velma V. Morrison, President
Initial approach: Proposal
Deadlines: March 1
Board meeting dates: May

CHC Foundation
P.O. Box 1644
Idaho Falls, ID 83403
(208) 522-2368

Restrictions: Grants for social services, community development, youth, and conservation.
Focus of giving: Southeast Idaho.
$ given: $399,420 for 52 grants.
Assets: $11 million
Contact: Joan C. Hahn, President
Initial approach: Letter or proposal
Deadlines: February 1 or September 1

ILLINOIS

Ameritech Foundation
30 South Wacker Drive, 34th Floor
Chicago, IL 60606
(312) 750-5223

Restrictions: Special project funding for economic revitalization, education, and culture in the Great Lakes region; additional funding for communications research and programs.
Focus of giving: Limited primarily to Illinois, Indiana, Michigan, Ohio, and Wisconsin.
$ given: $7.38 million for 134 grants; average range, $10,000–$25,000.
Assets: $64.6 million
Contact: Michael E. Kuhlin, Director
Application information: No application form required
Initial approach: Letter
Copies of proposal: 1
Deadlines: None
Board meeting dates: March, June, August, and December
Final notification: 3 months

The Aurora Foundation
111 West Downer Place, Suite 312
Aurora, IL 60506-5136
(708) 896-7800

Restrictions: Support for higher education, education, health, hospitals,
    social services, youth, and the arts. Grants for equipment, capital
    campaigns, seed money, student aid, building funds, and matching funds.
Focus of giving: Aurora, Illinois, area.
$ given: $240,771 for grants; $151,400 for grants to individuals.
Assets: $7.64 million
Publications: Annual report, application guidelines, and newsletter
Contact: Sharon Strede, Executive Director
Application information: Application form required
Initial approach: Telephone
Copies of proposal: 12
Deadlines: Varies; contact for current deadlines
Board meeting dates: May and November
Final notification: Varies

Continental Bank Foundation
231 South LaSalle Street
Chicago, IL 60697
(312) 923-5114

Restrictions: Special projects and renovation funding for economic develop-
    ment, low- and moderate-income housing, and education of economi-
    cally disadvantaged youth.
Focus of giving: Limited to Chicago, Illinois, area.
$ given: $1.87 million for grants; average range, $2,500–$10,000.
Assets: $24.5 million
Contact: Julie Chavez, Executive Director
Application information: No application form required
Initial approach: Proposal
Copies of proposal: 1
Board meeting dates: Quarterly
Final notification: Varies

Patrick and Anna M. Cudahy Fund
P.O. Box 11978
Milwaukee, WI 53211
(708) 866-0760

See full entry under Wisconsin.

Dillon Foundation
2804 West LeFevre Road
Sterling, IL 61081
(815) 626-9000
Application address: P.O. Box 537, Sterling, IL 61081

Restrictions: General and special project funding for community development and civic/urban affairs, libraries and historic preservation, education, hospitals, social services, and youth.
Focus of giving: Limited primarily to Sterling, Illinois, area.
$ given: $1.6 million for 80 grants; average range, $750–$8,000.
Assets: $30.6 million
Contact: Peter W. Dillon, President
Application information: No application form required
Initial approach: Letter
Copies of proposal: 1
Deadlines: None
Board meeting dates: February and August; committee meets quarterly
Final notification: As soon as possible after meetings.

Fannie Mae Foundation
3900 Wisconsin Avenue, NW
Washington, DC 20016
(202) 752-6500

See full entry under District of Columbia.

First National Bank of Chicago Foundation
One First National Plaza
Chicago, IL 60670
(312) 732-6948

Restrictions: Building funds and general support for human services, including housing programs, community development, civic affairs, law enforcement, education, and the arts.
Focus of giving: Limited to metropolitan Chicago, Illinois.
$ given: $748,174 for grants.
Assets: $1 million
Contact: David J. Paulus, President
Application information: No application form required
Initial approach: Letter
Copies of proposal: 1
Deadlines: None
Board meeting dates: March, June, September, and December
Final notification: 3 months

New Prospect Foundation
1420 Sheridan Road, Apartment 9A
Wilmette, IL 60091
(708) 256-3886

Restrictions: Seed money and special/general purpose funding for activities designed to improve housing, employment, health, welfare, and economic viability of urban neighborhoods; priority to organizations with modest budgets that may not qualify for traditional funding. Also, for pro-choice activities, AIDS advocacy, women's organizations, nuclear disarmament, human and civil rights.

Focus of giving: Limited to metropolitan Chicago area.

$ given: $613,485 for 147 grants; average range, $1,500–$7,500.

Assets: $10.4 million

Publications: Informational brochure and application guidelines

Contact: Frances Lehman, President

Application information: No application form required

Initial approach: Letter, proposal, or telephone

Copies of proposal: 1

Deadlines: 6 weeks prior to board meetings

Board meeting dates: March, June, October, and December

Final notification: 3 months

The Northern Trust Company Charitable Trust

c/o The Northern Trust Company, Community Affairs Division
50 South LaSalle Street
Chicago, IL 60675
(312) 444-4059

Restrictions: General purpose and special project funding for community development, urban development, education, health services, social services, cultural activities, youth agencies, women's organizations, minority student programs, literacy programs, performing arts, and theater.

Focus of giving: Limited to metropolitan Chicago, Cook County, area.

$ given: $1.36 million for 190 grants; average range, $2,000–$5,000.

Assets: $32 million

Contact: Marjorie W. Lundy, Vice President, The Northern Trust Co., or Eleanor Alcantara, Community Coordinator/Matching Gifts Manager

Application information: No application form required

Initial approach: Proposal

Copies of proposal: 1

Deadlines: February 1 for Health and Social Welfare; June 1 for Arts and Culture; April 1 for Education; and August 1 and December 1 for Community Revitalization

Board meeting dates: Bimonthly

Final notification: 2 months

INDIANA

Ameritech Foundation

30 South Wacker Drive, 34th Floor
Chicago, IL 60606
(312) 750-5223

See full entry under Illinois.

Fort Wayne Community Foundation, Inc.
709 South Clinton Street
Fort Wayne, IN 46802
(219) 426-4083

Restrictions: Land acquisition and several other types of support for projects that benefit Fort Wayne, including community development projects, demonstration projects, programs using community resources and volunteers, environmental programs, social/health service projects, the arts, and education.
Focus of giving: Limited primarily to Allen County, Indiana, area.
$ given: $1.2 million for 101 grants; average range, $3,000–$25,000.
Assets: $27.3 million
Contact: Mrs. Barbara Burt, Executive Director
Application information: No application form required
Initial approach: Letter, telephone, or proposal
Copies of proposal: 1
Deadlines: None
Board meeting dates: February, May, August, and November
Final notification: 3 months

Portland Foundation
411 North Meridian Street
Portland, IN 47371
(219) 726-4260

Restrictions: Seed money, capital campaign funding and other types of support for community development, youth, family services, child development, and cultural programs.
Focus of giving: Limited to Jay County, Indiana.
$ given: $209,944 for 20 grants; $123,500 for 61 grants to individuals.
Assets: $5.47 million
Publications: Newsletter, annual report, 990-PF
Contact: Jack Cole, Executive Secretary
Initial approach: Telephone or in person
Copies of proposal: 1
Deadlines: November 30
Board meeting dates: Quarterly
Final notification: January 15

IOWA

Marie H. Bechtel Charitable Remainder Uni-Trust
1000 Firstar Court
201 West Second Street
Davenport, IA 52801
(319) 328-3333

Restrictions: Grants for social services, youth, higher education, and community development.
Focus of giving: Limited primarily to Scott County, Iowa.
$ given: $512,100 for 16 grants.
Assets: $17.9 million
Contact: R. Richard Bittner, Trustee
Application information: Application form required
Deadlines: None

James W. and Ella B. Forster Charitable Trust
P.O. Box 549
Rock Rapids, IA 51246-0549
(712) 472-2537
Application address: First State & Trust Bank, Rock Rapids, IA 51246

Restrictions: Grants for community development, civic affairs, and hospitals.
Focus of giving: Limited to Iowa, with emphasis on Rock Rapids.
$ given: $118,000 to 7 grants; range, $1,400–$45,000.
Assets: $1.87 million
Contact: George Schneidermann, President and Trust Officer, First State & Trust Bank.
Application information: Application form required
Initial approach: Letter
Deadlines: September 30
Final notification: December 30

KANSAS

INTRUST Bank Charitable Trust
(formerly 1st National Bank in Wichita Charitable Trust)
c/o INTRUST Bank
P.O. Box 1
Wichita, KS 67201

Restrictions: General-purpose and building funds for higher education, youth, social services, and community funds.
Focus of giving: Kansas, with emphasis on Wichita.
$ given: $282,083 for 25 grants.
Assets: $306 million
Contact: Steven C. Woods, Sr., Vice President and Senior Trust Officer, INTRUST Bank
Application information: No application form required
Deadlines: None

Claude R. Lambe Charitable Foundation
4111 East 37th Street, North
Wichita, KS 67220
(316) 832-5404
Application address: P.O. Box 2256, Wichita, KS 67201; (316) 832-5227

Restrictions: Grants for education and the arts.
Focus of giving: No restrictions.
$ given: $2 million for 19 grants; average range, $25,000–$100,000.
Assets: $26 million
Contact: Mary Ann Fox, Secretary
Initial approach: Proposal
Deadlines: None

KENTUCKY

Foundation for the Tri-State Community
P.O. Box 2096
Ashland, KY 41105
(606) 324-3888
FAX: (606) 324-5961

Restrictions: Funding for charitable, scientific, cultural, and educational
  concerns. Support for general purposes, special projects, seed money,
  consulting services, and technical assistance.
Focus of giving: Limited to the tri-state area of Ashland, Kentucky; Ironton,
  Ohio; and Huntington, West Virginia.
$ given: $175,714 for grants.
Assets: $3.2 million
Publications: Annual report, 990-PF, and application guidelines
Contact: Theodore N. Burke, Jr., Chief Executive Officer and President
Application information: Application form required
Initial approach: Letter, telephone, or proposal
Copies of proposal: 1
Deadlines: September 15 for grants
Board meeting dates: Quarterly

Kentucky Foundation for Women, Inc.
The Heyburn Building, Suite 1215
Louisville, KY 40202
(505) 562-0045

Restrictions: Support for women artists and arts-related organizations.
  Funds for conferences and seminars, continuing support, fellowships, and
  grants to individuals.
Focus of giving: Kentucky and contiguous areas in Indiana, Ohio, West
  Virginia, and Tennessee.
$ given: $54,877 for 8 grants; $123,031 for 27 grants to individuals; $112,836
  for 2 foundation-administered programs.
Assets: $8.79 million
Contact: Ann Stewart Anderson
Application information: Application form required
Initial approach: Request application form
Copies of proposal: 2

Deadlines: October 1
Board meeting dates: November 1
Final notification: January

The Henry Vogt Foundation, Inc.
1000 West Ormsby Avenue
Louisville, KY 40210
Mailing address: P.O. Box 1918, Louisville, KY 40201-1918

Restrictions: Land acquisition, building/renovation funding, continuing
support, equipment, annual campaigns, and research funding for commu-
nity development, education, social services, youth agencies, business
education, and computer sciences.
Focus of giving: Limited to Kentucky, with emphasis on Louisville and
Jefferson County.
$ given: $238,850 for 26 grants.
Assets: $2.2 million
Contact: Kent Oyler, Manager
Application information: No application form required
Initial approach: Letter
Copies of proposal: 1
Deadlines: May 1
Board meeting dates: June 30
Final notification: Only to successful applicants

LOUISIANA

Baton Rouge Area Foundation
One American Place, Suite 610
Baton Rouge, LA 70825
(504) 387-6126

Restrictions: Renovation, special project, and other types of support for
secondary education, health, cultural programs, social services, youth, the
aged, child development, women, environment, and community develop-
ment. Preference for projects affecting a broad segment of the popula-
tion.
Focus of giving: Limited to the Baton Rouge, Louisiana, area.
$ given: $921,067 for grants.
Assets: $13.8 million
Contact: John G. Davies, President
Application information: Application form required
Initial approach: Letter, telephone or proposal
Copies of proposal: 1
Deadlines: February 15, May 15, August 15, and November 15
Board meeting dates: March, June, September, and December
Final notification: 1 week after board meetings

The Greater New Orleans Foundation
2515 Canal Street, Suite 401
New Orleans, LA 70119
(504) 822-4906

Restrictions: Funding for social services, education, health, cultural pro-
    grams, and the arts. Grants for emergency funds, technical assistance,
    seed money, special projects, equipment, and matching funds.
Focus of giving: Limited to southeast Louisiana.
$ given: $1.1 million for 272 grants; $50,000 for 1 program-related invest-
    ment.
Assets: $17 million
Publications: Program policy statement, application guidelines, annual
    report, newsletter, and informational brochure
Contact: Mrs. J. Thomas Lewis, Chairperson
Application information: Application form required
Initial approach: Proposal
Copies of proposal: 2
Board meeting dates: Quarterly

Poindexter Foundation, Inc.
P.O. Box 1692
Shreveport, LA 71165
(318)226-1040

Restrictions: General purposes and building funds for youth, health services,
    higher education, the handicapped, and cultural programs.
Focus of giving: Louisiana.
$ given: $84,000 for 37 grants.
Assets: $2 million
Contact: Roy W. James, Jr., Secretary-Treasurer
Initial approach: Letter
Deadlines: None

MAINE

Libra Foundation
P.O. Box 426
Portland, ME 04112
(207) 774-2635

Restrictions: General charitable giving.
Focus of giving: Limited primarily to Maine.
$ given: $867,073 for 29 grants.
Assets: $8.2 million
Contact: Owen W. Wells, Trustee

Application information: Application form required
Deadlines: None

UNUM Charitable Foundation
2211 Congress Street
Portland, ME 04122
(207) 770-2211

Restrictions: Support for AIDS, the aged, handicapped, family services, community development, the arts, and education. Grants for capital campaigns, employee matching gifts, matching funds, seed money, and special projects.
Focus of giving: Maine.
$ given: $1.37 million for grants.
Assets: $3.6 million
Publications: Corporate giving report with application guidelines, informational brochure, and grants list.
Contact: Janice Manning, Secretary
Application information: No application form required
Initial approach: Letter
Copies of proposal: 1
Deadlines: None
Board meeting dates: Quarterly; grants under $25,000 reviewed by staff on regular basis

MARYLAND

The Baltimore Community Foundation
The Latrobe Building
Two East Read Street, 9th Floor
Baltimore, MD 21202
(410) 332-4171

Restrictions: General-purpose, special project and other types of funding for youth, the aged, children and families, cultural programs, neighborhood programs, human services, and other community needs.
Focus of giving: Limited primarily to the Baltimore, Maryland, area.
$ given: $2.9 million for 263 grants; average range, $1,000–$10,000; $136,900 for grants to individuals; $112,149 for 1 foundation-administered program; and $6,000 for one loan.
Assets: $30.6 million
Contact: Timothy D. Armbruster, Executive Director
Application information: No application form required
Initial approach: Letter
Copies of proposal: 3
Deadlines: 60 days before board meetings
Board meeting dates: 3 times annually
Final notification: Within 2 weeks after board meetings

Morris Goldseker Foundation of Maryland, Inc.
The Latrobe Building
Two East Read Street, 9th Floor
Baltimore, MD 21202
(410) 837-5100
FAX: (410) 837-4701

Restrictions: Grants to nonprofit organizations with community affairs programs, neighborhood development projects, educational programs, services benefiting the economically disadvantaged, and for health and human services. Support for seed money, matching funds, technical assistance, and special projects.
Focus of giving: Limited primarily to the Baltimore, Maryland, area.
$ given: $1.7 million for 37 grants; average range, $700–$96,900.
Assets: $51.7 million
Publications: Annual report, application guidelines, and informational brochure.
Contact: Timothy D. Armbruster, President
Application information: No application form required
Initial approach: Submit preliminary letter as early as possible before deadlines
Copies of proposal: 2
Deadlines: April 1, August 1, and December 1
Board meeting dates: Distribution committee meets in March, June, and October.
Final notification: After board meetings

MASSACHUSETTS

The Boston Foundation, Inc.
One Boston Place, 24th Floor
Boston, MA 02108-4402
(617) 723-7415
FAX: (617) 589-3616

Restrictions: Grants for urban and community development, health, AIDS, child welfare, social services, youth, women, housing programs, the disadvantaged, and educational and cultural programs. Support for emergency funds, technical assistance, special projects, matching funds, seed money, and consulting services.
Focus of giving: Limited to metropolitan Boston area.
$ given: $18.5 million for grants; average range, $20,000–$40,000.
Assets: $276 million
Publications: Annual report, 990-PF, newsletter, grants list, and application guidelines.
Contact: Anna Faith Jones, President
Initial approach: Proposal
Copies of proposal: 1

Deadlines: 3 months prior to board meetings
Board meeting dates: March, June, September, and December
Final notification: 1 week–2 weeks after board meetings

Fidelity Foundation
82 Devonshire Street, 53
Boston, MA 02109-3614
(617) 570-6806

Restrictions: Building funds and special project funding for community development organizations, cultural affairs, education, and health organizations.
Focus of giving: Limited primarily to Massachusetts.
$ given: $2.2 million for grants; average range, $1,000–$20,000.
Assets: $40.7 million
Contact: Anne-Marie Soulliere, Foundation Director
Application information: Application form required
Initial approach: Letter requesting guidelines
Copies of proposal: 1
Deadlines: March 30 and September 30
Board meeting dates: June and December
Final notification: Immediately following board meeting

Gerondelis Foundation, Inc.
56 Central Avenue
Lynn, MA 01901
(617) 595-3311

Restrictions: Support for education, higher education, child development, Greece, medical education, hospitals, and civic affairs. Grants for scholarship funds.
Focus of giving: Massachusetts.
$ given: $201,550 for 20 grants; $51,000 for 17 grants to individuals of $3000 each.
Assets: $5 million
Contact: Charles Demakis, President
Application information: No application form required
Copies of proposal: 1
Deadlines: None
Board meeting dates: 1st Wednesday of January, April, July, and October
Final notification: Following board meetings

The George B. Henderson Foundation
c/o Henry R. Guild, Jr.
50 Congress Street, Suite 1020
Boston, MA 02109
Application address: c/o Palmer & Dodge, One Beacon Street, Boston, MA 02108
(617) 573-0100

Restrictions: Renovation and special project funding for community development, historic preservation, recreation, and the overall enhancement of the physical appearance of Boston.
Focus of giving: Limited to Boston, Massachusetts.
$ given: $244,097 for 11 grants; range, $2,000–$50,000.
Assets: $6.5 million
Contact: John T. Galvin, Secretary, Board of Designators
Application information: Application form required
Initial approach: Letter or proposal
Copies of proposal: 1
Deadlines: None
Board meeting dates: As needed
Final notification: 1 month–3 months

The Henry P. Kendall Foundation

176 Federal Street
Boston, MA 02110
(617) 951-2525

Restrictions: Funding focus on natural environment and its resources, arms control, peace, and museums. Grants for operating budgets, seed money, emergency funds, research, special projects, publications, conferences and seminars, continuing support, and loans.
Focus of giving: No geographic restrictions.
$ given: $1.1 million for 6 grants; average range, $5,000–$100,000.
Assets: $54.3 million
Contact: Salvatore F. Battinelli
Initial approach: Brief proposal
Copies of proposal: 1
Deadlines: February 15, May 15, August 15, and November 15.
Board meeting dates: March, June, September, and December
Final notification: 2 months

The Arthur D. Little Foundation

25 Acorn Park
Cambridge, MA 02140
(617) 498-5524

Restrictions: Support for higher education, science and mathematics research, innovative community programs, health care, and other scientific research. Grants for general purposes, seed money, special projects, conferences, and seminars.
Focus of giving: Limited primarily to areas of company operations.
$ given: $368,474 for 70 grants; average range, $2,000–$3,000.
Assets: $208 million
Publications: Biennial report and application guidelines
Contact: Ann Farrington, Secretary
Application information: No application form required
Initial approach: Letter

Copies of proposal: 1
Deadlines: None
Board meeting dates: 3 times–4 times a year
Final notification: After meetings

MICHIGAN

Ameritech Foundation
30 South Wacker Drive, 34th Floor
Chicago, IL 60606
(312) 750-5223

See full entry under Illinois.

Dayton Hudson Foundation
777 Nicollet Mall
Minneapolis, MN 55402-2055
(612) 370-6553

See full entry under Minnesota.

The Grand Rapids Foundation
209-C Waters Building
161 Ottawa, NW
Grand Rapids, MI 49503-2703
(616) 454-1751

Restrictions: Funding for local neighborhood development, the environment, social welfare, education, health, recreation, and cultural programs. Support for seed money, emergency funds, building funds, capital campaigns, equipment, land acquisition, matching funds, loans, renovation projects, special projects, scholarship funds, technical assistance, and consulting services.
Focus of giving: Limited primarily to Grand Rapids, Michigan, and surrounding community.
$ given: $2.2 million for 67 grants; $132,000 for 185 grants to individuals; $39,700 for 75 foundation-administered programs.
Assets: $46.4 million
Publications: Annual report, informational brochure, newsletter, and application guidelines
Contact: Marcia Rapp, Program Officer
Application information: Application form required
Initial approach: Letter or telephone
Copies of proposal: 10
Deadlines: 12 weeks prior to board meetings
Board meeting dates: February, May, August, and November
Final notification: 1 month

The Jackson Community Foundation
230 West Michigan Avenue
Jackson, MI 49201-2230
(517) 787-1321

Restrictions: Funding for local community development, historic preservation, the environment, education, and other programs for the benefit of
the residents of Jackson County. Grants for seed money, building funds,
equipment, land acquisition, matching funds, consulting services, techni-
cal assistance, loans, special projects, research, and capital campaigns.
Focus of giving: Limited to Jackson County, Michigan.
$ given: $205,571 for 61 grants; average range, $500–$18,000; $6,000 for 4
grants to individuals.
Assets: $8.6 million
Publications: Annual report with application guidelines
Contact: Herbert F. Spieler, President
Application information: No application form required
Initial approach: Letter or telephone
Copies of proposal: 20
Deadlines: January 15, April 15, July 15, and October 15
Board meeting dates: March, May, August, and November
Final notification: 6 weeks

Muskegon County Community Foundation, Inc.
Community Foundation Building
425 West Western Avenue
Muskegon, MI 49440
(616) 722-4538

Restrictions: Priority funding for pilot projects, health and human services,
the arts and culture, social services, and education. Grants for seed
money, special projects, matching funds, equipment, research, publications, conferences and seminars, scholarship funds, continuing support,
and renovation projects.
Focus of giving: Limited to Muskegon County, Michigan.
$ given: $1 million for 120 grants; average range, $25–$50,000; $166,800 for
265 grants to individuals.
Assets: $23.4 million
Publications: Program policy statement, application guidelines, annual
report, newsletter, financial statement, grants list, and informational
brochure
Contact: Patricia B. Johnson, President
Application information: Application form required
Initial approach: Telephone
Copies of proposal: 16
Deadlines: None
Board meeting dates: February, April, June, August, October, and December
Final notification: 2 weeks–3 weeks

MINNESOTA

Dain Bosworth Foundation
Dain Bosworth Plaza
P.O. Box 1160
Minneapolis, MN 55402-1160
(612) 371-2765

Restrictions: Seed money, building funds, general-purpose and other funds
for youth development and education programs, economic development,
community development, civic and cultural affairs, health, education,
social services, and the arts.
Focus of giving: Limited primarily to areas of company operations in
Minnesota.
$ given: $414,172 for 478 grants.
Assets: $85 million
Publications: Annual report and application guidelines
Contact: Sherry Koster, Executive Director
Application information: No application form required
Initial approach: Letter
Copies of proposal: 1
Deadlines: January 31 and July 31
Board meeting dates: February, March, August, and September
Final notification: 2 weeks–3 weeks after March and September meetings

Dayton Hudson Foundation
777 Nicollet Mall
Minneapolis, MN 55402-2055
(612) 370-6553

Restrictions: Funding priorities on social action programs promoting
individual socioeconomic progress and community-level socioeconomic
development, cultural and the arts programs, social services, and also for
the disadvantaged. Money for operating budgets, continuing support,
annual campaigns, matching funds, consulting services, technical
assistance, special projects, publications, and general purposes.
Focus of giving: Limited primarily to areas of company operations, including
California, Florida, Michigan, Minnesota, and Texas.
$ given: $9.69 million for 517 grants; average range, $5,000–$100,000.
Assets: $19.7 million
Publications: Program policy statement, application guidelines, informa-
tional brochure, and annual report
Contact: Cynthia Mayeda, Chairperson
Application information: Organizations located outside Minnesota should
apply to local headquarters office of Dayton Hudson Corporation
Initial approach: Letter with proposal
Copies of proposal: 1
Deadlines: None

Board meeting dates: March, June, and December
Final notification: Within 60 days, although decisions are generally not
   made between January 31 and April 15

The Minneapolis Foundation
A200 Foshay Tower
821 Marquette Avenue South
Minneapolis, MN 55402
(612) 339-7343

Restrictions: Funding to promote community development and equal
   access to resources; encourages participation of community leaders and
   constituents. Grants for seed money, emergency funds, equipment,
   technical assistance, special projects, loans, general purposes, and
   operating budgets.
Focus of giving: Limited primarily to the Minneapolis-St. Paul, Minnesota,
   seven-county metropolitan area.
$ given: $6.1 million for 602 grants; average range, $7,500–$35,000; $185,624
   for 14 grants to individuals.
Assets: $101 million
Publications: Annual report, newsletter, informational brochure, and
   application guidelines
Contact: Marion G. Etzwiler, President
Application information: Application form required; request guidelines for
   appropriate funds
Initial approach: Letter or telephone
Copies of proposal: 17
Deadlines: March 1 and September 1 for undesignated grants; January 10
   and July 10 for McKnight-Neighborhood Self-Help Initiatives Program.
Board meeting dates: Quarterly; distribution committee meets 8 times per
   year

The Prudential Foundation
Prudential Plaza
751 Broad Street
Newark, NJ 07102-3777
(201) 802-7354

See full entry under New Jersey.

MISSOURI

Harry Wilson Loose Trust
c/o The Greater Kansas City Community Foundation
1055 Broadway Street, No. 130
Kansas City, MO 64105-1595
(816) 842-0944

Restrictions: Special project funding and research for community development and civic affairs, health, social services, and culture and the arts.
Focus of giving: Limited to Kansas City, Missouri.
$ given: $205,850 for grants.
Assets: $3.4 million
Contact: Janice C. Kreamer, President, The Greater Kansas City Community Foundation
Application information: No application form required
Initial approach: Letter or proposal
Copies of proposal: 1
Deadlines: 4 months prior to full board meetings
Board meeting dates: March, June, September, and December
Final notification: 2 weeks after full board meetings

Sunnen Foundation
7910 Manchester Avenue
St. Louis, MO 63143
(314) 781-2100

Restrictions: Support for family planning, civil rights, child welfare, youth, family services, primarily for protection of reproductive and First Amendment rights. Grants for matching funds, special projects, capital campaigns, and endowment funds.
$ given: $664,942 for 24 grants.
Assets: $15 million
Contact: Helen S. Sly, President
Application information: No application form required
Copies of proposal: 5
Deadlines: August 1
Board meeting dates: Usually October
Final notification: Mid-November

MONTANA

Dennis R. Washington Foundation, Inc.
P.O. Box 7067
Missoula, MT 59807-7067
(406) 523-1300

Restrictions: Support for youth, education, delinquency, the disadvantaged, family planning, women, adult education, hunger, the aged, hospitals, fine arts, and theater. Grants for annual and capital campaigns, building funds, continuing support, and employee-related scholarships.
Focus of giving: Limited to areas of company operations.
$ given: $246,500 for 72 grants.
Assets: $4.18 million

Contact: Russell J. Ritter
Application information: Application form required
Initial approach: Letter
Copies of proposal: 1
Deadlines: None
Board meeting dates: Quarterly
Final notification: Within 30 days–45 days of receiving application

NEBRASKA

Omaha Community Foundation
Two Central Park Plaza
222 South 15th Street
Omaha, NE 68102
(402) 342-3458

Restrictions: Support for cultural programs, education, neighborhood and
community development, health, social services, women, and youth.
Grants for building funds, conferences and seminars, continuing support,
emergency funds, matching funds, publications, renovation projects, seed
money, technical assistance, and other types of support.
Focus of giving: Metropolitan Omaha, Nebraska, area.
$ given: $983,899 for 234 grants.
Assets: $9.5 million
Contact: W. Earl Taylor, Executive Director
Application information: Application form required
Copies of proposal: 7
Deadlines: April 1 and October 1
Board meeting dates: June and December
Final notification: June and December

Peed Foundation
6441 Ponderosa Drive
Lincoln, NE 68510

Restrictions: Grants for Catholic giving and Catholic welfare, and general
charitable giving.
Focus of giving: Lincoln, Nebraska.
$ given: $253,595 for 43 grants.
Assets: $794 million
Contact: Thomas Peed, Director, or Rhonda Peed, Director
Initial approach: Letter
Deadlines: None

NEVADA

Robert Z. Hawkins Foundation
One East Liberty St., Suite 509
Reno, NV 89501
(702) 786-1105

Restrictions: Special project grants for youth, child welfare, higher education, community development, social services, and Protestant giving.
Focus of giving: Nevada.
$ given: $442,425 for 79 grants.
Assets: $16.4 million
Contact: William H. Wallace, Chairman
Application information: No application form required
Initial approach: Proposal
Copies of proposal: 1

Robert M. Lee Foundation
1117 Gator Way
Sparks, NV 89431
(702) 356-7772

Restrictions: Grants for environment, conservation, and wildlife.
Focus of giving: No geographic restrictions.
$ given: $209,500 for 22 grants.
Assets: $841 million
Contact: James Crispino, Treasurer

NEW HAMPSHIRE

The New Hampshire Charitable Foundation
37 Pleasant Street
P.O. Box 1335
Concord, NH 03302-1335
(603) 225-6641

Restrictions: Funding for social and community services, the environment and conservation, and the arts; grants to start-up programs. Grants for seed money, loans, general purposes, special projects, technical assistance, and consulting services, fellowships, and college scholarships.
Focus of giving: Limited to New Hampshire.
$ given: $3.2 million for 813 grants; average range, $1,000–$5,000; loans totaling $118,000 to organizations; $394,931 for loans to individuals; $1.2 million for grants to individuals.

Assets: $73.8 million
Publications: Program policy statement, application guidelines, annual
   report, and informational brochure
Contact: Deborah Cowan, Associate Director
Application information: No application form required
Initial approach: Letter or telephone
Copies of proposal: 1
Deadlines: April 1, September 1, December 1; April 24 for student aid
   applications
Board meeting dates: February, June, and November
Final notification: 8 weeks

NEW JERSEY

The Prudential Foundation
751 Broad Street
Newark, NJ 07102-3777
(201) 802-7354

Restrictions: Program interests include business, AIDS, social services, civic
   affairs, child welfare, youth, community funds, urban and community
   affairs and education. Grants for operating budgets, continuing support,
   annual campaigns, seed money, equipment, matching funds, conferences
   and seminars, employee matching gifts, consulting services, technical
   assistance, special projects, and equipment.
Focus of giving: Primarily to areas of company operations, especially
   Newark, New Jersey, and including California, Florida, Minnesota, New
   Jersey, and Pennsylvania.
$ given: $13.2 million for grants; average range, $10,000–$75,000.
Assets: $125.7 million
Publications: Annual report and application guidelines
Contact: Barbara L. Halaburda, Secretary
Initial approach: Letter with brief description of program
Copies of proposal: 1
Deadlines: None
Board meeting dates: April, August, and December
Final notification: 4–6 weeks

Victoria Foundation, Inc.
40 South Fullerton Avenue
Montclair, NJ 07042
(201) 783-4450

Restrictions: Grants primarily for urban activities and educational programs,
   youth agencies, and education programs; support also for certain
   statewide environmental projects. Grants for operating budgets, continuing support, seed money, emergency funds, deficit financing, building

funds, matching funds, special projects, research, consulting services, technical assistance, land acquisition, and renovation projects.

Focus of giving: Limited primarily to the greater Newark, New Jersey, area; environmental grants statewide.

$ given: $6.9 million for 161 grants; average range, $20,000–$50,000; $1.5 million for 1 program-related investment.

Assets: $162 million

Publications: Annual report, informational brochure, and application guidelines

Contact: Catherine M. McFarland, Executive Officer

Application information: Application form required

Initial approach: Letter of 2 pages

Copies of proposal: 1

Deadlines: February 1 and August 1

Board meeting dates: June and November

Final notification: Within 3 weeks after board meeting if accepted

NEW MEXICO

Robert M. Lee Foundation
1117 Gator Way
Sparks, NV 89431
(702) 356-7772

See full entry under Nevada.

NEW YORK

Albany's Hospital for Incurables
P.O. Box 3628, Executive Park
Albany, NY 12203-0628
(518) 459-7711

Restrictions: Funding aimed at development for better health care, including grants to community health centers and regional health planning groups; also for AIDS programs, nutrition, and hunger programs. Money for general purposes, building funds, equipment, matching funds, renovation projects, seed money, and special projects.

Focus of giving: Limited to Albany, Schenectady, Rensselaer, and Saratoga counties, New York.

$ given: $272,103 for 19 grants; average award, $17,000.

Assets: $2.5 million

Publications: Program policy statement, application guidelines, and multiyear report

Contact: Arnold Cogswell, President

Application information: Application form required
Initial approach: Letter, telephone, or proposal
Copies of proposal: 1
Deadlines: 30 days before board meetings
Board meeting dates: January, April, June, and September
Final notification: 5 days after board meets

Bruner Foundation, Inc.

560 Broadway, 5th Floor
New York, NY 10012-3938
(212) 334-9844

Restrictions: Funds are for the evaluation of educational reform projects; the foundation is actively involved in improving the assessment of the impact of social programs. Also awards Rudy Bruner Award for Urban Excellence.
Focus of giving: Limited primarily to New York.
$ given: $462,019 for grants.
Assets: $6.5 million
Publications: Informational brochure, program policy statement, application guidelines, and newsletter
Contact: Janet Carter, Executive Director
Initial approach: Letter and brief outline of proposal
Copies of proposal: 1
Deadlines: None for most grants; November 30 for Rudy Bruner Award
Board meeting dates: As required
Final notification: 1 month

The Buffalo Foundation

601 Main-Seneca Building
237 Main Street
Buffalo, NY 14203-2781
(716) 852-2857

Restrictions: Funding for community development, charitable giving, educational and civic purposes, health, education, family services, AIDS, hospitals, child welfare, and the arts. Grants for operating budgets, seed money, emergency funds, building funds, equipment, land acquisition, special projects, matching funds, consulting services, technical assistance, research, publications, conferences and seminars, general purposes, and renovation projects.
Focus of giving: Limited primarily to Erie County, New York.
$ given: $1.59 million for 220 grants; average range, $1,000–$5,000; $371,188 for grants to individuals.
Assets: $43.7 million
Publications: Program policy statement, application guidelines, annual report, informational brochure, newsletter, and 990-PF
Contact: William L. Van Schoonhoven, Director
Initial approach: Proposal

Copies of proposal: 1
Deadlines: Last business day of March, June, September, and December
Board meeting dates: 1st Wednesday of February, May, August, and
   November
Final notification: 1st meeting after submission

Fund for the City of New York, Inc.
121 Sixth Avenue, 6th Floor
New York, NY 10013
(212) 925-6675

Restrictions: A private operating foundation supporting public and private
   projects designed to improve the effectiveness of government and
   nonprofit agencies. Emphasis on government, public policy, civic affairs,
   housing, urban environment, youth, and AIDS. Money for technical
   assistance, loans, seed money, special projects, general purposes, and
   consulting services.
Focus of giving: Limited to New York City area.
$ given: $460,550 for 63 grants; average range, $5,000–$10,000; $35,000 for
   7 grants to individuals; $9.5 million for 391 loans.
Assets: $12.1 million
Publications: Multiyear report, grants list, informational brochure, and
   application guidelines
Contact: Nancy Rivera, Program Assistant
Initial approach: Proposal
Copies of proposal: 1
Deadlines: None
Board meeting dates: Approximately 3 times a year in January, June, and
   October.

The Glens Falls Foundation
237 Glen Street
Glens Falls, NY 12801
(518) 792-1151
Application address: P.O. Box 311, Glens Falls, NY 12801

Restrictions: Promotion of the mental, moral, and physical improvement of
   the people of Glens Falls. Grants for seed money, emergency funds,
   building equipment, research, conferences and seminars, special projects,
   matching funds, land acquisition, student aid, and renovation projects.
Focus of giving: Limited to Saratoga, Warren Washington, and counties,
   New York.
$ given: $128,216 for 47 grants; $118,418 for grants to individuals.
Assets: $4.8 million
Publications: Annual report, application guidelines, and informational
   brochure
Contact: G. Nelson Lowe, Administrator
Initial approach: Letter or telephone
Copies of proposal: 8

Deadlines: March 20, June 20, September 20, and December 20.
Board meeting dates: 2nd Wednesday in January, April, July, and October
Final notification: 2 days after quarterly meetings

Stewart W. & Willma C. Hoyt Foundation
105-107 Court Street, Suite 400
Binghamton, NY 13901
(607) 722-6706

Restrictions: Funding for the arts, humanities, AIDS, social sciences, and
  education. Grants for general purposes, building funds, seed money, and
  several other types of support.
Focus of giving: Limited to Broome County, New York.
$ given: $344,898 for 33 grants; average range, $1,500–$30,000; $14,391 for
  2 loans.
Assets: $14 million
Publications: Annual report and application guidelines
Contact: Judith C. Peckham, Executive Director
Application information: Application form required
Initial approach: Letter or telephone
Copies of proposal: 1
Deadlines: 1st day of month prior to board meeting
Board meeting dates: Bimonthly, beginning in January; no grants awarded
  January, May, or September
Final notification: 1 to 3 days following board meetings

The Katzenberger Foundation, Inc.
c/o Muchnick, Golieb & Golieb
630 Fifth Avenue, Suite 1425
New York, NY 10111
(212) 315-5575

Restrictions: General purposes giving for the disadvantaged, welfare, higher
  education, secondary education, youth, child welfare and development,
  and community development.
Focus of giving: No geographic restrictions.
$ given: $579,500 for 40 grants.
Assets: $11.8 million
Contact: Abner J. Golieb, President
Application information: No application form required
Initial approach: Letter
Copies of proposal: 2
Deadlines: September 30
Board meeting dates: November and May
Final notification: November 30

The Lavanburg-Corner House, Inc.
130 East 59th Street, 15th Floor
New York, NY 10022
(212) 836-1358

Restrictions: Support for youth, child welfare, the disadvantaged, education, minorities and employment. Grants for seed money, matching funds, and special project funding.
Focus of giving: Metropolitan area of New York, New York.
$ given: $262,150 for 33 grants.
Assets: $1.69 million
Contact: Lauren Katzowitz, Staff Consultant
Application information: Application form required
Initial approach: Proposal with 1-page summary
Copies of proposal: 1
Deadlines: None
Board meeting dates: As needed
Final notification: 3 weeks after board meetings

The New York Community Trust

Two Park Avenue, 24th Floor
New York, NY 10016-9385
(212) 686-0010
FAX: (212) 532-8528

Restrictions: Interests in the following areas: (1) children and youth; (2) community development and the environment, including conservation, housing, economy, and revitalization; (3) education, the arts, and humanities; and (4) health and people with special needs. Grants for seed money, technical assistance, special projects, research, publications, and other types of support.
Focus of giving: Limited to New York, New York, area.
$ given: $100.8 million for 2947 grants; average range, $5,000–$35,000.
Assets: $1 billion
Publications: Annual report, newsletter, informational brochure, financial statement, occasional report, and application guidelines
Contact: Lorie A. Slutsky, Director
Application information: Application form required
Initial approach: Proposal with cover letter
Copies of proposal: 1
Deadlines: None
Board meeting dates: February, April, June, July, October, and December
Final notification: Up to 25 weeks

Rich Foundation, Inc.

1150 Niagara Street
P.O. Box 245
Buffalo, NY 14240
(716) 878-8000

Restrictions: Grants for community funds, religion: Christian education, higher education, youth, and Catholic giving.
Focus of giving: Limited to Buffalo and western New York area.
$ given: $307,203 for 150 grants.

Assets: $1 million
Contact: David A. Rich, Executive Director
Initial approach: Letter
Deadlines: None

The Frederick W. Richmond Foundation, Inc.

P.O. Box 33
Wantagh, NY 11793
(516) 579-3373

Restrictions: Grants for special projects and seed money for projects in
    education, the arts, and cultural programs, museums, and funding for
    AIDS.
Focus of giving: No geographic restriction.
$ given: $282,808 for 106 grants; average award, $2,000.
Assets: $3.3 million
Publications: Program policy statement
Contact: Pauline Nunen, Executive Director
Application information: No application form required
Initial approach: Letter
Copies of proposal: 1
Deadlines: None
Board meeting dates: Twice annually
Final notification: 3 months

Surdna Foundation, Inc.

1155 Avenue of the Americas, 16th Floor
New York, NY 10036
(212) 730-0030
FAX: (212) 391-4384

Restrictions: General purpose, seed money, technical assistance, continuing
    support, and special project funding for the environment, especially
    energy, transportation, urban/suburban, and cultural diversity issues; and
    for community revitalization. Interest in entrepreneurial programs
    addressing systemic problems.
Focus of giving: No geographic restrictions.
$ given: $11.47 million for 160 grants.
Assets: $380 million
Contact: Edward Skloot, Executive Director
Application information: No application form required
Initial approach: Letter and program outline, IRS certification letter, and
    audited financial statements
Copies of proposal: 1
Deadlines: None
Board meeting dates: February, May, September, and November
Final notification: 90 days

NORTH CAROLINA

Foundation for the Carolinas
301 South Brevard Street
Charlotte, NC 28202
(704) 376-9541

Restrictions: Funding to organizations serving Carolina citizens; support for
health, education, human services, and the arts. Grants for seed money,
matching funds, and scholarship funds.
Focus of giving: Limited primarily to North Carolina and South Carolina, with
emphasis on the Central Piedmont region.
$ given: $6.97 million for grants; average range, $1,000–$5,000.
Assets: $65.9 million
Publications: Program policy statement, application guidelines, annual
report, and newsletter
Contact: Marilyn M. Bradbury, Vice President
Application information: Application form required
Initial approach: Letter
Copies of proposal: 15
Deadlines: February 1, June 1, and October 1
Board meeting dates: Quarterly, with annual meeting in March; distribution
committee meets 3 times a year
Final notification: 2 months

Hillsdale Fund, Inc.
P.O. Box 20124
Greensboro, NC 27420
(919) 274-5471

Restrictions: General charitable giving.
Focus of giving: North Carolina and eastern seaboard.
$ given: $806,100 for 52 grants.
Assets: $18.5 million
Contact: Sion A. Boney, Administrative Vice President
Application information: No application form required
Initial approach: Proposal and 14 copies each of brochures and printed
materials
Copies of proposal: 1
Deadlines: 1 month–6 months prior to board meetings
Board meeting dates: Usually April, June, and November

OHIO

Ameritech Foundation
30 South Wacker Drive, 34th Floor
Chicago, IL 60606
(312) 750-5223

See full entry under Illinois.

The Dayton Foundation
2100 Kettering Tower
Dayton, OH 45423-1395
(513) 222-0410
FAX: (513) 222-0636

Restrictions: Funding for community development, civic affairs, conservation, environment, youth, social services, cultural programs, health
services, and other purposes beneficial to local citizens. Grants for seed
money, building funds, equipment, matching funds, and several other
types of support.
Focus of giving: Limited to the Dayton, Ohio, area.
$ given: $9.1 million for grants; $40,182 for 44 grants to individuals; $1.15
million for program-related investments.
Assets: $59.7 million
Publications: Program policy statement, application guidelines, annual
report, newsletter, and informational brochure
Contact: Judy Thompson, Director, Grants/Programs
Initial approach: Letter or telephone, proposal
Copies of proposal: 1
Deadlines: March, July, September, and November
Board meeting dates: 4 times a year
Final notification: 4 weeks–6 weeks

George H. Deuble Foundation
c/o Society National Bank, Trust Tax Department
Box 5937
Cleveland, OH 44101-0937
Application address: c/o DCC Corp., 5757 Mayfair Road, North Canton, OH
44720; (216) 445-0160

Restrictions: Support for youth agencies, education, hospitals, and cultural
programs. Grants for continuing support, building funds, and several other
types of support.
Focus of giving: Limited primarily to the Stark County, Ohio, area.
$ given: $840,019 for 103 grants.
Assets: $17.8 million
Contact: Andrew H. Deuble, Trustee
Initial approach: Letter
Copies of proposal: 1
Deadlines: None
Board meeting dates: Monthly
Final notification: 1 month

Foundation for the Tri-State Community
P.O. Box 2096
Ashland, KY 41105
(606) 324-3888
FAX: (606) 324-5961

See full entry under Kentucky.

Ferro Foundation
1000 Lakeside Avenue
Cleveland, OH 44114-1183
(216) 641-8580

Restrictions: Support for community funds, higher education, cultural programs, and hospitals. Grants for operating budgets, building funds, annual campaigns, and capital campaigns.
Focus of giving: Ohio.
$ given: $250,200 for 45 grants.
Assets: $30 million
Contact: James M. Hill, Secretary-Treasurer
Application information: No application form required
Board meeting dates: 4th Friday in April for annual meeting; board meets quarterly

David Meade Massie Trust
65 East Second Street
P.O. Box 41
Chillicothe, OH 45601
(614) 772-5070

Restrictions: Equipment for community development programs, especially volunteer fire departments, youth, and health; additional funding for social services, education, and cultural programs.
Focus of giving: Limited to Chillicothe and Ross counties, Ohio.
$ given: $274,451 for 63 grants.
Assets: $3.8 million
Contact: Marilyn J. Carnes
Application information: Application form required
Deadlines: March 1, June 1, September 1, and December 1

The Stark County Foundation
United Bank Building, Suite 350
220 Market Avenue South
Canton, OH 44702
(216) 454-3426

Restrictions: Funding for local civic improvement programs, including the Newmarket Project for downtown revitalization in Canton. Grants for seed money, emergency funds, building funds, equipment, land acquisition, matching funds, special projects, research, conferences and seminars, consulting services, and technical assistance.
Focus of giving: Limited to Stark County, Ohio.
$ given: $1.9 million for 251 grants; average range, $2,500–$20,000; $52,202 for grants to individuals; $105,845 for loans to individuals.
Assets: $46.4 million
Publications: Program policy statement, application guidelines, grants list, financial statement, and multiyear report.
Contact: James A. Bower, Executive Director

Initial approach: Letter or proposal
Copies of proposal: 8
Deadlines: None; March 1 for student aid
Board meeting dates: Monthly
Final notification: 60 days–90 days

OKLAHOMA

Tulsa Foundation
c/o Liberty Bank of Tulsa
P.O. Box One
Tulsa, OK 74193
(918) 586-5594

Restrictions: General charitable giving, funding for local community
   development and social services.
Focus of giving: Limited to the Tulsa, Oklahoma, area.
$ given: $882,391 for 26 grants.
Assets: $11.3 million
Contact: J. Michael Bartel, Vice President, Liberty Bank of Tulsa

OREGON

The Oregon Community Foundation
621 SW Morrison, Suite 725
Portland, OR 97205
(503) 227-6846

Restrictions: Statewide funding for civic affairs, education, culture, health,
   and social services. Grants for operating budgets, seed money, building
   funds, equipment, land acquisition, technical assistance, special projects,
   matching funds, and renovation projects.
Focus of giving: Limited to Oregon.
$ given: $6.4 million for 730 grants; average range, $1,000–$10,000; $547,038
   for 199 to individuals; $323,848 for 1 foundation-administered program.
Assets: $96 million
Publications: Program policy statement, application guidelines, newsletter,
   and annual report
Contact: Gregory A. Chaille, Executive Director
Application information: Application form required
Initial approach: Letter of 1 page
Copies of proposal: 12
Deadlines: April 1 and September 1
Board meeting dates: January, June, September, and November
Final notification: 3 months

Tektronix Foundation

P.O. Box 1000
Wilsonville, OR 97070-1000
(503) 627-7084

Restrictions: Support for education, community funds, health agencies, other social service programs, and some arts. Grants for operating budgets, continuing support, annual campaigns, seed money, building funds, and other types of support.
Focus of giving: Oregon
$ given: $1.37 million for 59 grants; average range, $10,000–$25,000.
Assets: $1.8 million
Contact: Jill Kirk, Executive Director
Application information: No application form required
Initial approach: Letter
Copies of proposal: 1
Deadlines: None
Board meeting dates: February, May, August, and November
Final notification: Following board meetings to recipients only

PENNSYLVANIA

Allegheny Foundation

Three Mellon Bank Center
525 William Penn Place, Suite 3900
Pittsburgh, PA 15219-1708
(412) 392-2900

Restrictions: Seed money and general-purpose funding for historic preservation, community development, economics, education, and public policy.
Focus of giving: Limited primarily to western Pennsylvania, with emphasis on Pittsburgh.
$ given: $7.67 million for 66 grants; average range, $5,000–$50,000.
Assets: $27.5 million
Contact: Joanne B. Beyer, President
Application information: No application form required
Initial approach: Letter
Copies of proposal: 1
Deadlines: None
Board meeting dates: December
Final notification: December

Aristech Foundation

600 Grant Street, Room 980
Pitsburgh, PA 15219-2704
(412) 433-7828

Restrictions: General-purpose and renovation project funding for community/urban development, youth, education, science and technology, the environment, wildlife, and the arts.
Focus of giving: Areas of company operations in Arkansas, Florida, Kentucky, Ohio, Pennsylvania, Texas, West Virginia, and.
$ given: $339,300 for 58 grants.
Assets: $1 million
Publications: Annual report
Contact: David G. Higie, Executive Director
Application information: No application form required
Initial approach: Letter of 1 page–2 pages
Copies of proposal: 1
Deadlines: November
Board meeting dates: January
Final notification: January

Fannie Mae Foundation
3900 Wisconsin Avenue, NW
Washington, DC 20016
(202) 752-6500

See full entry under District of Columbia.

The Greater Harrisburg Foundation
P.O. Box 678
Harrisburg, PA 17103-0678
(717) 236-5040

Restrictions: Seed money and special project funding for community development, education, health, human services, and the arts.
Focus of giving: Limited primarily to Pennsylvania, with emphasis on Dauphin, Cumberland, Franklin, and Perry counties.
$ given: $381,665 for 245 grants.
Assets: $5 million
Publications: Annual report, newsletter, application guidelines, and informational brochure
Contact: Diane Sandquist, President
Application information: Application form required
Initial approach: Telephone or proposal
Copies of proposal: 1
Deadlines: April 15 and September 1
Board meeting dates: June and November
Final notification: 2 weeks after board meetings

The R.K. Laros Foundation
c/o PNC Bank, N.A.
1632 Chestnut Street
Philadelphia, PA 19103
Application address: 3529 Magnolia Drive, Easton, PA 18042

Restrictions: General-purpose funding for civic affairs, education, and social services.
Focus of giving: Limited primarily to the Lehigh Valley area of eastern Pennsylvania.
$ given: $113,000 for 12 grants.
Assets: $3.2 million
Contact: Robert A. Spillman, Secretary
Initial approach: Proposal
Copies of proposal: 6
Deadlines: None
Board meeting dates: Summer

Mellon Bank Foundation
c/o Mellon Bank Corp.
One Mellon Bank Center, Room 1830
Pittsburgh, PA 15258-0001
(412) 234-2732

Restrictions: General and special-purpose funding for economic development, business development, and employment/training initiatives in local communities; additional funding for education, health, welfare, and cultural programs.
Focus of giving: Limited primarily to southwestern Pennsylvania.
$ given: $1 million for 34 grants; average range, $1,500–$10,000.
Assets: $8.9 million
Contact: James P. McDonald, Secretary
Application information: No application form required
Initial approach: Proposal
Copies of proposal: 1
Deadlines: None
Board meeting dates: Monthly
Final notification: 2 months

The Philadelphia Foundation
1234 Market Street, Suite 1900
Philadelphia, PA 19107-3794
(215) 563-6417
FAX: (215) 563-6882

Restrictions: Funding emphasis on health and welfare as well as education and culture. Grants for operating budgets, continuing support, seed money, and other types of support.
Focus of giving: Limited to Philadelphia; Bucks and Chester counties; Delaware and Mongomery county in southeastern Pennsylvania (except for designated funds).
$ given: $5.1 million for 464 grants; average range, $5,000–$25,000.
Assets: $76 million
Publications: Annual report, informational brochure, newsletter, and application guidelines

Contact: Carolle Perry, Director
Application information: Application form required
Initial approach: Proposal, cover sheet, and statistical form
Copies of proposal: 1
Deadlines: July 31 and January 15; proposals not accepted August–October
or February–April
Board meeting dates: April and November
Final notification: 3 months–4 months

The Prudential Foundation
Prudential Plaza
751 Broad Street
Newark, NJ 07102-3777
(201) 802-7354

See full entry under New Jersey.

Robert & Mary Weisbrod Foundation
c/o Integra Financial Corp.
Fourth Avenue & Wood Street
Pittsburgh, PA 15222

Restrictions: Support for hospitals, medical research, social services, child
welfare, music, historic preservation, and general charitable giving. Grants
for capital campaigns and equipment.
Focus of giving: Primarily Pittsburgh, Pennsylvania, area.
$ given: $443,000 for 25 grants
Assets: $9.3 million
Contact: The Distribution Committee
Application information: No application form required
Copies of proposal: 1
Deadlines: None
Board meeting dates: As required

Westinghouse Foundation
c/o Westinghouse Electric Corp.
11 Stanwix Street
Pittsburgh, PA 15222-1384
(414) 642-6033

Restrictions: Seed money, matching funds, operating budgets, and special
project funds for youth, the disadvantaged, minority education, social
services, and selected cultural grants in plant cities.
Focus of giving: Areas of company operations.
$ given: $5.2 million for 195 grants; $328,000 grants to individuals.
Assets: $3.7 million
Contact: G. Reynolds Clark, President or C.L. Kubelick, Manager, Contribution,
and Community Affairs
Application information: No application form required

Initial approach: Proposal
Copies of proposal: 1
Deadlines: None
Board meeting dates: March, June, September, and December
Final notification: 2 months

RHODE ISLAND

Citizens Charitable Foundation
c/o Citizens Bank
One Citizens Plaza
Providence, RI 02903
(401) 456-7285
FAX: (401) 456-7366

Restrictions: Building and land acquisition funds, special project and other funding for community/urban development, urban affairs, and the environment.
Focus of giving: Limited to Rhode Island.
$ given: $430,650 for 59 grants; average award, $2,500.
Assets: $1 million
Contact: D. Faye Sanders, Chairperson
Application information: No application form required
Initial approach: Letter
Copies of proposal: 6
Deadlines: No set deadline; proposals accepted in June
Board meeting dates: March, June, September, and December
Final notification: 3 months–6 months

The Henry P. Kendall Foundation
176 Federal Street
Boston, MA 02110
(617) 951-2525

See full entry under Massachusetts.

SOUTH CAROLINA

Foundation for the Carolinas
301 South Brevard Street
Charlotte, NC 28202
(704) 376-9541

See full entry under North Carolina.

TENNESSEE

East Tennessee Foundation
360 NationsBank Center
550 West Main Avenue
Knoxville, TN 37902
(615) 524-1223

Restrictions: Special project, renovation funding, and others for support in
   community development, children and youth, education, culture, and the
   arts and general charitable giving.
Focus of giving: Limited to Knoxville, Tennessee, and its 18 surrounding
   counties.
$ given: $600,721 for 234 grants.
Assets: $10 million
Contact: Katharine Pearson, Executive Director
Application information: No application form required
Initial approach: Letter or telephone
Copies of proposal: 1
Deadlines: April and October for unsolicited applications

TEXAS

Amarillo Area Foundation, Inc.
700 First National Place 1
801 South Fillmore
Amarillo, TX 79101
(806) 376-4521

Restrictions: Land acquisition, building funds, and special project funding for
   community development.
Focus of giving: Limited to the 26 northern most counties of the Texas
   Panhandle.
$ given: $1.17 million for 55 grants; average range, $1,000–$30,000; $40,280
   for grants to individuals.
Assets: $23.8 million
Publications: Annual report, newsletter, and application guidelines
Contact: Jim Allison, President and Executive Director
Application information: Application form required
Initial approach: Letter or telephone
Copies of proposal: 1
Deadlines: January 15, March 19, July 9, and September 17
Board meeting dates: Bimonthly

ARCO Foundation
515 South Flower Street
Los Angeles, CA 90071
(213) 486-3342

See full entry under California.

The Constantin Foundation
3811 Turtle Creek Boulevard, Suite 320- LB 39
Dallas, TX 75219
(214) 522-9300

Restrictions: Support for higher education, secondary education, libraries, humanities, cultural programs, social services, youth, health, rehabilitation, media, and communications. Grants for building funds, matching funds, renovation projects, land acquisition, equipment, capital campaigns, continuing support, and general support.
Focus of giving: Dallas, Texas, metropolitan area.
$ given: $2.3 million for 32 grants.
Assets: $32 million
Contact: Betty S. Hillin, Executive Director
Application information: No application form required
Initial approach: Request guidelines
Copies of proposal: 1
Deadlines: September 30; grants reviewed at quarterly meetings; grant meeting in December
Board meeting dates: February, May, August, November, and December
Final notification: January

Dayton Hudson Foundation
777 Nicollet Mall
Minneapolis, MN 55401-2055
(612) 370-6553

See full entry under Minnesota.

Fannie Mae Foundation
3900 Wisconsin Avenue, NW
Washington, DC 20016
(202) 752-6500

See full entry under District of Columbia.

Dresser Foundation, Inc.
P.O. Box 718
Dallas, TX 75221
(214) 740-6078

Application address: Scholarship Committee, One Gateway Center, Pittsburgh, PA 15222

Restrictions: Support for community funds, higher education, hospitals, health, youth, and cultural programs. Grants for general purposes, building funds, employee matching gifts, and employee-related scholarships.

Focus of giving: Areas of company operations in Marion, Ohio; Pittsburgh, Pennsylvania; Houston and Dallas, Texas, and Waukesha, Wisconsin.

$ given: $1.4 million for 226 grants; $54,405 for 80 grants to individuals.

Assets: $7.5 million

Publications: Application guidelines

Contact: Richard E. Hauslein, Chairman of Contribution Committee

Application information: Application form required for employee-related scholarship programs

Initial approach: Proposal

Copies of proposal: 1

Deadlines: None for general grants; February 14 for Harbison-Walker employee scholarship and June 1 for Dresser, Canada, employee scholarships

Board meeting dates: As required

Final notification: 3 months

Halliburton Foundation, Inc.

3600 Lincoln Plaza
500 North Ackard Street
Dallas, TX 75201-3391
(214) 978-2600

Restrictions: Support for higher education, computer sciences, and engineering. Grants for operating budgets, continuing support, annual campaigns, employee matching gifts, research, conferences and seminars, and special projects.

Focus of giving: Southwest, with emphasis on Texas.

$ given: $1 million for 79 grants; average range, $500–$25,000; $461,367 for 204 employee matching gifts.

Assets: $9.63 million

Contact: Karen S. Stuart, Vice President

Application information: No application form required

Initial approach: Letter

Copies of proposal: 1

Deadlines: None

Board meeting dates: February and September

Final notification: Within 3 months

The Luling Foundation

523 South Mulberry Avenue
P.O. Drawer 31
Luling, TX 78648-0031
(512) 875-2438

Restrictions: Special project funding to teach farmers new agricultural techniques and to help local 4-H and FFA students with marketing show animals; operates an agricultural demonstration farm.
Focus of giving: Limited to Caldwell, Gonzales, and Guadalupe counties, Texas.
$ given: $9,375 for 6 grants; $75–$3,150; $3,000 for 3 grants to individuals; $34,483 for foundation-administered program.
Assets: $5.6 million
Publications: 990-PF, application guidelines, informational brochure and occasional report
Contact: Archie Abramiet, Manager
Application information: Application form required
Initial approach: Letter
Copies of proposal: 1
Deadlines: May 15
Board meeting dates: January, April, July, October, and as required

The Moody Foundation
2302 Postoffice Street, Suite 704
Galveston, TX 77550
(409) 763-5333

Restrictions: Local funding for historic restoration projects, performing arts organizations, and cultural programs; for promotion of health, science, and education; for community/social services; and for religion. Grants for seed money, emergency, building funds, equipment, and several other types of support.
Focus of giving: Limited to Texas.
$ given: $62.1 million for grants; average range, $10,000–$150,000.
Assets: $538 million
Publications: Annual report, application guidelines, 990-PF, and financial statements
Contact: Peter M. Moore, Grants Officer
Initial approach: Letter or telephone
Copies of proposal: 1
Deadlines: 6 weeks prior to board meetings
Board meeting dates: Quarterly
Final notification: 2 weeks after board meetings

The Pineywoods Foundation
P.O. Box 3659
Lufkin, TX 75903
(409) 634-7444
Application address: 515 South First Street, Lufkin, TX 75901

Restrictions: Funds for community/rural development, civic affairs, historic preservation, social and health services, education, youth, and cultural programs. Grants for general purposes, equipment, seed money, matching funds, building funds, and other types of support.
Focus of giving: Limited to Angelina, Cherokee, Houston, Jasper,

Nacogdoches, Panola, Polk, Sabine, San Augustine, San Jacinto, Shelby,
Trinity, and Tyler counties, Texas.
$ given: $167,785 for grants.
Assets: $2 million
Contact: Bob Bowman, Secretary
Application information: Application form required
Initial approach: Proposal
Copies of proposal: 7
Deadlines: None
Board meeting dates: Quarterly
Final notification: Following board meetings

UTAH

Dr. W.C. Swanson Family Foundation
257 37th Street
Ogden, UT 84405
(801) 399-5837

Restrictions: Scholarship funds and operating budgets for education, youth,
the homeless, hospitals, historical preservation, and animal welfare.
Focus of giving: Utah; emphasis on Ogden.
$ given: $1 million for 67 grants.
Assets: $25.6 million
Contact: Lew Costley, Trustee
Initial approach: Letter
Deadlines: None

VERMONT

The Kelsey Trust
c/o Vermont Community Foundation
P.O. Box 30
Middlebury, VT 05753

Restrictions: Operating budgets for community development and conserva-
tion.
Focus of giving: Lake Champlain Valley Drainage Basin area, New York and
Vermont.
$ given: $114,800 for 2 grants.
Assets: $2.6 million
Application information: No application form required
Deadlines: None

VIRGINIA

Quincy Cole Trust
c/o NationsBank
P.O. Box 26903
Richmond, VA 23261
(804) 788-2143

Restrictions: Grants for higher education, historic preservation, cultural programs, museums, and performing arts.
Focus of giving: Richmond, Virginia, area.
$ given: $324,346 for 15 grants.
Assets: $6.5 million
Contact: Rita Smith
Initial approach: Letter
Deadlines: April 20
Board meeting dates: June

WASHINGTON

Benaroya Foundation
1001 4th Avenue Plaza, Suite 4700
Seattle, WA 98154

Restrictions: Equipment support for medical research, medical education, health, and museums.
Focus of giving: Seattle, Washington.
$ given: $665,000 for 6 grants.
Assets: $3.4 million
Contact: Jack A. Benaroya, President
Initial approach: Proposal
Deadlines: None

Louella Cook Foundation
c/o The Bank of California
P.O. Box 3123
Seattle, WA 98114
(206) 587-3623

Restrictions: Operating budgets for religion, social services, education, and the homeless; provides food, clothing, shelter for street people of Seattle, Washington.
Focus of giving: Washington, with emphasis on Seattle.
$ given: $118,200 for 28 grants.
Assets: $2.4 million
Contact: Michael G. Vranizan, Vice President and Trust Officer, The Bank of California, N.A.

Application information: No application form required
Initial approach: Letter
Copies of proposal: 1
Deadlines: None
Board meeting dates: August

Seafirst Foundation
P.O Box 34661
Seattle, WA 98124-1661
(206) 358-3443

Restrictions: General and special project funding for community develop-
  ment, youth training/employment, higher/economic education, human
  services, culture, and the arts.
Focus of giving: Limited to Washington.
$ given: $1.34 million for 64 grants; average range, $5,000–$25,000.
Assets: $367 million
Publications: Informational brochure and application guidelines.
Contact: Nadine H. Troyer, Vice President and Secretary
Application information: Application form required
Initial approach: Letter of 2 pages
Copies of proposal: 1
Deadlines: Before October 1 for consideration within calendar year
Board meeting dates: Quarterly
Final notification: 4 weeks–6 weeks

WEST VIRGINIA

Foundation for the Tri-State Community
P.O. Box 2096
Ashland, KY 41105
(606) 324-3888
FAX: (606) 324-5961

See full entry under Kentucky.

The Greater Kanawha Valley Foundation
1426 Kanawha Boulevard East
Charleston, WV 25301
(304) 346-3620
Application address: P.O. Box 3041, Charleston, WV 25331

Restrictions: Support for community development, recreation, the environment, medical research, social services, education, and the arts. Grants
  for operating budgets, continuing support, seed money, building funds,
  equipment, special projects, research, publications, conferences and
  seminars, technical assistance, and general purposes.

Focus of giving: Limited to the West Virginia area of the Greater Kanawha Valley.
$ given: $1.2 million for 245 grants; average range, $200–$15,000; $402,100 for 275 grants to individuals.
Assets: $41.4 million
Publications: Annual report, informational brochure, financial statement, and application guidelines
Contact: Betsy B. Von Blond, Executive Director
Application information: No application form required
Initial approach: Proposal
Copies of proposal: 1
Deadlines: Vary annually; write or call
Board meeting dates: Usually in April, June, September, and December
Final notification: Immediately after board action

WISCONSIN

Ameritech Foundation
30 South Wacker Drive, 34th Floor
Chicago, IL 60606
(312) 750-5223

See full entry under Illinois.

Patrick and Anna M. Cudahy Fund
P.O. Box 11978
Milwaukee, WI 53211
(708) 866-0760

Restrictions: Funding for the arts, education, youth, international relief, social services, the homeless, family services, and for national programs addressing environmental and public interest issues as well as cultural and civic affairs. Grants for general purposes, operating budgets, continuing support, annual campaigns, seed money, building funds, and several other types of support.
Focus of giving: Limited primarily to Chicago, Illinois, and Wisconsin.
$ given: $1.82 million for 166 grants.
Assets: $23 million
Publications: Grants list and application guidelines
Contact: Sr. Judith Borchers, Executive Director
Application information: Application form required
Initial approach: Telephone
Copies of proposal: 1
Deadlines: 8 weeks prior to board meetings
Board meeting dates: Usually in March, June, September, and December
Final notification: 2 weeks after meetings

Giddings and Lewis Foundation, Inc.
142 Doty Street
Fond du Lac, WI 54935-3310
Application address: P.O. Box 590, Fond du Lac, WI 54936-0590
(414) 929-4252

Restrictions: Building funds, research funds, and other types of funding for
community development, community funds, education, and social
services.
Focus of giving: Limited primarily to Wisconsin.
$ given: $396,270 for grants.
Assets: $2.9 million
Contact: Robert D. Kamphreis, President
Initial approach: Letter
Deadlines: May 15 and December 1

Fred J. Peterson Foundation, Inc.
101 Pennsylvania Street
Sturgeon Bay, WI 54235
(414) 743-5574

Restrictions: Special project and other types of funding for community
development, youth, cultural programs, scholarships, and child welfare.
Focus of giving: Limited primarily to Door County, Wisconsin.
$ given: $129,050 for 72 grants; average range, $100–$5,000.
Assets: $2.76 million guidelines
Contact: Marsha L. Kerley, Secretary-Treasurer
Application information: No application form required
Initial approach: Letter only
Copies of proposal: 1
Deadlines: September 1
Board meeting dates: As required
Final notification: September 10

WYOMING

Tom & Helen Tonkin Foundation
c/o Norwest Bank Wyoming, Casper, N.A.
P.O. Box 2799
Casper, WY 82602
(307) 266-1100

Restrictions: Support for youth, especially handicapped; child development,
child welfare, and the disadvantaged. Grants for operating budgets, seed
money, emergency money, deficit financing, matching funds, scholarship
funds, publications, conferences, and seminars.
Focus of giving: Wyoming; emphasis on Caspar area.

$ given: $91,825 for 27 grants; average range, $1,000–$10,000.
Assets: $2 million
Publications: 990-PF and application guidelines
Contact: Elona Anderson
Application information: No application form required
Initial approach: Letter
Copies of proposal: 7
Deadlines: None
Board meeting dates: As required
Final notification: 60 days

4

Flow-Through Funding by Type of Business

AGRICULTURE

The Luling Foundation
523 South Mulberry Avenue
P.O. Drawer 31
Luling, TX 78648-0031
(512) 875-2438

Restrictions: Special project funding to teach farmers new agricultural techniques and to help local 4-H and FFA students with marketing show animals; operates an agricultural demonstration farm.
Focus of giving: Limited to Caldwell, Gonzales, and Guadalupe counties, Texas.
$ given: $9,375 for 6 grants; $75–$3,150; $3,000 for 3 grants to individuals; $34,483 for foundation-administered program.
Assets: $5.6 million
Publications: 990-PF, application guidelines, informational brochure, and occasional report
Contact: Archie Abramiet, Manager
Application information: Application form required
Initial approach: Letter
Copies of proposal: 1
Deadlines: May 15
Board meeting dates: January, April, July, October, and as required

The Needmor Fund
1730 15th Street
Boulder, CO 80302
(303) 449-5801

Restrictions: Seed money, technical assistance, general purposes, and operating budgets for projects designed to empower traditionally disadvantaged populations. Emphasis on grassroots, member-controlled organizations with realistic strategies and goals. Funding interest includes the environment, agriculture, rural development, housing, community development, and minority populations.
Focus of giving: Limited to the United States.
$ given: $2.17 million for 243 grants; average range, $5,000–$25,000.
Assets: $17 million
Contact: Lynn Gisi, Coordinator
Application information: Application form required
Initial approach: Letter or telephone
Copies of proposal: 1
Deadlines: January 10 and July 10; call to confirm
Board meeting dates: May and November
Final notification: 2 weeks after board meetings

COMPUTER SCIENCES

Halliburton Foundation, Inc.
3600 Lincoln Plaza
500 North Ackard Street
Dallas, TX 75201-3391
(214) 978-2600

Restrictions: Support for higher education, computer sciences and engineering. Grants for operating budgets, continuing support, annual campaigns, employee matching gifts, research, conferences and seminars, and special projects.
Focus of giving: Southwest, with emphasis on Texas.
$ given: $1 million for 79 grants; average range, $500–$25,000; $461,367 for 204 employee matching gifts.
Assets: $9.63 million
Contact: Karen S. Stuart, Vice President
Application information: No application form required
Initial approach: Letter
Copies of proposal: 1
Deadlines: None
Board meeting dates: February and September
Final notification: Within 3 months

EMPLOYMENT

The Lavanburg-Corner House, Inc.
130 East 59th Street, 15th Floor
New York, NY 10022
(212) 836-1358

Restrictions: Support for youth, child welfare, the disadvantaged, education, minorities and employment. Grants for seed money, matching funds, and special project funding.
Focus of giving: Metropolitan area of New York, New York.
$ given: $262,150 for 33 grants.
Assets: $1.69 million
Contact: Lauren Katzowitz, Staff Consultant
Application information: Application form required
Initial approach: Proposal with summary of 1 page
Copies of proposal: 1
Deadlines: None
Board meeting dates: As needed
Final notification: 3 weeks after board meetings

Mellon Bank Foundation
c/o Mellon Bank Corp.
One Mellon Bank Center, Room 1830
Pittsburgh, PA 15258-0001
(412) 234-2732

Restrictions: General- and special-purpose funding for economic development, business development, and employment/training initiatives in local communities; additional funding for education, health and welfare, and cultural programs.
Focus of giving: Limited primarily to southwestern Pennsylvania.
$ given: $1 million for 34 grants; range, $1,500–$10,000.
Assets: $8.9 million
Contact: James P. McDonald, Secretary
Application information: No application form required
Initial approach: Proposal
Copies of proposal: 1
Deadlines: None
Board meeting dates: Monthly
Final notification: 2 months

Seafirst Foundation
P.O Box 34661
Seattle, WA 98124-1661
(206) 358-3443

Restrictions: General and special project funding for community development, youth training/employment, higher/economic education, human services, the arts, and culture.
Focus of giving: Limited to Washington.
$ given: $1.34 million for 64 grants; average range, $5,000–$25,000.
Assets: $367 million
Publications: Informational brochure and application guidelines
Contact: Nadine H. Troyer, Vice President and Secretary
Application information: Application form required
Initial approach: Letter of 2 pages
Copies of proposal: 1
Deadlines: Before October 1 for consideration within calendar year
Board meeting dates: Quarterly
Final notification: 4 weeks–6 weeks

ENVIRONMENT

ARCO Foundation
515 South Flower Street
Los Angeles, CA 90071
(213) 486-3342

Restrictions: Grants for education, higher education, engineering, business, social services, the aged, the arts, public policy, and the environment. "Programs that address causes of educational, social and cultural disparity in American life." Money for technical assistance, seed money, equipment, land acquisition, operating budgets, matching funds, and special projects.
Focus of giving: Areas of company operations: Anchorage, Alaska; Los Angeles, California; Dallas, Texas.
$ given: $70,000 for 2 grants.
Assets: $2 million
Contact: Eugene R. Wilson, President
Application information: No application form required
Initial approach: Proposal of 2 pages
Copies of proposal: 1
Deadlines: None
Board meeting dates: June and December
Final notification: 4 months–6 months

Aristech Foundation
600 Grant Street, Room 980
Pittsburgh, PA 15219-2704
(412) 433-7828

Restrictions: General-purpose and renovation project funding for community/urban development, youth, education, science and technology, the environment, wildlife, and the arts.

Focus of giving: Areas of company operations in Arkansas, Florida, Kentucky, Ohio, Pennsylvania, Texas, and West Virginia.
$ given: $339,300 for 58 grants.
Assets: $1 million
Publications: Annual report
Contact: David G. Higie, Executive Director
Application information: No application form required
Initial approach: Letter of 1 page–2 pages
Copies of proposal: 1
Deadlines: November
Board meeting dates: January
Final notification: January

Citizens Charitable Foundation
c/o Citizens Bank
One Citizens Plaza
Providence, RI 02903
(401) 456-7285
FAX: (401) 456-7366

Restrictions: Building and land acquisition funds, funding for special project funding and for community/urban development, urban affairs, and the environment.
Focus of giving: Limited to Rhode Island.
$ given: $430,650 for 59 grants; average award, $2,500.
Assets: $1 million
Contact: D. Faye Sanders, Chairperson
Application information: No application form required
Initial approach: Letter
Copies of proposal: 6
Deadlines: No set deadline; proposals accepted in June
Board meeting dates: March, June, September, and December
Final notification: 3 months–6 months

Columbia Foundation
One Lombard Street, Suite 305
San Francisco, CA 94111
(415) 986-5179

Restrictions: Seed money and special project funding for programs that make a significant positive impact in environmental preservation and conservation, urban community life/culture, intercultural relations, arms control, and protection of human rights.
Focus of giving: Funding focused primarily in the San Francisco Bay area.
$ given: $2.19 million for 180 grants; average range, $1,000–$50,000.
Assets: $44.6 million
Contact: Susan Clark Silk, Executive Director
Application information: Application form required
Initial approach: Letter

Copies of proposal: 1
Deadlines: February 1 and August 1
Board meeting dates: Twice a year
Final notification: 2 months–3 months

The Greater Kanawha Valley Foundation
1426 Kanawha Boulevard East
Charleston, WV 25301
(304) 346-3620
Application address: P.O. Box 3041, Charleston, WV 25331

Restrictions: Support for community development, recreation, the environment, medical research, social services, education, and the arts. Grants for operating budgets, continuing support, seed money, building funds, equipment, special projects, research, publications, conferences and seminars, technical assistance, and general purposes.
Focus of giving: Limited to the West Virginia area of the Greater Kanawha Valley.
$ given: $1.2 million for 245 grants; average range, $200–$15,000; $402,100 for 275 grants to individuals.
Assets: $41.4 million
Publications: Annual report, informational brochure, financial statement, and application guidelines
Contact: Betsy B. Von Blond, Executive Director
Application information: No application form required
Initial approach: Proposal
Copies of proposal: 1
Deadlines: Vary annually; write or call
Board meeting dates: Usually in April, June, September, and December
Final notification: Immediately after board action

The Henry P. Kendall Foundation
176 Federal Street
Boston, MA 02110
(617) 951-2525

Restrictions: Funding focus on the natural environment and its resources, arms control and peace, and museums. Grants for operating budgets, seed money, emergency funds, research, special projects, publications, conferences and seminars, continuing support, and loans.
Focus of giving: No geographic restrictions.
$ given: $1.1 million for 6 grants; average range, $5,000–$100,000.
Assets: $54.3 million
Contact: Salvatore F. Battinelli
Initial approach: Brief proposal
Copies of proposal: 1
Deadlines: February 15, May 15, August 15, and November 15
Board meeting dates: March, June, September, and December
Final notification: 2 months

The Needmor Fund
1730 15th Street
Boulder, CO 80302
(303) 449-5801

See full entry under Agriculture.

The New Hampshire Charitable Foundation
37 Pleasant Street
P.O. Box 1335
Concord, NH 03302-1335
(603) 225-6641

Restrictions: Funding for social and community services, the environment and conservation, and the arts; grants for start-up programs. Grants for seed money, loans, general purposes, special projects, technical assistance, consulting services, and fellowships and college scholarships.
Focus of giving: Limited to New Hampshire.
$ given: $3.2 million for 813 grants; average range, $1,000–$5,000; loans totaling $118,000 to organizations; $394,931 for loans to individuals; $1.2 million for grants to individuals.
Assets: $73.8 million
Publications: Program policy statement, application guidelines, annual report, and informational brochure
Contact: Deborah Cowan, Associate Director
Application information: No application form required
Initial approach: Letter or telephone
Copies of proposal: 1
Deadlines: April 1, September 1, December 1; April 24 for student aid applications
Board meeting dates: February, June, and November
Final notification: 8 weeks

The New York Community Trust
Two Park Avenue, 24th Floor
New York, NY 10016-9385
(212) 686-0010
FAX: (212) 532-8528

Restrictions: Interests in the areas of (1) children and youth; community development and the environment, including conservation, housing, economy, and revitalization; education and arts and humanities; and health and people with special needs. Grants for seed money, technical assistances, special projects, research, publications, and other types of support.
Focus of giving: Limited to New York, New York area.
$ given: $100.8 million for 2947 grants; average range, $5,000–$35,000.
Assets: $1 billion

Publications: Annual report, newsletter, informational brochure, financial statement, occasional report, and application guidelines.
Contact: Lorie A. Slutsky, Director
Application information: Application form required
Initial approach: Proposal with cover letter
Copies of proposal: 1
Deadlines: None
Board meeting dates: February, April, June, July, October, and December
Final notification: Up to 25 weeks

L.J. Skaggs and Mary C. Skaggs Foundation
1221 Broadway, 21st Floor
Oakland, CA 94612-1837
(510) 451-3300

Restrictions: Funding for ecology programs, historic preservation, and theater. Grants for special projects, general purposes, and continuing support.
Focus of giving: Limited to northern California for everything except historic preservation projects which are funded nationally.
$ given: $1.9 million for 140 grants; average range, $10,000–$30,000.
Assets: $4.4 million
Publications: Annual report, grants list, informational brochure, and application guidelines
Contact: Philip M. Jelley, Secretary; or David G. Knight, Program Director and Office Manager
Initial approach: Letter
Copies of proposal: 1
Deadlines: June 1 for letter of intent, September 1 for solicited proposals
Board meeting dates: November
Final notification: 2 weeks–3 weeks after board meeting

Surdna Foundation, Inc.
1155 Avenue of the Americas, 16th Floor
New York, NY 10036
(212) 730-0030
FAX: (212) 391-4384

Restrictions: General-purpose, seed money, technical assistance, continuing support, and special project funding for: (1) the environment, especially energy, transportation, urban/suburban, and cultural diversity issues; and (2) community revitalization. Interest in entrepreneurial programs addressing systemic problems.
Focus of giving: No geographic restrictions.
$ given: $11.47 million for 160 grants.
Assets: $380 million
Contact: Edward Skloot, Executive Director
Application information: No application form required
Initial approach: Letter and program outline, IRS certification letter, and audited financial statements.

Copies of proposal: 1
Deadlines: None
Board meeting dates: February, May, September, and November
Final notification: 90 days

HISTORIC PRESERVATION

Allegheny Foundation
Three Mellon Bank Center
525 William Penn Place, Suite 3900
Pittsburgh, PA 15219-1708
(412) 392-2900

Restrictions: Seed money and general-purpose funding for historic preservation, community development, economics, education, and public policy.
Focus of giving: Limited primarily to western Pennsylvania, with emphasis on Pittsburgh.
$ given: $7.67 million for 66 grants; average range, $5,000–$50,000.
Assets: $27.5 million
Contact: Joanne B. Beyer, President
Application information: No application form required
Initial approach: Letter
Copies of proposal: 1
Deadlines: None
Board meeting dates: December
Final notification: December

Fair Play Foundation
350 Delaware Trust Building
Wilmington, DE 19801
(302) 658-6771

Restrictions: Renovation projects, equipment, and land acquisition for historic preservation, museums, environment, and wildlife.
Focus of giving: Washington, DC, Delaware, and Maryland.
$ given: $492,722 for 32 grants; average, $20,000–$30,000.
Assets: $8 million
Contact: Blaine T. Phillips, President
Initial approach: Brief letter
Deadlines: October 1
Board meeting dates: December

The Hawaii Community Foundation
222 Merchant Street, 2nd Floor
Honolulu, HI 96813
(808) 537-6333
FAX: (808) 521-6286

Restrictions: Funding for families in crisis, youth problems, environmental concerns, historic preservation, community-based economic development, and family services. Grants for operating budgets, seed money, equipment, technical assistance, research, special projects, renovation projects, student aid, scholarship funds, consulting services, conferences, and seminars.
Focus of giving: Limited to Hawaii.
$ given: $8.5 million for 1261 grants; average range, $500–$50,000; $586,453 for 575 grants to individuals.
Assets: $166 million
Publications: Program policy statement, application guidelines, informational brochure, newsletter, and annual report
Contact: Jane Renfro Smith, Chief Executive Officer
Application information: No application form required
Initial approach: Letter requesting guidelines
Copies of proposal: 1
Deadlines: 2 months prior to board meetings
Board meeting dates: Monthly, except April and September
Final notification: 2 weeks after meetings

The George B. Henderson Foundation
c/o Henry R. Guild, Jr.
50 Congress Street, Suite 1020
Boston, MA 02109
Application address: c/o Palmer & Dodge, One Beacon Street, Boston, MA 02108
(617) 573-0100

Restrictions: Renovation and special project funding for community development, historic preservation, recreation, and the overall enhancement of the physical appearance of Boston.
Focus of giving: Limited to Boston, Massachusetts.
$ given: $244,097 for 11 grants; range, $2,000–$50,000.
Assets: $6.5 million
Contact: John T. Galvin, Secretary, Board of Designators
Application information: Application form required
Initial approach: Letter or proposal
Copies of proposal: 1
Deadlines: None
Board meeting dates: As needed
Final notification: 1 month–3 months

The Jackson Community Foundation
230 West Michigan Avenue
Jackson, MI 49201-2230
(517) 787-1321

Restrictions: Funding for local community development, historic preservation, the environment, education, and other programs for the benefit of

the residents of Jackson County. Grants for seed money, building funds, equipment, land acquisition, matching funds, consulting services, technical assistance, loans, special projects, research, and capital campaigns.
Focus of giving: Limited to Jackson County, Michigan.
$ given: $205,571 for 61 grants; average range, $500–$18,000; $6,000 for 4 grants to individuals.
Assets: $8.6 million
Publications: Annual report with application guidelines.
Contact: Herbert F. Spieler, President
Application information: No application form required
Initial approach: Letter or telephone
Copies of proposal: 20
Deadlines: January 15, April 15, July 15, and October 15
Board meeting dates: March, May, August, and November
Final notification: 6 weeks

The Moody Foundation
2302 Postoffice Street, Suite 704
Galveston, TX 77550
(409) 763-5333

Restrictions: Local funding for historic restoration projects, performing arts organizations, cultural programs; for promotion of health, science, and education; for community/social services; and for religion. Grants for seed money, emergency, building funds, equipment, and several other types of support.
Focus of giving: Limited to Texas.
$ given: $62.1 million for grants; average range, $10,000–$150,000.
Assets: $538 million
Publications: Annual report, application guidelines, 990-PF, and financial statements
Contact: Peter M. Moore, Grants Officer
Initial approach: Letter or telephone
Copies of proposal: 1
Deadlines: 6 weeks prior to board meetings
Board meeting dates: Quarterly
Final notification: 2 weeks after board meetings

The Pineywoods Foundation
P.O. Box 3659
Lufkin, TX 75903
(409) 634-7444
Application address: 515 South First Street, Lufkin, TX 75901

Restrictions: Funds for community/rural development, civic affairs, historic preservation, social and health services, education, youth, and cultural programs. Grants for general purposes, equipment, seed money, matching funds, building funds, and other types of support.
Focus of giving: Limited to Angelina, Cherokee, Houston, Jasper,

Nacogdoches, Panola, Polk, Sabine, San Augustine, San Jacinto, Shelby, Trinity, and Tyler counties, Texas.
$ given: $167,785 for grants.
Assets: $2 million
Contact: Bob Bowman, Secretary
Application information: Application form required
Initial approach: Proposal
Copies of proposal: 7
Deadlines: None
Board meeting dates: Quarterly
Final notification: Following board meetings

L.J. Skaggs and Mary C. Skaggs Foundation
1221 Broadway, 21st Floor
Oakland, CA 94612-1837
(510) 451-3300

See full entry under Environment in this section.

Quincy Cole Trust
c/o NationsBank
P.O. Box 26903
Richmond, VA 23261
(804) 788-2143

Restrictions: Grants for higher education, historic preservation, cultural programs, museums, and the performing arts.
Focus of giving: Richmond, Virginia, area.
$ given: $324,346 for 15 grants.
Assets: $6.5 million
Contact: Rita Smith
Initial approach: Letter
Deadlines: April 20
Board meeting dates: June

HOUSING

Continental Bank Foundation
231 South LaSalle Street
Chicago, IL 60697
(312) 923-5114

Restrictions: Special projects and renovation funding for economic development, low- and moderate-income housing, and education of economically disadvantaged youth.
Focus of giving: Limited to Chicago, Illinois, area.
$ given: $1.87 million for grants; average range, $2,500–$10,000.

Assets: $24.5 million
Contact: Julie Chavez, Executive Director
Application information: No application form required
Initial approach: Proposal
Copies of proposal: 1
Board meeting dates: Quarterly
Final notification: Varies

Fannie Mae Foundation

3900 Wisconsin Avenue, NW
Washington, DC 20016
(202) 752-6500

Restrictions: Seed money and general-purpose funding for housing and community development programs, as well as the arts, health, AIDS, media and communications, youth, public policy, and social concerns.
Focus of giving: Limited primarily to the Washington, DC, area and to cities with regional corporate offices, including Pasadena, California; Georgia; Chicago, Illinois; Philadelphia, Pennsylvania; Dallas, Texas.
$ given: $6.38 million for 554 grants; average range, $1,000–$10,000.
Assets: $17.5 million
Contact: Harriet M. Ivey, Executive Director
Application information: No application form required
Initial approach: Proposal
Copies of proposal: 1
Deadlines: None
Board meeting dates: Twice annually

Fund for the City of New York, Inc.

121 Sixth Avenue, 6th Floor
New York, NY 10013
(212) 925-6675

Restrictions: A private operating foundation supporting public and private projects designed to improve the effectiveness of government and nonprofit agencies. Emphasis on government, public policy, civic affairs, housing, urban environment, youth, and AIDS. Money for technical assistance, loans, seed money, special projects, general purposes, and consulting services.
Focus of giving: Limited to the New York City area.
$ given: $460,550 for 63 grants; average, $5,000–$10,000; $35,000 for 7 grants to individuals; $9.5 million for 391 loans.
Assets: $12.1 million
Publications: Multiyear report, grants list, informational brochure, and application guidelines
Contact: Nancy Rivera, Program Assistant
Initial approach: Proposal
Copies of proposal: 1
Deadlines: None

Board meeting dates: Approximately 3 times a year in January, June, and October.

The Lavanburg-Corner House, Inc.
130 East 59th Street, 15th Floor
New York, NY 10022
(212) 836-1358

Restrictions: Support for youth, child welfare, the disadvantaged, education, minorities, and employment. Grants for seed money, matching funds, and special project funding.
Focus of giving: Metropolitan area of New York, New York.
$ given: $262,150 for 33 grants.
Assets: $1.69 million
Contact: Lauren Katzowitz, Staff Consultant
Application information: Application form required
Initial approach: Proposal with 1 page summary
Copies of proposal: 1
Deadlines: None
Board meeting dates: As needed
Final notification: 3 weeks after board meetings

The Needmor Fund
1730 15th Street
Boulder, CO 80302
(303) 449-5801

See full entry under Agriculture in this section.

New Prospect Foundation
1420 Sheridan Road, Apartment 9A
Wilmette, IL 60091
(708) 256-3886

Restrictions: Seed money and special/general-purpose funding for activities designed to improve housing, employment, health, welfare, and economic viability of urban neighborhoods; priority to organizations with modest budgets that may not qualify for traditional funding. Also, for pro-choice activities, AIDS advocacy, women's organizations, nuclear disarmament, and human and civil rights.
Focus of giving: Limited to metropolitan Chicago area.
$ given: $613,485 for 147 grants; average range, $1,500–$7,500.
Assets: $10.4 million
Publications: Informational brochure and application guidelines
Contact: Frances Lehman, President
Application information: No application form required
Initial approach: Letter, proposal, or telephone
Copies of proposal: 1

Deadlines: 6 weeks prior to board meetings
Board meeting dates: March, June, October, and December
Final notification: 3 months

MEDIA

The Constantin Foundation
3811 Turtle Creek Boulevard, Suite 320- LB 39
Dallas, TX 75219
(214) 522-9300

Restrictions: Support for higher education, secondary education, libraries, humanities, cultural programs, social services, youth, health, rehabilitation, media, and communications. Grants for building funds, matching funds, renovation projects, land acquisition, equipment, capital campaigns, continuing support, and general support.
Focus of giving: Metropolitan area of Dallas, Texas.
$ given: $2.3 million for 32 grants.
Assets: $32 million
Contact: Betty S. Hillin, Executive Director
Application information: No application form required
Initial approach: Request guidelines
Copies of proposal: 1
Deadlines: September 30; grants reviewed at quarterly meetings; grant meeting in December
Board meeting dates: February, May, August, November, and December
Final notification: January

Fannie Mae Foundation
3900 Wisconsin Avenue, NW
Washington, DC 20016
(202) 752-6500

See full entry under Housing in this section.

MEDICAL RESEARCH

The Greater Kanawha Valley Foundation
1426 Kanawha Boulevard East
Charleston, WV 25301
(304) 346-3620
Application address: P.O. Box 3041, Charleston, WV 25331

See full entry under Environment in this section.

SCIENCE & TECHNOLOGY

Aristech Foundation
600 Grant Street, Room 980
Pittsburgh, PA 15219-2704
(412) 433-7828

Restrictions: General-purpose and renovation project funding for community/urban development, youth, education, science and technology, the environment, wildlife, and the arts.
Focus of giving: Areas of company operations in Arkansas, Florida, Kentucky, Ohio, Pennsylvania, Texas, and West Virginia.
$ given: $339,300 for 58 grants.
Assets: $1 million
Publications: Annual report
Contact: David G. Higie, Executive Director
Application information: No application form required
Initial approach: Letter of 1 page–2 pages
Copies of proposal: 1
Deadlines: November
Board meeting dates: January
Final notification: January

The Moody Foundation
2302 Postoffice Street, Suite 704
Galveston, TX 77550
(409) 763-5333

See full entry under Historic Preservation in this section.

Section III

Federal Money

The grants in this section consist primarily of awards made by government agencies. In addition to these sources, you may want to check with your local bank or Small Business Administration (SBA) office about the possibility of obtaining as SBA loan. The cost for this loan is not inexpensive; interest rates vary but the loan is above the prime rate. To meet the requirements of an SBA loan, you must have been turned down by a commercial lender and you must be able to collaterize the loan. The good news is that repayment note terms vary from 7 to 25 years; as SBA tries to keep their default rate at a minimum, they will structure the loan and work with the recipient in an effort to guarantee repayment. Most businesses are eligible for SBA assistance, with a few exceptions such as publishing, gambling, investment, or speculation in real estate.

Under the Small Business Investment Act, SBA licenses, regulates, and helps to provide financing of privately and publicly owned small business investment companies (SBICs). SBIC financing provides both start-up and expansion capital either in the form of a loan or for an equity position in the company.

Most buyers of this book will apply to receive financing from an SBIC, such as ITT in California. However, for those businesses that have some cash on hand–one million dollars minimum–creating an SBIC offers an interesting and lucrative possibility. For example, motion picture company XYZ would benefit as follow:

1. The SBIC can serve the XYZ Production Company's own interests. The SBIC could be used to acquire up to a 40 percent interest in companies that serve the needs of the XYZ Production Company. The SBIC could choose, for example, in invest in an ad agency, a media-buying service–existing or start-up businesses that have tremendous potential for growth and that directly relate to the motion picture industry. If the XYZ Production Company invested in a media placement service, it would receive 40 percent of the profits of that service. As the XYZ Production Company would assure 50 million dollars in billing per year, the agency would be guaranteed 7.5 million dollars in fees based on the standard 15 percent commission structure on the XYZ account alone. The XYZ Production Company would receive 40 percent earnings of said 7.5 million dollars or approximately 3 million dollars per year (less reasonable operating costs). The creation of the SBIC would save the XYZ Production Company 3 million dollars each year in their print and media costs alone.

2. The SBIC acts as a tax shelter for profits.

3. The SBIC would bring in additional revenues for the XYZ Production Company aside from its film revenues, thus assuring profitability for the XYZ Production Company to become a diversified corporation for minimal investment.

5

Federal Money

AGRICULTURE

AGRICULTURAL CONSERVATION PROGRAM (ACP)
Federal Program 10.063

Agricultural Stabilization and Conservation Service
U.S. Department of Agriculture
P.O. Box 2415
Washington, DC 20013
(202) 720-6221

Restrictions: Payments for the control of erosion and sedimentation to those in voluntary compliance with federal and state requirements to solve point and nonpoint source pollution, to improve water quality, and to assure a continued supply of necessary food and fiber. The program is directed toward the solution of critical soil, water, woodland, and pollution abatement problems on farms and ranches. The conservation practices are to be used on agricultural land and must be performed satisfactorily and in accordance with specifications.

Eligibility: Direct payments of up to $3,500 a year (average $990), up to $10,000 with a pooling agreement (average $1,600); usually made for projects lasting a year, but the possibility exists of obtaining up to ten years.

Contact: Local or state ASCS office.

COLORADO RIVER BASIN SALINITY CONTROL PROGRAM
(CRBSCP)
Federal Program 10.070

Conservation and Environmental Protection Division
Agricultural Stabilization and Conservation Service
U.S. Department of Agriculture
P.O. Box 2415
Washington, DC 20013
(202) 720-6221

Restrictions: Financial and technical assistance to decrease the salt load
and sedimentation level in the Colorado River and to enhance the water
quality in the United States and Mexico. Cost-share assistance to treat
salinity problems caused by agricultural irrigation activities, conduct
research, education, and demonstration projects.
Eligibility: Landowners or operators of eligible land in identified salt source
areas may apply for cost-share assistance. Program available in the
following areas: Delta, Dolores, Mesa, Montezuma, and Montrose counties,
Colorado; Clark County, Nevada; Duchesne and Uinta counties, Utah; and
Sweetwater County, Wyoming.
$ given: Cost-share assistance funded up to 70 percent of total cost on
long-term three- to ten-year contracts, average $20,000. For 1993, $15.4
million given.
Contact: Local or state ASCS office

COMMODITY LOANS AND PURCHASES
(Price Supports)
Federal Program 10.051

Cotton, Dairy, Grain, Rice, and Tobacco Price Support Division
Agricultural Stabilization and Conservation Service
U.S. Department of Agriculture
P.O. Box 2415
Washington, DC 20013
(202) 720-7641
or
Commodity Operations Division
ASCS
(202) 447-5074

Restrictions: Price support loans and purchases to improve and stabilize
farm income, to improve balance of supply and demand of commodities,
and to promote more orderly marketing by farmers. Commodities eligible
for purchase include feed grains, wheat, rice, rye, peanuts, tobacco, and
dairy products. Commodities eligible for loans include honey, cotton,
sugar, soybeans, canola, flaxseed, mustard seed, rapeseed, safflower, and
sunflower seed.

Eligibility: Owners, landlords, tenants, or sharecroppers on farms with a history of producing the eligible commodities; additional program requirements as announced by the Secretary of Agriculture.
$ given: Loans range from $50-$76 million; average loan, $24,288. In 1993, $9.4 billion given.
Contact: Local or state ASCS office

CONSERVATION RESERVE PROGRAM (CRP)
Federal Program 10.069

Agricultural Stabilization and Conservation Service
U.S. Department of Agriculture
P.O. Box 2415
Washington, DC 20013
(202) 720-6221

Restrictions: Payments to owners of private cropland to encourage them to protect the nation's long-term soil erosion, reduce sedimentation, improve water quality, create a better habitat for fish and wildlife, curb production of surplus commodities, and provide some needed income support for farmers.
Eligibility: Owners or operators of private croplands willing to place highly erodible land under a 10-15 year contract. The participants, in return for annual payments, agree to implement a conservation plan developed by the local conservation district for converting highly erodible cropland to a less intensive use.
$ given: Range of direct payments: $50–$50,000; average award, $5239. $1.77 billion given in 1993.
Contact: Local or state ASCS office

COTTON PRODUCTION STABILIZATION
(Cotton Direct Payments)
Federal Program 10.052

Commodity Analysis Division
Agricultural Stabilization and Conservation Service
U.S. Department of Agriculture
P.O. Box 2415
Washington, DC 20013
(202) 447-6734

Restrictions: Payments designed to stabilize cotton prices in order to attract the cotton production that is needed to meet domestic and foreign demand for fiber, to protect income for farmers, and to assure adequate supplies at fair and reasonable prices. Payments are used to provide producers with a guaranteed price whenever average prices drop below the established or "target" price.
Eligibility: Owners, landlords, tenants, or sharecroppers on farms where the

commodity is planted that meets program requirements as announced by the Secretary of Agriculture.
$ given: Direct payments may not exceed $75,000 per person for 1991-97 crops.
Contact: Local or state ASCS office

CROP INSURANCE
Federal Program 10.450

Crop Insurance
Manager
Federal Crop Insurance Corporation
U.S. Department of Agriculture
2101 L Street NW, Suite 500
Washington, DC 20250
(202) 254-8460
$ given: Insurance for up to 65 percent of appraisal and yield. Estimated $979 million given in 1993.
Contact: Regional Field Service Office

DAIRY INDEMNITY PROGRAM
Federal Program 10.053

Emergency Operations and Livestock Program Division
Agricultural and Stabilization and Conservation Service
U.S. Department of Agriculture
P.O. Box 2415
Washington, DC 20013
(202) 720-7673

Restrictions: To protect dairy farmers and dairy product manufacturers who, through no negligence or willful failure of their own, are required to remove their products from commercial markets because of contamination from approved government pesticides, chemicals, toxic substances, or nuclear radiation.
$ given: Direct payments range from $88 to $95,000; average payment is $40,000.
Contact: Local or state ASCS office

ECONOMIC INJURY DISASTER LOANS (EIDL)
Federal Program 59.002

Office of Disaster Assistance
Small Business Administration
409 3rd Street, SW
Washington, DC 20416
(202) 205-6734

Restrictions: Loans to assist small businesses suffering financially due to certain Presidential, Small Business Administration and/or Department of Agriculture declared disasters.

Eligibility: Limited to small business concerns and small agricultural cooperatives unable to obtain credit elsewhere; must be within disaster area.

$ given: Direct loans up to $1,5 million given at interest rates note to exceed 4 percent, with up to 30 years for repayment; average loan, $54,008.

Contact: Local Disaster Area Office

EMERGENCY CONSERVATION PROGRAM (ECP)
Federal Program 10.054

Agricultural Stabilization and Conservation Service
U.S. Department of Agriculture
P.O. Box 2415
Washington, DC 20013
(202) 720-6221

Restrictions: Payments designed to enable farmers to perform emergency conservation measures to control wind erosion on farmlands, or to rehabilitate farmlands damaged by wind erosion, floods, hurricanes, or other natural disasters, and to carry out emergency water conservation or water-enhancing measures during periods of severe drought.

$ given: For total amount of damage, payments up to 64 percent are made for the first $62,500 and 40 percent for the next $62,500 worth of damage, etc. Maximum payment limitation of $200,000 per person per disaster. Average award is $1,780; range, $50–$64,000.

Contact: Local or state ASCS office

EMERGENCY LIVESTOCK ASSISTANCE
Federal Program 10.066

Emergency Operations and Livestock Programs Division
Agricultural Stabilization and Conservation Service
U.S. Department of Agriculture
P.O. Box 2415
Washington, DC 20013
(202) 720-5621

Restrictions: Emergency feed assistance for eligible livestock owners in approved areas where emergency situations exist due to natural disasters.

Eligibility: Livestock owners who have suffered substantial loss of feed; must meet conditions determined by approving official.

$ given: Direct payments ranging from $10–$50,000; average payment, $3,400.

Contact: Local or state ASCS office

FARM LABOR HOUSING LOANS AND GRANTS
(Labor Housing)
Federal Program 10.405

Multifamily Housing Processing Division
Farmers Home Administration
U.S. Department of Agriculture
Washington, DC 20250
(202) 720-1604

Restrictions: Loans and grants to provide safe, decent, sanitary low-rent
housing for domestic farm laborers. Funding provided for construction,
repair, and purchase of housing; purchase of land for such housing;
development of support facilities, and etc.
Eligibility: Loans available to farmers and farm associations/corporations.
Grants available only to nonprofit farm worker corporations in pressing
need.
$ given: Initial grants range from $135,000 to $2.3 million.
$ loaned: Initial loans to individuals range from $20,000–$200,000; average
individual loan is $34,500. Initial loans to organizations range from
$165,000–$670,000; average, $292,750.
Contact: Local or state Farmers Home Administration office

FARM OPERATING LOANS
Federal Program 10.406

Farmer Programs Loan Making Division
U.S. Department of Agriculture
Washington, DC 20250
(202) 720-1632

Restrictions: To enable family farm owners to make efficient use of their
resources through loans and supervisory assistance. Loans may be used
for purchase of livestock or equipment, operating or family subsistence
expenses, minor real estate improvements, to finance youth projects, and
for payment of property taxes or insurance programs and others.
Eligibility: Applicants must be U.S. citizens with very small family farms and
farm experience.
$ given: Insured loans up to $200,000; average, $36,230; guaranteed loans
up to $400,000; average, $94,640.
National Contact: Director, Farmer Programs Loan Making Division
Local Contact: Local or state Farmers Home Administration office.

FEED GRAIN PRODUCTION STABILIZATION
(Feed Grain Direct Payments)
Federal Program 10.055

Commodity Analysis Division
Agricultural Stabilization and Conservation Service
U.S. Department of Agriculture
P.O. Box 2415
Washington, DC 20013
(202) 720-4418

Restrictions: Payments designed to stabilize the price of feed grain in order
to attract the production needed to meet domestic and foreign demand,
to protect income for farmers, and to assure adequate supplies at fair
and reasonable prices. Payments are used to provide producers with a
guaranteed price on their planted acreage in the event the average prices
drop below the established or "target" price.
Eligibility: Owners, landlords, tenants, or sharecroppers on farms where the
commodity is planted that meets program requirements as announced
by the Secretary of Agriculture.
$ given: Direct payments based on number of bushels produced to a
maximum of $50,000.
Contact: Local or state ASCS office

FORESTRY INCENTIVES PROGRAM (FIP)
Federal Program 10.064

Agricultural Stabilization and Conservation Service
U.S. Department of Agriculture
P.O. Box 2415
Washington, DC 20013
(202) 720-6221

Restrictions: A cost-sharing program designed to bring private non-
industrial forest land under intensified management, to increase timber
production, to assure adequate supplies of timber, and to enhance other
forest resources through a combination of public and private investment.
Eligibility: Individuals, tribes, or groups who own non-industrial private
forest lands capable of producing industrial wood crops.
$ given: Cost-sharing up to 65 percent of total cost is authorized, state may
set lower levels. Length of program is one–ten years. Average award is
$1,600; range, $50–$10,000.
Contact: Local or state ASCS office

GRAIN RESERVE PROGRAM
(Farmer-Held and-Owned Grain Reserve)
Federal Program 10.067

Cotton, Grain, and Rice Price Support Division
Agricultural Stabilization and Conservation Service
U.S. Department of Agriculture
P.O. Box 2415
Washington, DC 20013
(202) 720-9886

Restrictions: Payments to farmers designed to withhold sufficient quantities
   of grain from the market to increase price to farmers, to improve and
   stabilize farm income, and to assist farmers in the orderly marketing of
   their crops.
Eligibility: All producers or approved cooperatives having a CCC loan on
   wheat, corn, barley, oats, or sorghum who provide storage through loan
   maturity.
$ given: Direct payments range from $1.–$122,863; average, $2,660.
Contact: Local or state ASCS office

GREAT PLAINS CONSERVATION
Federal Program 10.900

Deputy Chief for Programs
Soil Conservation Services
U.S. Department of Agriculture
P.O. Box 2890
Washington, DC 20013
(202) 720-1868

Restrictions: Technical assistance and payments to farmers and ranchers to
   encourage them to conserve and develop the Great Plains soil and water
   resources. Cost-share funds are available only for soil and water conservation measures determined necessary to protect and stabilize a farm or
   ranch unit against climatic and erosion hazards. The program operates in
   the ten Great Plains states: Colorado, Kansas, Montana, Nebraska, New
   Mexico, North Dakota, Oklahoma, South Dakota, Texas, and Wyoming.
Eligibility: Applicant must have control of land for period of contract,
   minimum of three years to maximum of ten years.
$ given: Direct payments up to $35,000 per farm over a three- to ten-year
   contract period.
Contact: State Conservationists for the Soil Conservation Service in the ten
   Great Plain States

NATIONAL WOOL ACT PAYMENTS
(Wool and Mohair Price Support Payments)
Federal Program 10.059

Deputy Administrator, Policy Analysis
Agricultural Stabilization and Conservation Service
U.S. Department of Agriculture
P.O. Box 2415
Washington, DC 20013
(202) 720-6734

Restrictions: Price support payments for wool and mohair to encourage
  increased domestic production at prices fair to both producers and
  consumers, and to encourage producers to improve the quality and
  marketing of their wool and mohair.
Eligibility: Any person who owns sheep or lambs for 30 days or more and
  sells shorn wool or unshorn lambs during the marketing year. Any person
  who owns angora goats for 30 days or more and sells mohair produced
  therefrom.
$ given: Direct Payments average $2,034 for wool and $4,701 for mohair.
Contact: Local or state ASCS office

RICE PRODUCTION STABILIZATION
(Rice Direct Payments)
Federal Program 10.065

Commodity Analysis Division
Agricultural Stabilization and Conservation Service
U.S. Department of Agriculture
P.O. Box 2415
Washington, DC 20013
(202) 447-7923

Restrictions: To assure adequate rice production to meet domestic and
  foreign demands, to protect farmer's income, to enhance competitiveness
  of U.S. exports, and to conserve U.S. natural resources. These goals are
  met by setting "target" crop prices.
Eligibility: Owners, landlords, tenants, or sharecroppers on farms where the
  commodity is planted that meets program requirements as announced
  by the Secretary of Agriculture.
$ given: Direct payments of up to $50,000 per person. Average payments
  were $14,997 for 1991 crop. $608 million estimated for 1992 crop.
Contact: Local or state ASCS office

RURAL CLEAN WATER PROGRAM (RCWP)
Federal Program 10.068

Conservation and Environmental Protection Division
Agricultural Stabilization and Conservation Service
U.S. Department of Agriculture
P.O. Box 2415
Washington, DC 20013
(202) 720-6221

Restrictions: Financial and technical assistance to private landowners in
   approved project areas. Assistance is provided through three- to ten-year
   contracts designed to solve critical water quality problems resulting from
   agricultural nonpoint source pollution.
Eligibility: Any landowner (individual, tribe, or operator in irrigation district)
   in an approved project area whose land or activity contributes to the
   water problem and who has an approved water quality plan may enter
   into an RCWP contract.
$ given: Maximum payment is $50,000 per individual per contract.
Contact: Local or state ASCS office

SMALL BUSINESS INNOVATION RESEARCH
(SBIR Program)
Federal Program 10.212

SBIR Coordinator
Office of Grants and Program Systems
Cooperative State Research Service
U.S. Department of Agriculture
Aerospace Building, Room 2243
14th and Independence Avenue, SW
Washington, DC 20250-2243
(202) 401-6852

Restrictions: To stimulate technological innovation in the private sector, to
   encourage small businesses to meet federal research and development
   needs and to foster minority participation in technological research. The
   SBIR program operates in three stages and addresses specific areas of
   research, including forests, agriculture, animal production and protection,
   and rural community development; air, water, soils; industrial applications, food sciences, and nutrition.
Eligibility: Limited to United States-owned and -operated independently
   owned small businesses with fewer than 500 employees.
$ given: Awards range form $25,687–$220,000; average, $89,325.
Contact: SBIR Coordinator

VERY LOW INCOME HOUSING REPAIR LOANS AND GRANTS
(Section 504 Rural Housing Loans and Grants)
Federal Program 10.417

Director, Single-Family Housing Processing Division
Farmers Home Administration
U.S. Department of Agriculture
Washington, DC 20250
(202) 720-1474

Restrictions: Grants to very low-income rural homeowners to give them an opportunity to make essential repairs to their homes in order to make them safe and to remove health hazards to the family or the community. This may include repairs to the foundation, roof, or basic structure, as well as water and waste disposal systems and weatherization.

$ given: Grants range from $200–$5,000 over homeowner's lifetime; average, $3,481

$ loaned: Loans range from $200–$15,000; average, $3966. (Section 504 loans and/or grants are for very low-income homeowners; Section 502 loans are for the purchase, construction, or repair of low-income housing.)

Contact: Local or state Farmers Home Administration office

WHEAT PRODUCTION STABILIZATION
(Wheat Direct Payments)
Federal Program 10.058

Commodity Analysis Division
Agricultural Stabilization and Conservation Service
U.S. Department of Agriculture
P.O. Box 2415
Washington, DC 20013
(202) 720-4418

Restrictions: Payments designed to stabilize the price of wheat in order to assure adequate production for domestic and foreign demand, to protect income for farmers, and to assure adequate supplies at fair and reasonable prices.

Eligibility: Owners, landlords, tenants, or sharecroppers on farms where the commodity is planted that meets program requirements as announced by the Secretary of Agriculture.

$ given: Direct cash payment of up to $250,000 per person.

Contact: Local or state ASCS office

AIRLINES

PAYMENTS FOR ESSENTIAL AIR SERVICES
Federal Program 20.901

Director
Office of Aviation Analysis
P-50
U.S. Department of Transportation
400 Seventh Street, SW
Washington, DC 20590
(202) 366-1030

Restrictions: Direct government subsidy payments to airlines providing
essential air transportation to eligible communities. Subsidy payments
are made to air carriers to provide essential air services that could not be
provided without a subsidy.
Eligibility: Carriers must be approved by Department of Transportation.
$ given: For Continental United States, average $365,989 annually per point.
Contact: Director, Office of Aviation Analysis

BUSINESS

EMPLOYMENT AND TRAINING RESEARCH AND
DEVELOPMENT PROJECTS
Federal Program 17.248

Chief, Division of Research and Demonstration
Employment and Training Administration
U.S. Department of Labor
Washington, DC 20210
(202) 219-5677

Restrictions: Project grants for employment and training studies that
develop policy and programs for optimal use of the nation's human
resources; for improving the nation's employment and training system;
for developing new approaches to facilitate employment of the difficult-
to-employ; and for conducting research and development into long-term
socio-economic trends and their effects on the employment market.
Eligibility: Colleges, organizations, and individuals fulfilling the program
objectives.
$ given: Project grants from $10,000–$1 million; average award, $175,000.
Contact: Lafayette Grisby

COMMUNITY DEVELOPMENT

AMERICAN INDIAN PROGRAM (AIP)
Federal Program 11.801

Office of Operations
Room 5063
Minority Business Development Agency
U.S. Department of Commerce
14th and Constitution Avenue, NW
Washington, DC 20230
(202) 377-8015

Restrictions: To provide business development services to American Indians entering the marketplace by selecting and funding American Indian business consultants and development centers. Funding recipients provide management and technical assistance to American Indian clients across the country.
Eligibility: Assistance emphasis is on Native Americans.
$ given: Awards range from $157,500–$303,000 depending upon fund availability.
National Contact: Mr. Bharat Bhargava, Assistant Director, Office of Operations
Local Contact: Minority Business Development Agency Regional Office

BUSINESS AND INDUSTRIAL LOANS
Federal Program 10.768

Administrator, Rural Development Administration
U.S. Department of Agriculture
Washington, DC 20250-0700
(202) 690-1553

Restrictions: To assist for-profit or nonprofit organizations and individuals in rural areas in obtaining loans for the purpose of improving, developing, or financing businesses and industries that will contribute to the economic and environmental improvement of the rural communities.
Eligibility: Individuals and for-profit/nonprofit entities are eligible. Preference to open country areas and towns with populations of 25,000 or less.
$ given: Guaranteed loans range from $30,000–$7.5 million; average, $1.1 million.
National Contact: Administrator, Farmers Home Administration
Local Contact: Local or state Farmers Home Administration office

INDIAN COMMUNITY DEVELOPMENT BLOCK GRANT PROGRAM
Federal Program 14.223

Office of Native American Programs
Office of Public and Indian Housing
U.S. Department of Housing and Urban Development
451 7th Street, SW
Washington, DC 20410
(202) 708-1015

Restrictions: Project grants to Indian tribes and Alaskan native villages to
assist in the development of viable Indian communities, i.e., to improve
housing, provide community facilities, improve infrastructure, create job
opportunities, and support ongoing economic development.
Eligibility: Indian tribes, bands, groups, and nations, including Alaskan
Indians, Aleuts, and Eskimos.
$ given: The average grant in 1990 was $276,000.

SMALL BUSINESS INNOVATION RESEARCH
(SBIR Program)
Federal Program 10.212

SBIR Coordinator
Office of Grants and Program Systems
Cooperative State Research Service
U.S. Department of Agriculture
Aerospace Building, Room 2243
14th and Independence Avenue, SW
Washington, DC 20250-2243
(202) 401-6852

See full entry under Agriculture.

TENNESSEE VALLEY REGION—RURAL DEVELOPMENT
Federal Program 62.004

Resource Group
Tennessee Valley Authority
Knoxville, TN 37902
(615) 632-4765

Restrictions: Counseling and advice to promote the development of
economies in the Tennessee Valley through commercial business
assistance, industrial and navigation development, technology commer-
cialization, regional planning, and industrial skills development. Limited
financial assistance is available to help cover local-level administrative
costs.

Eligibility: Business firms and individuals, as well as local governments within the Tennessee Valley area.

$ given: Advisory services and counseling only; very limited financial assistance.

Contact: Norman A. Zigrossi, President

COLORADO RIVER BASIN SALINITY CONTROL PROGRAM (CRBSCP)
Federal Program 10.070

Conservation and Environmental Protection Division
Agricultural Stabilization and Conservation Service
U.S. Department of Agriculture
P.O. Box 2415
Washington, DC 20013
(202) 720-6221

See full entry under Agriculture.

CONSERVATION

GREAT PLAINS CONSERVATION
Federal Program 10.900

Deputy Chief for Programs
Soil Conservation Services
U.S. Department of Agriculture
P.O. Box 2890
Washington, DC 20013
(202) 720-1868

See full entry under Agriculture.

RURAL CLEAN WATER PROGRAM (RCWP)
Federal Program 10.068

Conservation and Environmental Protection Division
Agricultural Stabilization and Conservation Service
U.S. Department of Agriculture
P.O. Box 2415
Washington, DC 20013
(202) 720-6221

See full entry under Agriculture.

WATER BANK PROGRAM
Federal Program 10.062

Agricultural Stabilization and Conservation Service
Department of Agriculture
P.O. Box 2415
Washington, DC 20013
(202) 620-6221

Restrictions: Payments to eligible landowners to enter ten-year agreements to conserve surface waters, preserve and improve migratory waterfowl breeding and nesting areas, preserve wetland areas, and secure other environmental benefits. In return for annual payments, the participants agree not to drain, burn, fill, or otherwise destroy the wetland character of such areas and not to use areas for agricultural purposes.
$ given: Direct payment ranging from $7–$66 per acre; average, $15 per acre.
Contact: Local or state ASCS office

CONSTRUCTION

CAPITAL CONSTRUCTION FUND (CCF)
Federal Program 20.808

Associate Administrator for Maritime Aids
Maritime Administration
U.S. Department of Transportation
Washington, DC 20590
(202) 366-0364

Restrictions: Payments in the form of tax benefits for replacement vessels, additional vessels, or reconstructed vessels, built and documented under the laws of the United States for operation in the United States' foreign, Great Lakes, or noncontiguous domestic trade.
Eligibility: U.S. citizens who own or lease one or more eligible vehicles and demonstrate financial capability to complete program.
$ given: Tax benefits for depositing assets.
Contact: Associate Administrator for Maritime Aids

CONSTRUCTION RESERVE FUND (CRF)
Federal Program 20.812

Associate Administrator for Maritime Aids
Maritime Administration
U.S. Department of Transportation
Washington, DC 20590
(202) 366-0364

Restrictions: Payments designed to encourage the construction, reconstruction, reconditioning, or acquisition of merchant vessels needed for national defense and the development of U.S. commerce.
$ given: Tax benefits for depositing assets.
Contact: Associate Administrator for Maritime Aids

FEDERAL TRANSIT CAPITAL IMPROVEMENT GRANTS
(Capital Grants, Section 3)
Federal Program 20.500

Federal Transit Administration
U.S. Department of Transportation
400 Seventh Street, SW
Washington, DC 20590

Restrictions: Project grants to help finance the acquisition, construction, reconstruction, and improvement of facilities and equipment for use (by operation, lease, or otherwise) in mass transportation service in urban areas, and to assist in coordinating such service with other forms of transportation in such areas.
Eligibility: Open to public agencies, instrumentalities, and public corporations.
$ given: Project grants ranging from $9,450 to $1.6 billion; average, $7 million.

EMERGENCY & DISASTER FUNDING

ECONOMIC INJURY DISASTER LOANS (EIDL)
Federal Program 59.002

Office of Disaster Assistance
Small Business Administration
409 3rd Street, SW
Washington, DC 20416
(202) 205-6734

See full entry under Agriculture.

EMERGENCY LIVESTOCK ASSISTANCE
Federal Program 10.066

Emergency Operations and Livestock Programs Division
Agricultural Stabilization and Conservation Service
U.S. Department of Agriculture
P.O. Box 2415
Washington, DC 20013
(202) 720-5621

See full entry under Agriculture.

PHYSICAL DISASTER LOANS
(7[b] Loans [DL])
Federal Program 59.008

Office of Disaster Assistance
Small Business Administration
409 3rd Street, SW
Washington, DC 20416
(202) 205-6734

Restrictions: Direct loans to victims (homeowners, renters, and businesses)
of designated physical disasters for losses.
Eligibility: Individuals, businesses, and nonprofit organizations are eligible;
must demonstrate ability to repay loan; must have suffered loss in
eligible area.
$ loaned: Direct business loans of up to $1.5 million with interest rate not
to exceed eight percent; average, $58,821. Average loans for homes was
$22,290.
Local Contact: Field office of Disaster Area Offices

EMPLOYEE BENEFITS

COMMERCIAL DRIVERS EDUCATION
Federal Program 84.247

Division of National Programs
Office of the Assistant Secretary for Vocational and Adult Education
U.S. Department of Education
400 Maryland Avenue, SW
Washington, DC 20202-7242
(202) 205-5864

Restrictions: Project grants to establish and operate adult education
programs to improve literacy skills of commercial drivers.
Eligibility: Educational agencies, colleges, universities, and labor organizations that include commercial drivers, and private businesses employing
commercial drivers in partnership with educational agencies are eligible.
$ given: Grants from $83,952 to $427,944; average, $177,448. At least 50
percent of the total project cost must be borne by the applicant. (May be
from direct funding or in-kind contributions to the program.)
Contact: Paul Geib

ENGINEERING

COMPUTER AND INFORMATION SCIENCE AND ENGINEERING
(CISE)
Federal Program 47.070

Computer and Information Science and Engineering
National Science Foundation
4201 Wilson Boulevard
Arlington, VA 22230
(703) 306-1900

Restrictions: Funding to support research to improve the fundamental
understanding of computer and information processing; to improve
the training and education of scientists, engineers, and other personnel
in the field; to provide access to advanced computer networking
capabilities.
Eligibility: Small businesses as well as academic institutions and government agencies.
$ given: Project grants range from $15,000 to $5 million; average, $145,000.
Contact: Assistant Director, Computer and Information Science and Engineering

BIOPHYSICS AND PHYSIOLOGICAL SCIENCES
Federal Program 93.821

National Institute of General Medical Sciences
National Institutes of Health
Public Health Service
Department of Health and Human Services
Bethesda, MD 20892
(301) 594-7813

Restrictions: Grants for research that applies concepts from mathematics,
physics, and engineering to biomedical problems, especially AIDS, trauma,
and burn injury, or that uses engineering principles in the development
of computers for patient monitoring.
Eligibility: Individuals and qualifying small businesses (through SBIR), profit
or nonprofit universities, hospitals, academic institutions, or others in
biomedical research.
$ given: Phase I awards range from $21,000 to $1.09 million; Phase II awards
up to $500,000; SBIR award is $75,000.
Contact: Dr. W. Sue Shafer, (301) 594-7751 for SBIR or Ms. Carol Tipery,
Grants Management Officer, NIH, (301) 594-7813

ENGINEERING GRANTS
Federal Program 47.041

Directorate for Engineering
National Science Foundation
4201 Wilson Boulevard
Arlington, VA 22230
(703) 306-1302

Restrictions: Funds for research in engineering and technology, including
funds for laboratory improvement and for research opportunities for
women, minorities, and disabled scientists and engineers.
Eligibility: Small businesses, universities, nonprofit organizations, and
government agencies.
$ given: Grants range from $1,000 to $5 million; average, $79,000.
Contact: Paul Herer, Senior Advisor, Directorate for Engineering

GENERAL BUSINESS

BUSINESS SERVICES
(Counseling on Doing Business with the
Federal Government)
Federal Program 39.001

Office of Small and Disadvantaged Business Utilization (AU)
General Services Administration
Washington, DC 20405
(202) 501-1021

Restrictions: Provides small and disadvantaged business firms with advice
and counseling on taking advantage of government contracting opportunities. Procurement and surplus sales contracts are available as are
concession and construction contracts.
Eligibility: Any business is eligible, especially small and disadvantaged firms.
$ given: Advisory services and counseling only; resulting government
contracts can be lucrative, however.
National Contact: Director, (AU)
Local Contact: Business Service Center, General Services Administration

LOANS FOR SMALL BUSINESSES
(Business Loans 7[a][11])
Federal Program 59.003

Loan Policy and Procedures Branch
Small Business Administration
409 3rd Street, SW
Washington, DC 20416
(202) 205-6570

Restrictions: Direct loans to small businesses owned by low-income persons or employing a high percent of low-income persons, or located in an area of high unemployment. Excludes publishing, radio, television, nonprofit businesses, investment enterprises, gambling enterprises, and real estate investment.
Eligibility: Credit-worthy individuals or businesses which are independently owned or operated, which meet the above criteria, and have been denied financing elsewhere.
$ given: Direct loans up to $150,000; average, $68,000.
National Contact: Director, Loan Policy and Procedures Branch
Local Contact: Field office of Small Business Administration

MANAGEMENT AND TECHNICAL ASSISTANCE FOR SOCIALLY AND ECONOMICALLY DISADVANTAGED BUSINESSES
(7[J] Development Assistance Program)
Federal Program 59.007

Associate Administrator
Minority Small Business and Capital Ownership Development
Small Business Administration
409 3rd Street, SW
Washington, DC 20416
(202) 205-6423

Restrictions: Project grants to give technical and management assistance to individuals, public and private organizations to help them succeed with existing or potential businesses that are socially or economically disadvantaged and are located in areas of high unemployment.
Eligibility: Any government agency, academic institution, public or private organization or individual with ability to provide the required assistance.
$ given: Grants range from $1,800 to $388,000; average, $79,000.

PROCUREMENT ASSISTANCE TO SMALL BUSINESSES
Federal Program 59.009

Associate Administrator
Procurement Assistance
Small Business Administration
409 3rd Street, SW
Washington, DC 20416
(202) 205-6460

Restrictions: Assistance to small businesses (often through special set-aside programs) to help them obtain contracts and subcontracts for federal government supplies and services and to help them obtain property sold by the federal government.
Eligibility: Existing and potential small businesses, i.e., those that are independently owned and operated but are not dominant in their fields.
$ given: Special consideration and consultation services only; resulting government contracts can be lucrative, however.
Local Contact: Field office of Small Business Administration

SALE OF FEDERAL SURPLUS PROPERTY
(Sales Program)
Federal Program 39.007

Director
Property Management Division
Office of Transportation and Property Management
Federal Supply Services
General Services Administration
Washington, DC 20406
(703) 305-7807

Restrictions: Sale of surplus government property to businesses, individuals, and organizations by competitive bidding. Property includes vehicles, aircraft, hardware, electrical equipment, paper products, office supplies, etc.
$ given: Items sold to the general public through competitive bidding process.
National Contact: Director, Property Management Division

SMALL BUSINESS INNOVATION RESEARCH
(SBIR Program)
Federal Program 10.212

SBIR Coordinator
Office of Grants and Program Systems
Cooperative State Research Service
U.S. Department of Agriculture
Aerospace Building, Room 2243
14th and Independence Avenue, SW
Washington, DC 20250-2243
(202) 401-6852

See full entry under Agriculture.

SMALL BUSINESS LOANS
(Regular Business Loans—7[a] Loans)
Federal Program 59.012

Loan Policy and Procedures Branch
Small Business Administration
409 3rd Street, SW
Washington, DC 20416
(202) 205-6570

Restrictions: Guaranteed loans to small businesses for construction,
   expansion, or conversion of facilities, purchase of equipment or materials,
   or working capital. Includes loans to low-income business owners,
   businesses located in areas of high unemployment, nonprofit sheltered
   workshops, businesses owned by handicapped persons, and businesses
   involved in the use of specific energy measures.
Eligibility: Small businesses independently owned and operated but not
   dominant in their fields may apply.
$ loaned: Guaranteed loans of up to $750,000; average, $192,000.
National Contact: Director, Loan Policy and Procedures Branch
Local Contact: District office of Small Business Administration

WOMEN'S BUSINESS OWNERSHIP ASSISTANCE
Federal Program 59.043

Small Business Administration
Office of Women's Business Ownership
409 3rd Street, SW
Washington, DC 20416
(202) 205-6673

Restrictions: Grants for demonstration projects to benefit small businesses
  owned and controlled by women; demonstration projects will provide
  financial, management and marketing training and counseling services to
  both start-up and established women's businesses.
Eligibility: Organizations qualified to train and counsel business women
  effectively.
$ given: Project grants from $35,000 to $1.03 million; average, $150,000.
Contact: Harriett Fredman

HANDICAPPED BUSINESS OWNERS

HANDICAPPED ASSISTANCE LOANS
(HAL-2)
Federal Program 59.021

Loan Policy and Procedures Branch
Small Business Administration
409 3rd Street, SW
Washington, DC 20416
(202) 205-6570

Restrictions: Direct loans to assist in the establishment, acquisition, and
  operation of small businesses owned by handicapped individuals. Funds
  may be used for construction/renovation of facilities, for purchase of
  equipment or materials, or for working capital.
Eligibility: Small businesses must be independently owned and operated,
  not dominant in its field, meet SBA (Small Business Administration) size
  standards, and be 100 percent owned by handicapped individuals.
$ loaned: Direct loans from $500 to $350,000; average, $95,300.
National Contact: Director, Loan Policy and Procedures Branch
Local Contact: District office of SBA

SMALL BUSINESS LOANS
(Regular Business Loans—7[a] Loans)
Federal Program 59.012

Loan Policy and Procedures Branch
Small Business Administration
409 3rd Street, SW
Washington, DC 20416
(202) 205-6570

See full entry under General Business.

HEALTH

BIOLOGICAL MODELS AND MATERIALS RESEARCH
Federal Program 93.198

Office of Grants and Contract Management
National Center for Research Resources
National Institutes of Health
Public Health Service
Bethesda, MD 20892

Restrictions: Project grants and SBIR grants to fund biomedical research in non-mammalian models.
Eligibility: Hospitals, educational institutions, and other organizations compete for research funds. SBIR grants are awarded to small domestic businesses with fewer than 500 employees.
$ given: Grants from $80,000 to $1.49 million; average, $247,200.
Contact: Grants Management Officer, Office of Grants and Contract Management, (301) 594-7955; Director, Biological Models and Materials Research Program, (301) 594-7906; SBIR Contact, (301) 496-6023.

HUMAN GENOME RESEARCH
Federal Program 93.172
Grants Management
National Center for Human Genome Research
National Institutes of Health
Public Health Service
Department of Health and Human Services
Bethesda, MD 20892

Restrictions: Research project grants and SBIR program grants to study the DNA sequences of genomes.
Eligibility: Hospitals, educational institutions, and other organizations compete for research funds. SBIR grants are awarded to small domestic businesses with fewer than 500 employees.
$ given: Phase I SBIR grants average $50,000; Phase II grants up to $500,000.
Contact: Program contact, (301) 496-0844; SBIR contact, (301) 496-7531; Grants Management Officer, (301) 402-0733.

RESEARCH RELATED TO DEAFNESS AND COMMUNICATION DISORDERS
Federal Program 93.173

Grants Management
National Institute on Deafness and Communication Disorders
NIH–PSH–HSS
Executive Plaza South, Room 400-B
Bethesda, MD 20892

Restrictions: Project grants for research to investigate solutions to problems related to deafness and disorders of human communication, including the senses, speech, and language.
Eligibility: Public, private, nonprofit, and for-profit institutions may apply for research funds; proposals reviewed for scientific merit. SBIR grants are awarded to small domestic businesses with fewer than 500 employees.
$ given: Grants from $72,500 to $458,300; average, $186,000.
Contact: Grants Management Officer, (301) 402-0909 or Program Contact, (301) 496-1804.

MENTAL HEALTH PLANNING & DEMONSTRATION PROJECTS
Federal Program 93.125

Division of Demonstration Projects
Center for Mental Health Services
SAMHSA–PHS–HHS
Parklawn Building, Room 16-86
5600 Fishers Lane
Rockville, MD 20857

Restrictions: To develop community support systems for long-term mentally ill people, for children and youth, and homeless persons. Service and research demonstration projects for crisis support, case management, housing, rehabilitation, etc.

Eligibility: State and local governments, nonprofit and private agencies, Indian tribes and organizations.

$ given: Project grants from $1,600 to $2.5 million; average, $243,000.

Contact: Director, Division of Demonstration Programs. Adult Community Support, (301) 443-3653; Child and Adolescent Services, (301) 443-1333; Research of Child and Adolescents Studies, (301) 443-1333; Homeless, (301) 443-3653; Grants Management, (301) 443-4456.

HOUSING

FARM LABOR HOUSING LOANS AND GRANTS
(Labor Housing)
Federal Program 10.405

Multifamily Housing Processing Division
Farmers Home Administration
U.S. Department of Agriculture
P.O. Box 2415
Washington, DC 20013
(202) 720-1604

See full entry under Agriculture.

OPERATING ASSISTANCE FOR TROUBLED MULTIFAMILY
HOUSING PROJECTS
(Flexible Subsidy Fund/Troubled Projects)
Federal Program 14.164

Director
Office of Multifamily Housing Management
Department of Housing and Urban Development
Washington, DC 20410
(202) 708-3730

Restrictions: Flexible subsidy to assist in restoration and maintenance of physical/financial stability of structure; to assist with ongoing management and operating costs of low- to moderate-income projects approved under the National Housing Act or under the HUD Act of 1965.

Eligibility: Private owners and cooperative owners.

$ given: Based on specific needs of project; owner required to contribute at least 25 percent of total estimated costs; average, $1.69 million.

National Contact: Director, Program Support Branch

VERY LOW INCOME HOUSING REPAIR LOANS AND GRANTS
(Section 504 Rural Housing Loans and Grants)
Federal Program 10.417

Director, Single-Family Housing Processing Division
Farmers Home Administration
U.S. Department of Agriculture
Washington, DC 20250
(202) 720-1474

See full entry under Agriculture.

HUMANITIES

PROMOTION OF THE HUMANITIES—CENTERS FOR
ADVANCED STUDY
Federal Program 45.122

Centers for Advanced Study
Division of Research Programs
National Endowment for the Humanities, Room 318
Washington, DC 20506
(202) 606-8210

Restrictions: Support to independent research centers, American research
centers overseas, and independent libraries and museums for interrelated
scholarly research in well-defined subject areas. Funding provided allows
these research centers to offer fellowships stipends.
Eligibility: Open to centers for advanced study that are financed and
directed independently of institutions of higher learning.
$ given: Grants range from $20,000–$240,000; average, $66,000.

PROMOTION OF THE HUMANITIES—REFERENCE
MATERIALS/TOOLS
Federal Program 45.145

Reference Materials/Tools
Division of Research Programs
Reference Materials/Tools
National Endowment for the Humanities, Room 318
Washington, DC 20506
(202) 606-8358

Restrictions: Whole and partial funding for projects to create research tools

important to scholarly research, including grants for the preparation of basic reference works.
Eligibility: U.S. citizens and residents, minority organizations, nonprofit organizations, government agencies, etc.
$ given: Grants from $30,000–$300,000; average, $125,000.

IMPORT/EXPORT

EXPORT PROMOTION SERVICES
Federal Program 11.108

Office of the Director General
U.S. and Foreign Commercial Service
U.S. Department of Commerce, Room 3804
Washington, DC 20230
(202) 377-5777

Restrictions: Counseling and advice to encourage U.S. firms to increase exports.
Eligibility: U.S. citizens, firms, and organizations needing assistance with international business matters.
$ given: Only advisory and counseling services are provided; information may lead to increased overseas trade contacts, opportunities, and financial gain.

FOREIGN-TRADE ZONES IN THE UNITED STATES
(Foreign Trade Zones)
Federal Program 11.111

Executive Secretary
Office of the Executive Secretary
Foreign-Trade Zones Board
USDC
14th and Pennsylvania Avenue, NW, Room 3716
Washington, DC 20230
(202) 377-2862

Restrictions: Zone procedure services to encourage exports and to shift processing and production work from foreign sites to domestic sites; facilities sponsored by local public corporations and designated as foreign trade zones and subzones may enact zone procedures to reduce business and production costs.
Eligibility: Public and private for-profit corporations.

$ given: Only specialized services provided.
Contact: John J. DaPonte, Executive Secretary, Foreign-Trade Zones Board

TRADE ADJUSTMENT ASSISTANCE–WORKERS
Federal Program 17.245

Director
Office of Trade Adjustment Assistance
Employment and Training Administration
Department of Labor
200 Constitution Avenue, NW, Room C-4318
Washington, DC 20210
(202) 219-5555

Restrictions: Adjustment assistance for workers adversely affected by increase of imports of articles similar to or directly competitive with articles produced by such workers' firms.
Eligibility: Workers in groups of 3 or more must file petitions with the Secretary of Labor through union representative. Other requirements exist.
$ given: Specialized services and direct weekly payments equal to state unemployment compensation.
National Contact: Marvin Fooks, Director, Office of Trade Adjustment Assistance
Local Contact: Local union representative or regional office of the Employment and Training Administration, Department of Labor

TRADE DEVELOPMENT
Federal Program 11.110

International Trade Administration
U.S. Department of Commerce
14th and Constitution Avenue, NW
Washington, DC 20230

Restrictions: Counseling and advice to encourage competitiveness and growth of U.S. industries and to foster their participation in international markets.
Eligibility: Any citizen, business, or organization may request information.
$ given: Only advisory services and counseling are provided; services may improve business, however.
Contact: Aerospace & Technology (202) 482-1872; Textile Apparel & Consumer Goods, (202) 482-3737; Basic Industries, (202) 482-5023; Service Industries & Finance, (202) 482-5261; Export Trading Company Affairs, (202) 482-5131; Trade and Economic Analysis, (202) 482-5145; Export Promotion Coordination, (202) 482-4501

INVESTMENT

SMALL BUSINESS INVESTMENT COMPANIES
(SBIC; SSBICC)
Federal Program 59.011

Investment Division
Small Business Administration
409 3rd Street, SW
Washington, DC. 20416
(202) 205-6510

Restrictions: Direct loans to privately owned and managed investment
companies which, in turn, provide equity capital, long-term loans, and
advisory services to small businesses.
Eligibility: Any chartered small-business investment company with at least
$3 million in combined paid-in capital and paid-in surplus and with
qualified management.
$ loaned: Guaranteed loans range from $50,000–$90 million; average, $1.48
million.
National Contact: Director, Office of Investments
Local Contact: Small Business Administration field office

MINORITIES

AMERICAN INDIAN PROGRAM (AIP)
Federal Program 11.801

Office of Operations
Minority Business Development Agency
U.S. Department of Commerce, Room 5063
14th and Constitution Avenue, NW
Washington, DC 20230
(202) 377-8015

See full entry under Community Development.

INDIAN COMMUNITY DEVELOPMENT BLOCK GRANT PROGRAM
Federal Program 14.223

Office of Native American Programs
Office of Public and Indian Housing
U.S. Department of Housing and Urban Development
451 7th Street, SW
Washington, DC 20410
(202) 708-1015

See full entry under Community Development.

MANAGEMENT AND TECHNICAL ASSISTANCE FOR MINORITY
BUSINESS ENTERPRISES
(M&TA for MBEs)
Federal Program 81.082

Office of Minority Economic Impact (EDI)
Department of Energy
Forrestal Building, Room 5B-110
Washington, DC 20585
(202) 586-1594

Restrictions: Services to encourage increased participation of minority and
women business enterprises (MBEs) in the Department of Energy's high-
technology research and development activities.
Eligibility: Limited to minority business enterprises.
$ given: Advisory and counseling services only; resulting Department of
Energy contracts can be lucrative, however.

MANAGEMENT AND TECHNICAL ASSISTANCE FOR SOCIALLY
AND ECONOMICALLY DISADVANTAGED BUSINESSES
(7[J] Development Assistance Program)
Federal Program 59.007

Associate Administrator
Minority Small Business and Capital Ownership Development
Small Business Administration
409 3rd Street, SW
Washington, DC 20416
(202) 205-6423

See full entry under General Business.

MINORITY BUSINESS DEVELOPMENT CENTERS (MBDC)
Federal Program 11.800

Office of Operations
Minority Business Development Agency
U.S. Department of Commerce, Room 5096
14th and Constitution Avenue, NW
Washington, DC 20230
(202) 377-8015

Restrictions: Project grants for businesses willing to provide free management and technical assistance to economically and socially disadvantaged individuals who need help in starting and/or operating businesses. Primary objectives of the assistance are to increase the gross receipts and decrease the failure rates of the client firms. Clients must be minority individuals in designated Metropolitan Statistical Areas throughout the country.
$ given: Project grants range from $165,000–$1.8 million; average, $212,000.
National Contact: Associate Director, Office of Operations

SMALL BUSINESS INNOVATION RESEARCH
(SBIR Program)
Federal Program 10.212

SBIR Coordinator
Office of Grants and Program Systems
Cooperative State Research Service
U.S. Department of Agriculture
Aerospace Building, Room 2243
14th and Independence Avenue, SW
Washington, DC 20250-2243
(202) 401-6852

See full entry under Agriculture.

OCCUPATIONAL SAFETY

OCCUPATIONAL SAFETY AND HEALTH (OSHA)
Federal Program 17.500

Occupational Safety and Health Administration
Department of Labor
200 Constitution Avenue, NW
Washington, DC 20210
(202) 219-9361 or -8677

Restrictions: Assistance services designed to assure safe and healthful working conditions. Cooperative agreement with states to provide consultation services to small businesses.
Eligibility: Any employer, employee, or representative concerned with occupational health and safety problems, state agencies, or nonprofit organizations designated by the governor.
$ given: Dissemination of technical information, investigation of complaints, worker and employer safety training, and consultation services to small businesses.
National Contact: Assistant Secretary, OSHA-DOL, (202) 219-9361 or (202) 219-8677

OCCUPATIONAL SAFETY AND HEALTH RESEARCH GRANTS
Federal Program 93.262

Grants Management Officer
Procurement and Grants Office
Centers for Disease Control
Public Health Service
Department of Health and Human Services
255 East Paces Ferry Road, NE, (MS-E13)
Atlanta, GA 30305
(404) 842-6798

Restrictions: Grants for research designed to study the underlying charac-teristics of occupational safety and health problems; to discover effective solutions in dealing with them; to eliminate or control factors in the work environment that are harmful to the health and safety of workers; and to demonstrate technical feasibility or application of new safety and health procedures, methods, techniques, or systems. SBIR awards are given to stimulate technological innovation.
$ given: Grants from $10,000–$300,000; average, $160,000.
Contact: Mr. Henry Cassell, Grants Management Officer

PUBLISHING

PROMOTION OF THE HUMANITIES—TEXT/PUBLICATION
SUBVENTION
Federal Program 45.132

Subventions
Division of Research Programs
Room 318
National Endowment for the Humanities
Washington, DC 20506
(202) 606-0207

Restrictions: Project grants to publishing entities for the dissemination of works of scholarly distinction that, without support, could not be published.
Eligibility: Nonprofit and commercial scholarly presses and publishers.
$ given: Project grants of $7,000 each.

RANCHING

COLORADO RIVER BASIN SALINITY CONTROL PROGRAM
(CRBSCP)
Federal Program 10.070

Conservation and Environmental Protection Division
Agricultural Stabilization and Conservation Service
U.S. Department of Agriculture
P.O. Box 2415
Washington, DC 20013
(202) 720-6221

See full entry under Agriculture.

GREAT PLAINS CONSERVATION
Federal Program 10.900

Deputy Chief for Programs
Soil Conservation Services
U.S. Department of Agriculture
P.O. Box 2890
Washington, DC 20013
(202) 720-1868

See full entry under Agriculture.

REAL ESTATE: RENT SUPPLEMENTS

RENT SUPPLEMENTS—RENTAL HOUSING FOR LOWER INCOME
FAMILIES
(Rent Supplement Program)
Federal Program 14.149

Office of Multifamily Housing Management
Department of Housing and Urban Development
Washington, DC 20410
(202) 708-3730

Restrictions: Financial assistance designed to make good quality rental housing affordable to low-income families by making payments to owners of approved multifamily rental housing projects to supplement the partial rental payments of eligible tenants. No new projects are being approved, but tenants many apply for admission to existing projects.
Eligibility: Cooperative, nonprofit, builder-seller, investor-sponsor, and limited mortgagors.
$ given: Assistance shall not exceed 70 percent of the market rental.
National Contact: Director, Office of Multifamily Housing Management

RESEARCH

BIOLOGICAL MODELS AND MATERIALS RESEARCH
Federal Program 93.198

Office of Grants and Contract Management
National Center for Research Resources
National Institutes of Health
Public Health Service
Bethesda, MD 20892

See full entry under Health.

ENGINEERING GRANTS
Federal Program 47.041

Directorate for Engineering
National Science Foundation
4201 Wilson Boulevard
Arlington, VA 22230
(703) 306-1302

See full entry under Engineering.

GENERAL RESEARCH AND TECHNOLOGY ACTIVITY
Federal Program 14.506

Assistant Secretary
Policy Development and Research
Budget, Contracts and Program Control Division
Department of Housing and Urban Development
451 7th Street, SW
Washington, DC 20410
(202) 708-1796

Restrictions: Project grants for research and demonstration projects preselected by the Department of Housing and Urban Development as high priority projects designed to improve HUD program operations.
Eligibility: Academic institutions, government agencies, private and/or public profit and nonprofit organizations may apply.
$ given: Grants from $23,000–$1 million; average, $240,000.

HUMAN GENOME RESEARCH
Federal Program 93.172

Grants Management
National Center for Human Genome Research
National Institutes of Health
Public Health Service
Department of Health and Human Services
Bethesda, MD 20892

See full entry under Health.

PROMOTION OF THE HUMANITIES—CENTERS FOR ADVANCED STUDY
Federal Program 45.122

Centers for Advanced Study
Division of Research Programs
National Endowment for the Humanities, Room 318
Washington, DC 20506
(202) 786-0204

See full entry under Humanities.

PROMOTION OF THE HUMANITIES—REFERENCE MATERIALS/TOOLS
Federal Program 45.145

Reference Materials
Division of Research Programs
National Endowment for the Humanities, Room 318
Washington, DC 20506
(202) 606-8358

See full entry under Humanities.

RESEARCH RELATED TO DEAFNESS AND COMMUNICATION DISORDERS
Federal Program 93.173

Grants Management
National Institute on Deafness and Communication Disorders
NIH–PHS–HSS
Executive Plaza South, Room 400-B
Bethesda, MD 20892

See full entry under Health.

SMALL BUSINESS INNOVATION RESEARCH
(SBIR Program)
Federal Program 10.212

Office of Grants and Program Systems
Cooperative State Research Service
U.S. Department of Agriculture
Aerospace Building, Room 323
14th and Independence Avenue, SW
Washington, DC 20250-2200
(202) 401-6852

See full entry under Agriculture.

SHIPPING

OPERATING-DIFFERENTIAL SUBSIDIES (ODS)
Federal Program 20.804

Associate Administrator for Maritime Aids
Maritime Administration
Department of Transportation
400 Seventh Street, SW
Washington, DC 20590
(202) 366-0364

Restrictions: Subsidy payments to promote the development and maintenance of the U.S. Merchant Marine by equalizing the cost of operating a
U.S. flagship with the cost of operating a competitive foreign flagship.
$ given: Direct subsidy payments ranging from $8,000–$14,000 per day per
ship; average, $9,700.
Contact: Associate Administrator for Maritime Aids

TECHNOLOGY

ADVANCED TECHNOLOGY PROGRAM (ATP)
Federal Program 11.612

Advanced Technology Program
National Institute of Standards and Technology
USDC
Gaithersburg, MD 20899
(301) 975-5187; application kit (301) 975-2636

Restrictions: To aid U.S. businesses in creating and using generic technology and research results to commercialize new discoveries rapidly and to refine manufacturing technologies.
Eligibility: U.S. businesses, joint research ventures, and independent research organizations.
Contact: Director, Advanced Technology Program

COMPUTER AND INFORMATION SCIENCE AND
ENGINEERING
(CISE)
Federal Program 47.070

Computer and Information Science and Engineering
National Science Foundation
4201 Wilson Boulevard
Arlington, VA 22230
(703) 306-1900

See full entry under Engineering.

ENGINEERING GRANTS
Federal Program 47.041

Directorate for Engineering
National Science Foundation
4201 Wilson Boulevard
Arlington, VA 22230
(703) 306-1302

See full entry under Engineering .

UTILITIES

RURAL ECONOMIC DEVELOPMENT LOANS AND GRANTS
Federal Program 10.854

Administrator
Rural Electrification Administration
U.S. Department of Agriculture
Washington, DC 20250-1500
(202) 720-9552

Restrictions: Direct loans and project grants to promote economic development and job creation.
Eligibility: Limited to electric and telephone utilities with current REA or Rural Telephone Bank loans or guarantees.
$ given: Loans and grants from $10,000–$400,000; average, $89,000.

RURAL TELEPHONE BANK LOANS
(Rural Telephone Bank)
Federal Program 10.852

Governor
Rural Telephone Bank
U.S. Department of Agriculture
Washington, DC 20250
(202) 720-9540

Restrictions: Direct loans and guaranteed loans to supplement long-term financing to extend/improve rural telephone service.
Eligibility: Organizations which are loan recipients under Section 201 of the Rural Electrification Act or which have been certified as qualified by the administrator.
$ loaned: Direct loans from $276,000–$39.1 million; average, $5.1 million; guaranteed loans from $3.3 million–$35.2 million; average, $22 million.

VETERAN-OWNED BUSINESSES

VETERANS LOAN PROGRAM
(Veterans Loans)
Federal Program 59.038

Loan Policy and Procedures Branch
Small Business Administration
409 3rd Street, SW
Washington, DC 20416
(202) 205-6570

Restrictions: Direct loans to small businesses owned by Vietnam-era and
disabled veterans. Funds may be used for the construction, expansion, or
conversion of facilities, for purchase of equipment, or for working capital.
Eligibility: Limited to small business concerns with a minimum of 51
percent ownership by the applying veteran(s).
$ loaned: Direct loans range from $1,000–$150,000; average loan is $75,900
National Contact: Director, Loan Policy and Procedures Branch

Index

Page numbers in italics refer to cross entries. Use roman page numbers to locate full entries.